BELIZE
The Journey to Paradise

Will Wesley P.E.
and
Deloris Stamm

authorHOUSE

AuthorHouse™
1663 Liberty Drive
Bloomington, IN 47403
www.authorhouse.com
Phone: 1 (800) 839-8640

© 2017 Will Wesley P.E. and Deloris Stamm. All rights reserved.

No part of this book may be reproduced, stored in a retrieval system, or transmitted by any means without the written permission of the author.

Published by AuthorHouse   10/27/2017

ISBN: 978-1-5246-2011-0 (sc)
ISBN: 978-1-5246-2012-7 (hc)
ISBN: 978-1-5246-2010-3 (e)

Library of Congress Control Number: 2016911814

Print information available on the last page.

Any people depicted in stock imagery provided by Thinkstock are models, and such images are being used for illustrative purposes only. Certain stock imagery © Thinkstock.

This book is printed on acid-free paper.

Because of the dynamic nature of the Internet, any web addresses or links contained in this book may have changed since publication and may no longer be valid. The views expressed in this work are solely those of the author and do not necessarily reflect the views of the publisher, and the publisher hereby disclaims any responsibility for them.

Contents

Introduction vii
Chapter 1 1
Chapter 2 9
Chapter 3 17
Chapter 4 91
Chapter 5 115
Chapter 6 141
Chapter 7 159
Chapter 8 171
Chapter 9 177
Chapter 10 189
Chapter 11 197
Chapter 12 223
Chapter 13 239
Chapter 14 263
Chapter 15 271

Introduction

This is the story of the little-known country, Belize, in Central America and how it changed one American couple's life forever. Belize has been known to capture the heart and soul. In this case, it certainly did! Alan and Deloris, inadvertently take a journey that leads them on a path of mystery, confusion and excitement.

Even though, Alan's family roots were in Mississippi, he grew up all over the world because his father was in the military. He and his brother, Morris, were both adopted and raised in a strict home, with a stay at home mother, which was traditional in those days, his father was a military man and his word was law. When his father retired from the Army, they returned to Meridian, Mississippi and Alan attended the local junior college. After beginning, he soon realized that college was not for him, Alan knew he wanted to start his life sooner, rather than later and saw no reason for a college degree. He was eager to start on the life of adventure that he had always dreamed of. Despite his parents' protest, he left college and headed to Jacksonville, Florida for a job. He was accompanied by a longtime friend. Alan was determined to live the carefree, bachelor life and no one was ever going to tell him what to do, again.

Deloris grew up in Columbia, South Carolina, in a single-parent home with a loving,

hardworking mother. She had the love of saintly grandparents who instilled in her the values of hard work and the virtues of following the rules. Deloris was always a good student and graduated from high school with several scholarship offers. Even so, there was never any doubt in her mind that she would become a nurse. She left her family and friends, to study nursing at the county hospital in Atlanta, Georgia. There she saw the worst cases and the most severe injuries; people who lived on the streets, couldn't afford to pay and only came to the hospital when they were faced with death. She realized then that not all Americans were able to afford regular medical care, she had not been exposed to these types of cultural differences as she was growing up. Because she had always been taught that people take care of each other. She found that although it appeared that she would have a promising career in nursing, she couldn't bear all the pain and suffering that she saw each day; so, three months prior to graduation, she walked away from that career and returned to her home in Columbia, South Carolina. Always drawn to numbers, she took an accounting job and learned that she was greatly satisfied balancing the numbers and having everything end with neat and tidy conclusions.

But wait, I'm getting ahead of myself a bit… My name is Will and I am Deloris' nephew. My mother was Deloris' sister and they were very close growing up. When I lost my Mother, my Aunt Deloris and Uncle Alan were all that I had left. They never had children and Aunt Deloris and I were as close as mother and son. My mother could always take comfort in knowing, that if anything were to happen to her, Deloris would be more than happy to watch over me, as she has. A true blessing, Aunt Deloris is and always has been.

She is a remarkably strong woman. I call her my "Lighthouse" and she has kept me from crashing into the rocky shores many times in my life. If you have a lighthouse in your life, thank them for being a constant beacon to save you from certain doom. I love hearing the stories about their adventures and misfortunes, as well as their success stories and this book is all about that. I want to tell you about the adventures that they've had in Belize. They hated Belize the first time they visited on a cruise ship. They would have never gone back if Alan had not gotten cancer.

Many people don't know much about Belize, I didn't until I researched it. It is a beautiful country, placed exactly in the perfect Caribbean location. I've often wondered how many things in Belize are missed by visitors because they don't take time to look. How many secrets are there still waiting to be found? How many ancient Mayan ruins are still left to be discovered in Belize? How many ancient battles took place there that no one even knows about? How many places in Belize still have never had a footprint from a human? If you are ever in Belize, you will see what I mean. It is almost untouched by civilization in many of the rural areas that are hidden in the jungle, its mountains and beneath its ocean. I for one enjoy that aspect of it and I suspect that most of you would too. After going through a rough divorce, Deloris asked me to come and visit them in Florida for a while. I had some time that I could take away from work, so I agreed. I ended up staying a week longer than I originally planned because I had so much fun. Alan, who is a gruff man, laughed more while I was there than I think I had ever heard before. Deloris was always fussing over whether we had enough to drink while we were sitting out on the patio. It was nice to have a family atmosphere again. I agreed to come and visit more often and Deloris promised to call more often and force to me talk because she knew that I wouldn't as often as I should. She knew that I had admittedly avoided the pain and frustration of a failed marriage and the strains of a diminishing industry that I am tied to forever. I just preferred not to talk about it. I guess I remembered hearing a wise old man talking to another when one said, "You don't seem worried. Why don't you worry?" the other, clearly wiser man, simply replied, "Would it help?" Those words ring true to me still to this day. I now know that we can't change anything that we can't control. The people of Belize seem to have intrinsically adopted this attitude. Worry does not seem high on their list of priorities. Deloris has hinted to me many times that I should find love and settle down. I had no desire to even look for love. She refused to lose hope and simply smiled when I told her that I didn't want a girlfriend. Maybe she knew something I didn't, because when I met my wife, she told me that is where I belonged.

I want to tell you this story of my aunt and uncle's journey because it is an amazing story and must be told. Not for him or her, or even for me, but for the people who have always wanted to know what it would be like to live in or visit another country. I still laugh out loud when I hear of some of the stories they tell and it isn't just them, I have heard many expats tell similar stories. The cultural clash is very real. Belize, for me, is a tropical paradise that is inexplicable without experiencing it first-hand. Yes, the Red Macaws are there and many species of monkeys also call Belize home. The elusive Jaguar is there as well as a multitude of species of birds just waiting to be seen. There are four indigenous races there. I am a large Caucasian man and in Belize I stick out like a barking cat. I'd say that the average height in Belize for men is around five-foot-eight and I am six-foot-five. Most people welcomed me with loving arms, as they do most people who come to their paradise, but they don't welcome those who come to "fix them". They simply live. We are so busy making a living that we sometimes forget to actually live. That is exactly what separates the rural Belizean cultures from our westernized way of life, where we are always insisting on having the newest and best of everything. People in Belize are simply happy to watch their families interact, have get-togethers and discuss what has happened that week. We westerners have forgotten those traits and values and place much more emphasis on the things we want, rather than being thankful for the things that we already have.

However, you'd also notice that their world comes down to what affects their family or their village. There is little interest in the world culture aside from how the economy affects the number of foreigners who visit and the flow of tourist dollars into their villages. They can get cells phones and other technology but very often it is through the generosity of tourist or expats who live in the village. When it comes to building practices or repairing an item, foreigners are always amazed at the techniques used because they still do things the same way they have for decades and at times, for centuries. Can you imagine for a moment watching a person use a stick that they have formed into a tool, rather than using the newest and best tools available? The lack of training in the newer, more efficient way of doing things is noticeability missing, but you come to wonder if they would be willing to learn the newer ways. Some social media is used and in fact there was an incidence that occurred when someone needed a doctor; a local resident placed a social media message on a forum and the doctor received the message before he could be physically located in the village.

Belizean's attitude toward time and deadlines is completely different from most of the North Americans who come to visit. Use of time and planning for the future have a completely different priority among most of the Belizean people. They simply use their time for what presents itself at the moment. Perhaps they use their time more wisely and they see no need to multi-task. Humph... Multi-task? I believe that is an excuse for focusing on so many things at once that we can ignore what is right in front of us. I am just as guilty as the next guy, but seeing the people of Belize has made me understand that there is a whole world out there just waiting to be discovered. When I first visited Belize, Deloris and

Alan both watched as I had my nose buried in my phone; checking emails, answering texts and checking on my social media networks, so that I didn't miss anything, that I thought, at that time, were the most important things in the world. Alan finally asked, "What is so important about that darn phone that you can't see the mountains?" I looked up and suddenly I realized that we were approaching the Mayan Mountain range and let me tell you folks, the beauty of that rock, clay and sand has been molded for millions of years and I would have missed it if Alan hadn't told me to look up. How often this is the case, when we are so enthralled with our phones and computers?

An attitude that is particularly appreciated by Deloris, is the fact that most Belizean women, regardless of whether they are heavy or pencil thin, are equally proud of their bodies. The fact that a size is not important, but, if they are able to squeeze into something, it fits! The women of Belize don't seem to be taunted day in and day out with a billboard, every other mile, telling them they need to look like this model or that model. They don't seem to be demoralized by the media monster and the vision of beauty that the United States and other countries try so hard to instill into their young girls. They are proud to look like a woman and they show it.

Nothing happens quickly in Belize and this book is a demonstration of that. Taking American's, Canadian's or any other idealism to Belize and implementing it onto the indigenous people, has never worked and I believe that it never will. The Belizeans have a different concept of time and prioritizing their time than we do. I have watched many people come into Belize and when trying to make sense of what they believe, is the logical way to do something, become so frustrated with the attitude they are confronted with, that they simply stomp their feet. When you think about it, why would they change their culture and ways of doing things for us?

To think that we have a better way of life than the Belizean people who have lived the same way for thousands of years is narcissistic at best. We must learn to appreciate the reason that they have held fast to their beliefs as long as they have and perhaps we could learn a bit from them. I for one have learned many things from the Belizean, Mayan and Meso-American cultures that I would love to implement in American society. Don't worry, I don't believe in human sacrifice or anything as drastic as that. I am referring to the idealisms and traditions of community gatherings and social bonding. I have never been hugged as much as I was when I was in Belize and I have honestly never relaxed as much as I did when I was there. There is just something about the water, the air, the temperature and the people that make that world seem right.

Being in the oil & gas industry so long has made me understand that the world has become so dependent upon carbon based fuels that if the pumps all stopped tomorrow, the people and cultures such as those in Belize would continue without fault and the U.S. would slow to a crawl, industrially. Countries like Belize have held onto the idealism of, 'If it is natural, it's okay', we on the other hand, modify almost everything to make it bigger and better or to make it grow faster. I've also learned that Belizeans avoid conflict with their neighboring countries, in most cases. Perhaps we could all learn from that. They are minimally political and for good reason. Belize was under British control for many generations and when they gained their independence (Belize was granted its full independence from British rule on September 21st, 1981) they wanted to make their government as simplistic as possible. We began that way in the United States, but somewhere along the line of history, our government complicated things to a voting advantage. In Belize there are many, many people who don't know what is happening in their parliament and, on the other hand, there are also many people who know the Prime Minister personally. We don't have that here in the United States because during most of our history, the Congressmen, Senators and President in power are too afraid to get near enough to the people to get to know them, this is where the United States' electoral vote law came into being. I'm not a political man, but I remember reading somewhere that Benjamin Franklin held town meetings every week with an open venue so that anyone who wanted to come and voice his opinion, was welcome to do so. You think that our leaders would do that, other than during an election year? I have worked in many states in the U.S. and I have worked in many different countries since I've been in the oil & gas industry. I have drilled oil wells in new production zones and I have been in some of the oldest fields in the world. I have yet to see a person who never uses any oil or gas in their lives. I have tried in many areas to improve the environmental impact that oil & gas exploration plays on mother earth and I will continue to do so as long as I am able. The Belizean people have solved this problem by stopping exploration of new areas offshore and in many areas onshore. If the world was this simple and a decision was as easily met, what a different world it would be.

One reason that Deloris insisted on writing this book, is that she wants the world to, not only know about Belize, but to share in their journey in this country that is appealing to so many foreigners. A wonderful adventure that has made us all shake our heads in disbelief, sometimes even stomping our feet in frustration, as well as, shed tears of joy for the people we have come to know as friends in Belize. It is a beautiful, slow paced paradise and I am happy to tell the stories and share the adventures of Deloris and Alan Stamm and their love affair with Belize, particularly the village of Placencia, Belize.

Chapter 1

The first-time Alan and Deloris went to Belize, they hated it. It was nothing like the travel books had promised or what they had imagined. They were on a cruise ship that stopped in Belize City. Their longtime friends, Cindy and Greg Thompson were with them on this cruise. Deloris found Belize City dirty, scary, and crowded. While the ship was anchored off the coast of Belize City, Alan and Cindy went diving the famed Blue Hole. Greg and Deloris chose to go on a Mayan Ruin tour to Lamanai (derived from Yucatec Maya word "Lama'anayin" which means submerged crocodile) about fifty miles north of Belize City. The Mayan ruin tour included what was billed as a "Jungle Cruise" up the New River. The trip up the river may have been beautiful, but the tiny boat kept breaking down in the middle of the river and the area was deserted and seemed a million miles from anywhere. You will come to know how much Deloris dislikes having to be in a boat, but there was no other way that the cruise line offered to get to the ruin. Her love for these ancient structures outweighed her dislike for having to ride in a boat. The two other boats that were part of the group, simply left them to fend for themselves when the motor on their boat refused to run. The boat was a tiny little thing with no cover and the boat driver, she simply refused call him a captain, had to change the spark plugs before they could catch up with the others. Once they were at the ruins, Deloris couldn't enjoy them because she was afraid the boat would not make it back after the tour. Even Greg who was experienced with boats, expressed concern that it had been necessary for him to help the "captain" change the spark plugs two times on the trip up. He strongly suspected they were not using new spark plugs. Since he was also anxious to begin the journey back up the river, Deloris had a hard time enjoying the sights.

In addition, when the cruise ship began to leave their mooring off the coast of Belize City, it ran aground on a sand bar. This was a demonstration of how shallow a large portion of the ocean is around Belize. This area is covered with small cays that rise out of the ocean with little warning. While stuck on this sandbar the ship was leaning at such an angle the elevators wouldn't operate and the dishes wouldn't stay on the tables. Then to top it all off, they were ordered to drink bottled water, even though the cruise staff kept telling them that there were no problems. Still, if they took a shower they smelled like gasoline. They stayed on that sandbar for about twelve hours before tugboats freed them. That was their first impressions of Belize. They would never have returned if Alan's battle with cancer had not left him a changed man whose love of adventure was honed by this experience.

For now, let's get to know a little about the small Central American country of Belize. It is comprised of six Districts. They are Belize, Cayo, Corozal, Orange Walk, Stann Creek and Toledo. As of 2016, the estimated population of residents was about 370,000. That is much less than the state of Wyoming and just a little larger than the population of the City of Tampa, Florida.

Belize is an unorthodox country, by US standards. The need to be bigger and better in all things has not come to Belize. There is very little interest in most world affairs. They do not feel the need to be involved in all things global. The use of cell phones has progressed and most homes have a functional television set, but there is no need for upgrading every few months. The vehicles are mostly imported from Asian countries and the occasional wealthy businessman who moved there to escape the mundane happenings in their home country, import a vehicle from the states or Canada. Although the Belizeans have modern technology available to them, their opinion of "Being and staying connected" is unlike many other countries. Social media is a huge part of their daily communications; however, you are much more likely to find a post asking where someone can get a needed part or item that is unavailable in the village, than to see opinions of world or even national issues. Of course, personal opinions about local situations are abundant, because their world revolves around things that are happening right in the village. People in Belize still sit around a table or a bar and visit with one another on a daily basis. In fact, that pastime seems to be one that expats adopt as soon as they arrive in Belize. If the world's problems could be solved by talking, the expats in Belize would have solved all of them because the activity of sitting around with a beer or rum drink occupies the majority of the hours in many of their days. The Kroil (Creole) word for gossip is "shush" and is the lifeblood of the villages. (Kroil is the shortened version of English that is spoken as the primary language in the homes of most Belizeans even though proper English is the official language.) Everyone knows what is going on at their neighbor's house and who is mad at whom and usually the reason for the dispute. I was very captivated by the country's simplicity and beauty, its people, and its slow, enchanting life style. Sometimes, when people from other countries spend time in Belize, they seem to lose their logical thinking ability and do the most unorthodox things. Logical thinking seems to vanish when visitors are immersed in the beauty and tranquility of the Caribbean land of Belize.

The journey to Paradise began in Jacksonville, Florida. Alan and Deloris Stamm were both in their very early sixties when they first came to Placencia. Coming from meager beginnings, they are very appreciative of what they have earned. They are the rare couple who have been married for more than forty-five years and still seem to really like each other. They are childless, and it seems that this is by choice. They have experienced many successful business adventures.

Their story began much like that of many couples, a friend of a friend and so on... Alan's friend asked Deloris to invite him and Alan over for a home-cooked meal. Deloris agreed because this nice Mississippian boy told her a sad tale of how he and his friend were craving a southern-cooked meal. Thus, the meeting of Deloris and Alan. From that first dinner, they were inseparable friends. They were the odd couple; Alan, who intended to remain footloose and fancy free for the rest of his life and have an adventure every day and the planner and rule-follower who assumed that someday her prince charming would ride up on a white horse and take her to the house with the white picket fence and they'd live happily ever after.

After several months, Alan told Deloris that he thought she would make someone a very good wife, and he thought she should be married. Deloris laughed at Alan's attempt to solve all problems, even if that meant he had missed the obvious. The friendship had reached the point that Alan decided that marriage did not mean that one person was the boss all the time. He thought that Deloris would be the wife who would let him live his life the way he wanted. He knew she worried when he did crazy things, but she did not insist that he not do them. He decided that with Deloris, he could have a home and still be allowed to follow his dream of fortune and adventure, so he proposed to her. She could not have been happier because Alan's wild nature was the perfect balance to her steadiness. Balance was what Deloris thought life should be about. Soon they were married, and Alan found that he was not cut out to climb the corporate ladder. With that way of life, he could not keep his promise to himself, that no one would tell him what to do. Therefore, corporate life was not for him. Alan would have to start businesses for himself, in order for them to be successful. Deloris found jobs she loved in accounting and rapidly progressed in the companies she chose to work for. She was confident that someday Alan would need her to do the accounting when he discovered the idea for the business of their future. As most couples do, they faced good times and bad times financially, but Deloris always seem to have a plan when things turned bad. Alan could try his ideas and he always seemed to have another. They both became insurance agents and open their agency while still pursuing building a dog breeding business where they raised and sold show quality Chow Chows all over the world. Alan traveled showing the dogs and Deloris remained at home and dealt with customers and maintaining the insurance agency. They always tried to give the customer what they would want if they were using that service. Both businesses were relatively successful. A friend, Ernie Bennett, was a veterinarian that they had met while establishing the successful Chow-Chow breeding and showing program. Ernie and Alan shared the love of adventure and became friends quickly. Never a couple to just do one thing at a time, Deloris and Alan started buying houses, remodeling and reselling. This appealed to Deloris's love of designing and decorating. There was never a dull or slow moment. Alan loved to fish and he loved to dive even more. Deloris didn't enjoy either but always loved to accompany him. Their friends Greg and Cindy Thompson, usually went along and while the others were out on whatever adventure had been planned, Deloris would read a book and take a break from their hectic lifestyle. She often laughed and called Alan an adrenalin junkie, telling him that if he went on a dive and something did not try to eat him, he classified it as just an alright dive but not a great one. He loved to dive with sharks and did so whenever he had the chance. His main complaint about Deloris was that she worried too much when he was on one of his adventures. However, it was not something she could control, and he knew it. Deloris is a tall, dark-eyed woman with dark hair and skin much more suited to taking the sun than Alan's, but he was the one who always wanted to be in the sun, and she was content with sitting in the shade and reading to escape their whirlwind life.

Lots of their friends were from the dive community, as members of these clubs, they had the chance to go all over the Caribbean to tropical dive sites. They did not have much free time to travel but made the most of the time they had. They were always going to new places because Alan tired quickly of doing the same dives over and over. He dove not for the beauty of the dive but for the adventure of diving into the unknown. They had been to most of the Caribbean countries and none had met their expectations, or captured their imagination. Alan and Ernie's friendship grew with Alan often going out and spending the day at his animal hospital and helping him when he needed an extra pair of hands. If he took one of their Chows in for treatment, he would spend the whole day helping in the animal hospital. Alan and Ernie often went fishing together as well and the conversation always came back to Ernie telling Alan how he was building his business. One night, after a full day at the animal hospital, Alan came in and said to Deloris, "Why don't we build an animal hospital on the land that we bought next door to this house."

Deloris, smiled patiently and said, "Why would we do that? Between the insurance agency, dog breeding and showing and work on the house our calendar is full." Alan apparently had been thinking about this for some time. Deloris, always the one to present the problem side of any idea, so that Alan would focus on the details, asked, "But neither of us are vets so who would you hire as the veterinarian? Neither of us are practice managers, so who would run it?" Nonetheless, Alan was ready.

"We will get the building up and then we will advertise for a young vet that wants to someday own his own practice. I have been working with Ernie and I basically know what's required to give good customer service. I know what it takes to manage an Animal Hospital. We'll set up our hospital so that the clients get the kind of service they want. We will be different from most hospitals. We will be customer oriented."

Deloris knew that look in his eye when Alan had an idea that he thought would lead them to the type of business he was seeking. He was like a little boy trying to talk his parents into a new bike for his birthday. To discourage him at this point would be hopeless, he sensed that this could be their next big adventure. It was her duty to plan step by step, how they could accomplish this next goal. Alan depended on Deloris, the rule follower, to never say no, but to point out all the possible problems. Sometime her observations would deter him and sometimes they seemed to fuel his dreams. Deloris had great faith in Alan's ideas and faith that he would work as hard as it was necessary to bring success to anything that he did. So, the adventure that Deloris thought would be the wildest idea they would ever tackle, began.

This adventure would just begin to prepare them for their plunge into the world of Belize, years later. Even this unorthodox project, did little to prepare the couple for situations like one that happened to them once they were in Placencia, Belize; when the Belizean police inspector, asked Alan to take the local drug taskforce out on his boat looking for drug smugglers. This story was actually one that occurred on their journey to Paradise, but I am getting ahead of myself.

Ernie helped the couple establish their animal hospital by providing advice and tutoring the vets they hired. The new venture proved to be the successful business they had been seeking. Soon it was very busy and they started a second hospital. Alan and Deloris sold the insurance agency and curtailed their breeding program. Deloris handled the financial side of both animal hospitals, while still managing the placement of their Chows into show homes around the world. Life was always interesting and there was not much relaxation for either of them. Although, they often worked seven-day weeks and ten to twelve hours a day, they loved the hectic life they were living. They even found their dream home on a small island on the St. John's River with a boat dock for Alan to keep one of his prized boats. It was a beautiful home with lots of windows and a tropical feel to the yard, which Deloris loved. Then tragedy struck!

Chapter 2

At age 55, Alan was diagnosed with esophageal cancer. The prognosis was that without experimental surgery he had no more than eighteen months to live. He also had only a fifty/fifty chance of surviving the surgery. However; if he did survive, he had a good chance of a full recovery. It did not take Alan long to make the decision to have the experimental surgery. Alan had a planned diving trip just three days after he received his diagnosis. Deloris was shocked when he told her that he was going diving and would have the surgery a week after he returned from his weeklong stay in Cozumel. This was one of the rare times that the two did not plan to travel together. She regretted the decision not to go with the group when she realized that they would be separated for a whole week, probably the most stressful week of their marriage. However, nothing that Deloris said would deter him from going and it was too late for her to accompany him. Alan promised Deloris that they would talk each day and that he would be fine.

It was the longest week of Deloris's life. Even so, when he returned he surprised her once again by saying that she had four days to plan a big party. She was shocked. Alan was unorthodox in most things he did, but a party, just before he underwent a procedure that only gave him a 50/50 chance of surviving. There was no deterring Alan from his party. Alan invited sixty people to what he called his, "Going Away Party." He left the planning and food details to Deloris. As he created a new will, and attended to the details that he thought needed to be taken care of, if he wasn't going to be around. Deloris suspected that the party was to keep her busy until the surgery. However, she was wrong. At the end of the party, Ernie approached Alan and said, "Man, I knew you were a gutsy dude, but to hold a "Going Away Party" when you are facing death is unheard of. Why are you doing it, really?" Alan, walked Ernie a short distance away from the rest of the group and said quietly, "Because if I die, I want you all to remember to look after Deloris. I know she will try to do everything herself and I thought if we were all here together, y'all wouldn't forget to take care of her." Then in typical Alan style, he wisecracked in a voice loud enough for the entire group to hear, "I wanted y'all to see my beautiful new home and I knew this was a way to get you all over here, so I only had to give one tour. Ha!"

Ernie, not to be outdone, jested, "Well if you don't kick the bucket, you'll have to agree to come to Belize with Amy and me. We'll show you what a real adventure is like." Everyone laughed and the night continued to be a happy one rather than a morbid one.

Alan survived the surgery and even though the surgery was now over, the rough road was not. Many weeks dragged by as he lay in the hospital bed with machines laboring for him. I can only imagine, as he must have felt like an inanimate robot. Aunt Deloris was constantly by his side and would run to the office only when she was sure that Alan would sleep until she could get back. For weeks Alan was unable to speak because of all the tubes that they inserted into his throat. But, he and Deloris communicated well without words. He lost seventy-eight pounds and was so weak that he couldn't walk. Whenever the tubes were finally removed and Alan could talk one of the first things that he told Deloris was, "This has made me want to do more, live more, experience more and not hold back."

Deloris, looked at him in mock despairs and laughed as she said, "You've been holding back? No one would have ever noticed!"

"I want a Hummer" Alan retorted after looking sharply at his wife.

"Why on earth would you want a Hummer? They are gas hogs and far too big to be practical,"

"I'm finished with being practical. I promised myself that if I survived cancer I would stop worrying about all that stuff and live a little. I don't want to have survived that and then die in an auto accident because I am in an unsafe vehicle." Alan quipped with a snarl.

Deloris listened to his rant and then with a big smile, replied, "With the way you drive, I guess you've got a point." The matter was settled. Alan would have his Hummer, but first he had to be able to walk again and, more importantly, be able to swallow again. He had to regain enough strength to stand. He had been given another chance at life.

For the next year it was a long slow battle for Alan. Tube feeding progressed to learning to swallow and then how to eat small amounts of things he was able to swallow. He never saw Deloris cry although he knew she did and he never complained of the intense pain and discomfort that he was certainly going through. Alan, refused to let this defeat him. Together they could conquer anything. Losing was simply not acceptable to a man like Alan. As soon as Alan was up and about, he told Deloris he was going to look for a Hummer. Her response was, "Just promise me it won't be yellow, because they look like a school bus."

He and Deloris went to a dealership where a black one, a blue one and a bright canary yellow H2 sat there next to one another. Alan looked at the black one immediately. He acted as if he was only partially interested, but after a while said, "I will take this one. Can you have it ready by morning?" But, that one was already sold. Alan was ready for a Hummer right then.

The purchase of the Hummer was not easy since they were in demand, but after several failed attempts at purchasing a Hummer, any color other than yellow, the day came that Deloris relented and the Stamm's purchased the yellow Hummer. When the question of price came up, Alan was told that he would have to pay sticker price. Now, I can tell you, my uncle Alan, under normal conditions would have stormed out of that dealership until he got a discount, however; on this day, for this purchase, he didn't. He simply asks, "Will you hold it until we can go to the bank and bring you a check?"

The couple had always owned practical, dependable vehicles, but this was certainly not practical. Deloris only hoped it was dependable. Alan was making good on his promise to himself that he was going to live life to the fullest, understandably so, after his brush with death.

I can tell you this, you would be hard pressed to find my Aunt Deloris allowing herself something personal that seemed that extravagant. She'd walk before she would have bought it for herself. But she knew how hard Alan had worked all of their life and it didn't seem so extravagant since he had been through such a rough battle with cancer. This was the first change in their lifestyle, soon to be followed by the change that Belize would cause. The yellow Hummer was destined to follow them on their Journey to Paradise.

That evening when they got the Hummer home, Alan said, "I'm calling Ernie to let him know that I have the Hummer and ask them to dinner, is that alright with you?"

"Sure, it is." Deloris said. She didn't know the Bennett's that well, but Alan really liked Ernie and the few times she had met Amy, she had been impressed by how well she handled everything with so little effort. She was an attorney, but she did not take many cases. She had the luxury of choosing only the cases that interested her. She was involved in a multitude of activities with their children and their community and no matter how busy, always seemed to be perfectly put together and in control. She seemed confident in everything she did. One morning both Alan and Deloris were at the Animal Hospital and Ernie took them to their house without notifying Amy and everything was perfectly in place, not an unmade bed or a dirty dish in sight. Everything looked like it had been placed by an interior designer.

When Alan called Ernie, they agreed to meet at an upscale restaurant that evening. Amy was in a beautiful and obviously expensive outfit. Each time that Deloris saw Amy the phrase 'Southern Belle' came to mind. Amy and Ernie were talking excitingly as Alan and Deloris entered the restaurant. They had not even looked out to see the Hummer. Alan ask what all the excitement was about. Ernie said, "We have been trying to purchase a home in Belize and the deal just got approved. We just got the call from the realtor that our offer has been accepted."

Deloris knew of Amy and Ernie's love of Belize, but her impression of Belize had been formed on that one trip and Belize had not made a good first impression. Amy immediately noticed Deloris's lack of excitement and ask, "Have you ever visited Belize?"

Deloris paused before describing the trip to Belize City- on the cruise that got stuck on a sand bar. Amy stared at her for a moment and then started laughing. "That sounds about right. I always tell people not to go to Belize on a cruise ship and I guess you proved my point." Amy always wanted to immerse herself into any culture that she could and thought that cruise lines hurt the ability to do so.

Ernie said, "The house we have purchased is in a little village in Southern Belize. The village is called Placencia and it's not anything like Belize City. You two would love it. You simply have to come visit as soon as we get the house set up. We would love to have you."

At this point, Amy, always the perfect hostess, remembered why they were meeting and asked to see the Hummer. Alan was delighted to show off his new toy.

After having the Hummer for a couple of years, the day came that the Hummer proved its worth, even to Deloris. On their way to lunch one day, Alan carefully pulled out from their Animal Hospital and right into the path of two racing hot rods. After the shaking was over, Alan shouted, "Are you alright, Deloris? It was clear when I pulled out!"

The accident had actually left the massive machine upright, but teetering on the edge of a massive drainage ditch. The front wheel was knocked off and the impact had been directly on Deloris's passenger door. Although obviously in shock, Deloris nodded her head and said, "I'm fine, I think. What happened?"

Charli, the Practice Manager of the hospital who had been in the parking lot when the accident happened, came running out to the street to check on them. Charli, a non-excitable woman in her late forties was at her best during emergencies. She ran to the front of the Hummer and peered through the window as Alan opened his door to get out. She shouted, "Are you sure Deloris is alright. That was an incredible hit!"

At that moment, Charli and Alan both realized that the car that hit them had gone through the massive ditch and then proceeded to hit a fence. Alan, knowing that Deloris was alright, went over to check on the occupants of the other car. They had not been as lucky as Alan and Deloris. Both were bleeding and in need of serious medical attention. The Emergency Units arrived and took both racing teenagers to the hospital. As the paramedics talked to Deloris they told her how lucky she was to have had the reinforced bar in the passenger side door. After the police report was done and everyone had left, Charli looked at Deloris and said, "I think you'd better be glad you were in the Hummer. If you had been in your Suburban, you may not have survived. The Hummer probably saved your life! Those kids were really flying and that was a terrible hit."

The other car was a pile of twisted metal, barely recognizable as a car. It was leaning against a telephone pole and it was clear from the way the front seats were crushed, that the driver and passenger probably had been seriously injured. At that point, Deloris realized that Alan's reward for having survived cancer, may have saved her life as well.

On the day of his "Going Away Party", Alan had committed to going to Belize with Ernie and Amy if he survived cancer. The time had come to honor that commitment.

Chapter 3

Deloris and Alan have always enjoyed watching me accomplish my goals. When I graduated High school, they were there. When I graduated college, they were there as well. You know, looking back now, they have always been there when something big happened in my life. They've always been proud of me and never pointed out my faults. I guess my mom knew that they thought of me as a son and loved me like their own. She picked some pretty good people to help mentor me and guide me. I don't know what I would do without them now and hope it is a very long time before I must find out. It has been important for me to try to understand what they were feeling at the time that Belize first came into their lives.

I have been in the oil & gas industry for many years now and when I first learned about their interest in Belize I wanted to know how Belizeans felt about drilling in their country. I was able to travel to Belize and I found that despite the fact that there is lots of oil there and could enrich the country; the average citizen is uninformed, but generally against progress being made in the production of oil in Belize. It seems that the things they know about drilling have come from the adversaries of drilling, but it is their country and they are the ones to make that decision. This attitude told me a lot about Belize. They are happy with their situation in life or at least are happy enough not to make major changes. Fear of the unknown, maybe.

Amy and Deloris had really become friends when Amy handled a legal case for the Stamms when a grammatical error in a contract with one of the veterinarians working for them, allowed him to attempt a takeover of the hospital. When Amy got involved the veterinarian and his lawyers soon realized that this 'Southern Belle' had a tough side and was as relentless as Alan in fighting if the case was justified.

During this case Deloris found that she worked better with Amy than Alan did, because he would get so angry that making his point took too much time. She and Amy worked out a system where Deloris gave Amy the facts and Amy handled the case without Alan having to be personally involved. This drove the other side wild because they had counted on having the volatile Alan in depositions and instead were faced with the very calm, analytical Deloris backed by a competent and tough Amy. The case was soon settled in the Stamm's favor and they obtained a sizeable settlement from the veterinarian for his actions. Both Deloris and Alan knew they owed a great deal to the Bennett's. First Ernie had mentored the veterinarians and now Amy had established the point that their business plan was valid. Deloris had learned that Amy, while appearing to be a 'Southern Belle' from a seemingly dying age of forgotten plantations and beautiful landscapes, actually had a multi-faceted personality. She clearly appreciated the finer things in life. She had aged gracefully and was the most confident person Deloris had ever known. Deloris would soon know that in Belize Amy showed still another side to her personality.

The thing that was exciting the Bennett's now, was the Country of Belize. Ernie and Amy had been traveling to the Central American Country of Belize for several years now. They had discovered it after one of their sons had done a trip with a school class. He raved about it so much, that the Bennett's traveled there and fell in love with it. Deloris knew she should not be closed minded about the entire country just because of her one experience with the incompetency of the tour company taking them to the ruins from the cruise ship. Lots of people have never even heard of Belize. I had to look it up on a map to find exactly where it was located the first time Deloris told me about it.

Let me tell you a few facts about Belize: It lies directly below the Mexican Yucatan Peninsula and borders Guatemala and Mexico on land and Honduras by sea. English has remained the official language of Belize and it has a parliamentary representative democratic monarchy form of government. Queen Elizabeth serves as head of state and is featured on the currency. There is a prime minister who is the head of the government and it is a multi-party system. The two largest parties are the Blue and Red parties. Exports from Belize consist of mainly sugar, bananas, oranges and pineapples. Most recently the chocolate in Belize is now being exported. Belize has a rich and colorful history from the Ancient Maya civilizations that resided there between 3,000 B.C. and 800 A.D. There is a large population that trace their roots back to this Maya heritage. Belize is also occupied by many other Meso-American cultures. These cultures enrich the country of Belize as well as other Central American countries. There was the declaration of Colonization by the British in 1840, after it was discovered by a ship on patrol. It was known as the Colony of British Honduras and more people seem to remember that name, than the current name of Belize. The name was officially changed to Belize in June 1973 and full independences was granted on September 21st, 1981.

Deloris thought that the September 10th was part of the Independence Day celebration but with research I learned that holiday is to celebrate the 1798 Battle of St. George's Cay. In 1638 a group of British sailors were shipwrecked on the land that was later to be known as Belize. These men were called the Bay Men and became loggers. These were rough and tough men. They were buccaneers and pirates and they had first settled on the Bay of Honduras, thus the name Bay men.

In 1719 Captain Nathaniel Uring described them in his memoirs in this way, *"The wood-cutters are generally a rude drunken crew, some of which have been pirates, and most of them sailors; their chief delight is in drinking; and when they broach a quarter cask or a hogshead of wine, they seldom stir from it while there is a drop left. Ozenbrigs is their general wear and it will be easily believed, that I had but little comfort living among this crew of ungovernable wretches, where there was little else heard but blasphemy, cursing and swearing."*

I learned that the Ozenbrigs that Captain Uring refers to is a type of fiber similar to cotton that is made into cloth. Captain Uring, on a British ship, is credited with delivering the first loads of mahogany to Europe. This started the popularity of the mahogany wood that is used in so much of the beautiful furniture worldwide.

When Spain tried to take the settlement of the Bay Men during one of the battles between England and Spain, the Spanish commander sent a huge invasion fleet to attack the tiny settlement. Despite the odds, the Bay Men prevailed. Thus, the celebration on September 10th of St. George's Cay. This holiday commemorates the first Belizeans and the defense of their country. September 21st is the day which they celebrate their independence from the British.

Deloris has often shown her dismay at the number of holidays that Belize seems to have. There are 15 official holidays. Belize knows how to celebrate a holiday. The entire country seems to close down on these days. Schools close, no public services, reduced transportation service and even news services are suspended.

The Easter holiday is actually four days and is probably the most celebrated holiday of the year. Another holiday is called "Baron Bliss Day". It is celebrated on March 9th. Baron Bliss was an eccentric

German financier who, although he never set foot on Belizean soil, left the government of Belize a large endowment. He fell in love with Belize when he anchored his yacht in a harbor off the coast of Belize. Because of his gift to Belize there is now a holiday in his name. Holidays are very important to the people of Belize. They celebrate them all. Of course, January 1st is New Year's Day and May 1st is Labor Day. There is also May 24th which is "Commonwealth Day" and this is adopted from Britain. Belize was not willing to give up this holiday when they were granted their Independence so they held on to it. They celebrate the two holidays in September and then Columbus Day on October 12th. November brings "Garifuna Settlement Day" on the 19th. The other major holidays are Christmas Day and the day after which is "Boxing Day". Boxing Day is also held over from the former "British" days.

Each time the Stamm's and Bennett's got together for dinner, the Bennett's sang the praises of Belize. Deloris took all this raving with a grain of salt and never put much stock in any of it. Alan and Deloris were not sheltered by any means or land locked to the U.S. They'd taken many cruises and been to almost all of the Caribbean spots that sported good diving. However, they were always under the control and protection of their Cruise Masters and guides. They enjoyed traveling and all the new adventures, but Belize just did not sound like a place that would appeal to them, especially to Deloris. The sound of limited availability of foods in the grocery stores, no telephone access, limited T.V. and walking being the primary way of making your way around the village, and boats being more numerous than people did not make her excited to visit this new-found love of the Bennett's.

Deloris and Amy were quite a bit different, but that did not stop them from forming a comfortable friendship. Amy would often talk about their property in Belize and Deloris would listen with amusement when told how the 'locals' acted or treated Americans. Deloris assumed that Amy often livened up the stories for the sake of being funny. But little did she know; the stories weren't as painted as she once thought. Deloris couldn't imagine the indigenous living in such a simplistic way. She found it hard to believe that their lives did not suffer if they did not even have cable T.V. to keep up with the happenings in the world. Amy told her that cable T.V. would reach most of the people in the village shortly but she was not sure if that was a good thing. Amy often explained Placencia to Deloris by telling her that it was a place where things were just simpler and better. Deloris loved the idea, but thought the reality of being in a place such as that would be much different.

When Ernie called to collect on Alan's promise to accompany them to Belize he reminded Alan that he had promise. "You said you would go to Belize if you survived the surgery and I have let you delay fulfilling your promise way too long. Don't worry, you'll love it and I suspect that Deloris will like it as well." Said Ernie.

"That is very nice, Ernie, but there's no way..." Alan trailed off as Ernie interrupted.

"Look Alan, I'd consider it a personal favor if you'd reconsider and make time to join us. We had another couple who were planning to go with us but they had to cancel this morning. I've talked to Amy and she wants to share this experience with you and Deloris. She is convinced that Deloris will love it."

Alan paused for a moment and remembered all that Ernie and Amy had done for them. He took a deep breath and accepted the offer, "We've heard so much about Belize we would love to see it with you and Amy." He knew that this statement was true for him, but he seriously doubted that his wife would share his enthusiasm. In fact, he was absolutely sure there would be a lot of resistance.

"Okay, we will get together soon and confirm all the plans. I will have Amy call Deloris with our flight information so you two can get on the same flight as we are." With that, Ernie hung up.

Alan looked up at the latest picture of the sharks that he had taken, as the tigers of the sea circled him. He only hoped he would survive convincing Deloris, that this was a good thing, as easily as he had photographed those sharks.

Deloris was sitting at her desk in her office building next door to the hospital when Alan walked in.

"I need to talk to you about something and you are not going to be pleased." Alan quickly got it out. He told her about Ernie's call and the fact that he had agreed to go.

"Why on God's green earth would you say yes? I don't think I would enjoy Belize at all!" Deloris whined.

Alan told her that Ernie had invited them to share their house and they had promised to show them around. "Where is your sense of adventure", Alan plead.

"We don't know them well enough to share a house... and I can't take time away from work and... Well, I can give you a thousand other reasons not to go if you will just give me a few minutes to think of them." snapped Deloris.

She thought she had made it quite clear that she had no desire to visit that "God Forsaken" country again. She refused to believe that someone like Amy could possibly be seduced by a foreign land, like Belize.

"Yes, but I've already confirmed." admitted Alan logically.

"Then you go and I will stay here." reasoned Deloris.

"I don't want to go without you."

"Well, I don't want to go to Belize, okay?"

Alan took a slow, deep breath and said, "Okay, I will call him back and cancel. You know I'm not going without you."

"I'm sorry Alan, it just sounds awful to me." said Deloris. She felt so badly for saying no, but she just couldn't picture herself in Belize again. She had grown to know Amy a little better now and she honestly couldn't see this educated, successful woman, with the perfect house and the perfect family and all the perfect outfits, enduring a place like they had described in this mysterious village in Belize. She had learned firsthand that all was not perfect in Belize.

Alan reluctantly called and after a few moments of waiting, got Ernie on the line.

"Hey, Alan! Couldn't wait to talk about going to Belize?" joked Ernie.

"Ernie, I know I said we would go, but I checked my calendar and I just can't make it happen."

"I thought we were all set." grumbled Ernie.

Deloris listened to the two friends on the speaker phone and knew that both men shared the same disappointment.

"Look Alan, I understand that things are different since your cancer but that is exactly why you need to go. Belize is changing fast and will soon be a different place than what you will find if you go now. I want you and Deloris to see it unchanged and raw, the way it was meant to be. You owe it to yourself to go, Alan. You beat death and you deserve to enjoy life. Belize will change your life. I promise!"

Alan laughed at his friend's unconcealed love of this foreign place and said, "Let me talk to Deloris and see if she has any suggestions of how we can pull this off and I will let you know tomorrow."

"Okay, but you really need this, Alan!" reiterated Ernie.

Alan laughed again and replied, "If you say so, Dude. I will call you tomorrow." He looked at Deloris and sighed as he pressed the speaker button to disconnect the call. She knew he felt obligated to Ernie and Amy and so did she, but she also knew that she did not like roughing it. She didn't like sand, she didn't fish, she hated boats and from what Amy had told her there wasn't a comfortable chair in Belize for anyone who weighed over a hundred pounds, so she would not even have a comfortable place to read. Nonetheless, she listened to Alan's arguments for going and finally agreed to go. However, she stipulated that they would only go for one week. The Bennett's were planning to stay for two weeks and would like them to do the same. Yet, Deloris was to win the battle to stay only a week.

The predestined day in June 2006 finally arrived and the four of them flew into Belize City's, Samuel Goldman Airport. The airport was smaller than one would see as a Municipal airport in the U.S., but is Belize's only International Airport. They were met by a large black man with an infectious smile. He 'bear hugged' both Amy and Ernie. They quickly introduced him to Deloris and Alan as Phil. Phil lives with his wife and two children in the village of Burrell Boom, on the Belize River about twenty miles from Belize City. He was a very energetic and happy person. He escorted them through the Belizean customs and immigration lines with little hassle. As they walked out of the Airport the heat and humidity of tropical Belize hit them. Phil expertly stowed the luggage into the bed of a four-seater Nissan pick-up truck that had been delivered to the airport for the Bennett's. Ernie explained that he had recently purchased the vehicle here in Belize so that he would have a way to get around and not depend on the sorts of general transportation that we'll soon come to know as "iffy" at best. Previously they simply flew from Belize City to Placencia on one of the small regional airlines. It was about a forty-minute flight. Phil produced several black garbage bags and quickly secured the luggage into the bags. Deloris and Alan looked questioningly at Amy. She explained that it was the beginning of the rainy season and there was the possibility of encountering showers; especially as they traveled through the mountains, so it was just a precaution. Amy and Ernie both exchanged inquiries with Phil about his family and he, in turn, asked about theirs. Ernie removed a small package from his carry-on bag and gave it to Phil. "Here is something I thought you would enjoy, Phil." Ernie said excitedly as he handed the package to the man.

The man's face lit up and he thanked them extensively. Ernie explained that they had met Phil on one of their early trips to Belize. Phil has been an employee of the airport, handling the baggage of the visitors when they arrive. He assists arriving passengers with their luggage, to either a connecting flight on one the only two airlines in Belize, or their ground transportation. The two airlines fly to many points in Belize, but there are many areas of Belize that driving is a must. Strangely enough there was no flight from Belize City to the country's capital, Belmopan. It is fifty-two miles between the Belize City International airport and Belmopan. Ernie explained that when they had met Phil, they had been too late to catch a flight to Placencia and Phil had befriended them, helping them find a hotel and a reliable cab driver to take them to the hotel. He had also arranged for the cab driver to retrieve them from their hotel and bring them back to the airport the following morning.

Since becoming so close to Phil, he had taken on the duty of making sure that the Nissan truck was delivered to the airport when the Bennett's arrived. It was stored at the dealership between trips. Phil would get a call or email from them and he'd check to see that the insurance sticker was up to date and that the gas tank had been filled before he delivered it to the airport for them. Ernie went on to explain that Phil was the type of guy who knew the ropes and could assist with any problem that you encountered once you arrived in the Belize City. This type of relationship is common between expats and Belizeans. For this type of service, the expats always remember to bring gifts and to tip handsomely. Yet, the service from Phil is done as much out of friendship, as it is for the money. Very often Belizeans end up traveling to the homes of the expats in the U.S., to visit the states. Belizeans have learned that most foreigners will reward well for these types of personal services, so it benefits all the parties involved.

With everything secure in the bed of the truck and a quick goodbye to Phil, they were off to the famed village of Placencia. As they left the airport, Alan asked Ernie what he had brought Phil. Ernie explained that Phil had visited them in Placencia on their last trip and stayed with them for a few days. Phil admired one of the flies used for fly-fishing that Ernie used regularly. But because it was also Ernie's favorite, he had not been able to give it to Phil at the time they last spoke in person. Nonetheless, he remembered how much Phil had admired that fly so he had brought him one on this trip.

Determining the distances between towns in Belize is confusing. On a map, I could tell that the distance as "the crow flies", is only 60 or 70 miles between Belize City and Placencia. However, I was told that the road trip was a 160-mile journey that took up to 4 hours. The answer to the discrepancy is that there are so few paved roads it is impossible to take a direct route. To get from Belize City International airport to Placencia you must take the Western Highway and that means going through Belmopan. You end up going about fifty miles due west away from the coast and Belize

City when your destination is due south of Belize City. The total paved road system in Belize consist of the Northern Highway, the Western Highway, the Hummingbird Highway and the Southern Highway. There is a dirt road that runs north and south connecting the Western Highway to the Hummingbird Highway which would shorten the trip between Placencia and Belize City considerably, because it would eliminate that fifty-mile western drive. This is known as, the Coastal Highway or the Manatee Highway, however; it washes out in heavy rain, is deserted and is not considered safe by most travelers and certainly not a comfortable ride due to the condition of the road.

The four traveled the fairly well paved Western Highway out of Belize City. The Western Highway runs from Belize City all the way to the western border of Belize. It runs through the twin towns of San Ignacio and Santa Elena in the far west of Belize before ending at the Guatemalan border. After traveling about 15 miles on the Western Highway, they abruptly pulled off the main road into a dirt driveway that lead passed several small one room thatch-roofed buildings, ending in a small parking lot. Only a small sign located, not on the road, but near the larger open-air thatch roofed building, designating that as a restaurant serving lunch. Deloris breathed a sigh of relief. Ever since they had left the airport, Deloris had been looking for a place that they might eat. She was getting hungry and knew that Alan was too. However, all the places she had spotted that advertised food, were not enticing. They either did not look clean, had trash scattered around the entrances, unkempt exteriors, or they looked dark and menacing. What she had seen of Belize City on this trip so far had not changed her first impression of Belize City. It was still as scary as she had remembered. She just hoped that this mysterious village of Placencia would change her impression of Belize. The restaurant was an open-air design with an aged thatched roof of weaved palm leaves which rested on hand carved beams and poles that were tied together with ropes. It was quaint and surprisingly cool for not having air conditioning. The foursome made their way to a wooden table with heavy wooden chairs near the counter. Their table was in the center of the restaurant and Deloris and Alan both had swivel heads as they'd never experience this type of place without a professional guide in tow. A large black woman approached the table, and greeted both Ernie and Amy and was introduced as Marta. She had worked for the restaurant for many years and obviously enjoyed her the work. She asks, "You want some'tin to drink?" as she handed out the four menus. Amy and Ernie ordered water and red Fanta and so Deloris and Alan followed suit. Deloris opened her menu and saw a handwritten list with these items as the offerings.

Lunch Specials

Stew Chicken with rice and beans $ 8.00
Gibnut with stew beans and rice $10.00
Stew Pork with rice and beans $10.00
Cow Foot Soup $7.00
White rice, stew beans and pigtail $ 8.00

As Marta went to get their drinks, they all looked at the single sheet of paper menus. Deloris asks quietly "So what are you guys having?"

Amy chimed in "I think I will have the chicken, but I want the green sauce on the side like we had last time, Ernie."

"Yes, that was good!" he agreed.

"Okay I will have the same Deloris said, with some reluctance. Amy looked at Deloris and with a straight face and asked, "Deloris do you want rice and beans or beans and rice with your chicken?"

"I know there is a joke here somewhere, but this is my first time, so you are going to have to explain that one to me." laughed Deloris.

"Well, said Amy, it is important for you to learn that rice and beans is a dish consisting mostly of rice with a few beans mixed in with it and you will probably consider it dry for your taste. However, if you ask for stew beans and rice you will be served a bowl of rice and a bowl of stewed beans which are quite good."

"Okay, that is valuable information." Deloris said with a smile. "Well neither of them sound very good to me." complained Alan, who's not a bean eater.

As Marta returned to the table with the drinks, Amy ask, "Marta? Do you have fries today? My friend doesn't like beans"

The large black waitress, with obvious distaste for someone who did not like beans, said happily to Amy, "For you, miz Amy, I sure de cook will make a 'ception if him really need fries instead of dem beans." Marta, then scratched on her pad as she read out, "Tre Stew Chick'n wit beans and rice and 1 Stew Chick'n with fries. Green Sauce too."

When Ernie nodded his head in agreement she moved toward the kitchen at a leisurely pace. Amy touched Deloris's arm and whispered, "It is called Stew Chicken but it has lots of flavor and is quite good, I think you will enjoy it."

Alan asked, "What is Gibnut?" Ernie and Amy started laughing and Ernie said, "We were hoping that you wouldn't ask about that until we got you to taste it. I guess it to too late now. It is the "Royal Rat" and yes, it is a large rodent. It grows up to 25 pounds. It got the nickname when it was served to Queen Elizabeth on one of her visits to Belize." "I guess then I don't have to ask what Cow Foot soup is, do I", said Deloris. Amy said, "Not that you will need it Deloris, but Alan you need to know that Cow Foot soup is touted to be the best Goma cure there is and by the way, Goma, is hangover in Kroil. (Creole). Kroil is a version of shortened English that Belizeans commonly speak.

Deloris realized that she would spend this week learning a new culture and was certain that she wouldn't fit in. At least the chicken did have wonderful flavor. Deloris immediately thought that if she had been serving this chicken, she would have thought of some much more exotic name for it. 'Stew Chicken' did not do justice to the wonderful flavor that it had; much like one would imagine a slow roasted chicken with a wonderful rich gravy. The spicing and seasonings that had been used were unfamiliar to her but ones that she liked and by the way Alan was eating, she could tell he agreed. She had not realized how hungry she was. The Fanta was a sweet soft drink and they come in many flavors. When they were all finished their lunch, Ernie told everyone that they should use the restrooms because there would not be another for quite a while. The restroom was a small dimly lit room with basic faculties, no amenities, and marginally clean.

Deloris ask Amy, "Just how far is it to another restroom?"

Amy thought for a moment and then said, "Well for someone like you, we could stop in Belmopan, but after leaving Belmopan it will be about 56 miles to the next restroom."

Deloris ask, "Why did you say for someone like me?"

Amy laughed and said, "Well for the guys and some of us girls who travel a lot on Belizean roads the next restroom is the next tree or thick patch of brush." The cultured 'Southern Belle' that Deloris knew from the states had disappeared before her very eyes. This was an Amy she had not seen before. As the four met back at the table, Ernie glanced at the bill on the table and took out a $20.00 and a $10.00 U.S. and placed them on the table. Alan proceeded to do the same. Ernie touched his hand and said, "That is way too much! The bill was only $24.00."

"I thought it was $48.00." said Alan as he looked again at the ticket.

"Yeah, that was $48.00 Belize and that makes it $24.00 U.S. The Belize dollar is one half of the U.S. dollar or two for one. Just divide all the prices in half." Ernie explained.

"Okay that seems easy enough" said Alan and smiled.

The four of them climbed back into the truck and Ernie wasted no time as he made his way toward Belmopan. Although the road was relatively straight and there was not a lot of traffic, the speed which Ernie was driving surprised even Alan. It was apparent that Ernie did not fear getting a speeding ticket as he would have done it the states. Alan knew that Deloris would be watching the road instead of enjoying the scenery, so he asks, "Hey dude, are we in a hurry?"

"Yes, I'm trying to make up some time so we can stop at the market in Belmopan." Ernie said as he sped around a school bus loaded with people. Deloris realized she hadn't been looking at the scenery because she had been staring at the road. She really didn't think Ernie would drive this speed if he had been in the states. The land here was flat but off in the distance you could see the large rocks and a few of the low-lying mountains. The trees seemed greener, the grass seemed thicker and the sky seemed even bluer than in Jacksonville. The land here seems to be a little more elevated. Deloris had noticed that there seemed to be a lot of standing water on the sides of the road as they had travel out and away from Belize City. Amy explained that was because Belize City is at sea level, but

Belmopan is about 249 feet above sea level. That is the main reason that Belmopan is now the capital, instead of it still being in Belize City. They soon arrive at the market in Belmopan and parked along the side of the road and removed the luggage from the rear, put it into the back seat and then locked the truck. Deloris noted that Amy and Ernie seemed so comfortable doing these small things. In the states, Ernie would have installed a cover on his Pickup or driven an SUV that had luggage storage inside. He would have never inconvenienced himself like this in the states, but seemed happy to do so in Belize. It was like he had returned to a previous point in his life when he did not have the money for all the luxuries and he seemed happy to do so. Just because you had money here in Belize, apparently it did not mean that everything was available. Ernie did not seem to mind forgoing these little inconveniences for the chance to live in Belize. Ernie was more like the carefree young man that he had prided himself for outgrowing. Making silly choices and not worrying about the consequences, at the moment seem to be his way of life while he was in Belize.

The market in Belmopan consisted of approximately fifty vendors, set up much like a farmer's market in the U.S. The vendors were housed under permanent roof structures. Some vendors were there daily while others only came in one or two days a week. Vendors apparently were located in the same spots consistently, as Amy seemed to know exactly where to go to get what they needed. Displayed were items from eggs to pineapples and bacon to coconuts. Here Deloris learned about many fruits that grow in Belize, many that she had never tasted. Fruits such as egg fruit, bread fruit, cocoa, and the golden plum. Deloris noticed that the vendor sat talking and visiting with one another when there were not active buyers at their stalls. It was lively and happy and all the people seemed to be carefree. Deloris, always the practical one, realized that many of these people must have traveled long distances to sell their products and a lot of work was required to display the produce items and keep it as fresh as possible. Most of these were perishable items so they needed to be sold or they would spoil. As Amy picked up a cardboard 'flat' that contained eggs, Deloris immediately noticed that they were not refrigerated. She decided to hold her comments until later when she could ask Amy about the dangers of purchasing unrefrigerated eggs. Amy purchased a bunch of bananas and as they walked away, she peeled one of the bananas and handed Deloris half. It was unlike any banana that Deloris had ever tasted. Its flavor was much more intense. This was what a banana should taste like. They gathered up several other items. Deloris loved fresh fruit and was amazed and intrigued with the variety. Deloris saw a fruit that resembled a Passion Fruit and asked about it.

"It is a Mamey fruit and they are very good! I think they taste like a candied yam." answered Amy. She asks the vendor to help her chose two that would be ripe and ready to eat by tomorrow. Amy explained that she had trouble telling which were ready to eat and that choosing it at just the right time was important because once ripe they spoil quickly, but if not quite ripe, they were dry and the unique sweetest was lost. It was about 8 inches in diameter and had a rough brown skin. Amy told her that it had a single seed in the middle and that the flesh was a bright orange. Deloris was like a kid in a candy store as she looked at all the new things that were being introduced to her. As familiar as a farmer's market was to her in the states, this was so different. Just before they left Amy purchased a bunch of small bananas and when Deloris ask her about them, Amy just winked and told her to wait. These were part of breakfast tomorrow.

The four repeated their routine of moving the luggage, then Alan and Ernie got into the front seats as Deloris and Amy climbed into the rear seats. As they drove out of Belmopan, they came to a round-about and took a left. Ernie said," Now for the mountain portion of our trip."

Now the four were on the Hummingbird Highway, which runs from Belmopan to the town of Dangriga on the coast.

Alan remarked, "I haven't seen a red light since we left Belize City and I only saw a couple of them there. I haven't quite gotten the hang of the idea of a roundabout. Do they have a lot of them here?"

Ernie said, "Remember this was a British colony for many years and the British influence remains. However, they do have the good sense to drive on the right side of road." A short distance after the roundabout they found that smooth pavement gave way to a lot more potholes and the road had narrowed. There was low mountain scenery on either side. Some of the potholes were quite sizeable. Their backside protested the lack of shocks in the truck. Alan ask Ernie, "How often do you have to replace shocks on this thing?"

Ernie laughed, "Why replace the shocks, they would only need to be replaced again in three months."

Alan stared at Ernie in disbelief. This was the man who had his car serviced before it was needed, who would not have entered a vehicle without proper shocks and always checked his tires before he got into his vehicles in the states. "What about tires?" asked Alan, since he had not looked at the tires before they left and could not imagine where you would pull off the road to change a tire on this road that had no shoulders and no guardrails even in the steepest areas.

"Oh, don't worry, I am still a fanatic about tires. I have the dealership check them routinely while it is stored there and they let me know if there is any problem with them. I don't want to change a tire on this road." Proclaimed Ernie.

There were no road lighting signs, nor reflectors for safety. Nonetheless, Deloris tried to relax and enjoy the scenery, since she loved mountains, waterfalls and caves. Deloris spotted a sign that said Ian Anderson's Cave Branch and a small road on the left leading away from the highway. "What is that?" Deloris asked.

"Oh, that is an adventure resort. It is very nice! We go and do cave tubing there fairly often. In fact, I know you love waterfalls and the resort advertises six of them." said Amy. Deloris realized that this was a place she would really like to visit, but she realized that only staying a week there would not be time to do that.

"Have you seen the waterfalls?" ask Deloris excitedly.

"No." said Amy. Her reason for never having tried that tour, was that the guide books said that to get to their destination, some rock climbing and a dive into a mountain pool was required and not easily negotiated. "That sounds too difficult for me." she laughed.

Deloris continued to look at the area that hid those elusive waterfalls and imagined the years of history and the amount of water that must have moved past each rock over the years. They continued along the Hummingbird Highway and Deloris took in the mountains and greenery and wondered what it would be like to wander those mountains in search of hidden wonders. Just as Deloris's body was relaxing, she spotted what appeared to be a one lane bridge, coming up fast. Ernie did not appear to be slowing. Deloris's fingernails dug into the upholstery of the back seat as Ernie raced to cross the bridge. She opened her eyes and clinched the seat in front of her. Alan felt her grip moving the seat. He glanced back at her, knowing full well that Deloris was filled with panic. He had to admit that he wished Ernie would slow down on these mountain roads. As they flew across the bridge they found a car waiting to enter the bridge. Alan ask, "How did you know that car would wait for you to cross the bridge before entering?"

"Oh, it is the rules of the road here. You each judge who will enter the bridge first and then the other waits until you have cleared before they start." Answered Amy.

"Well, where did you learn this little piece of information." asked Alan with a laugh.

"From trial and error." chuckled Ernie as he glanced at Amy with a secret smile.

"Yeah, if you stop when you should have proceeded, you will be there a while. If you are stopped, each car coming up from the other side will enter the bridge ahead of you and then you have to wait until all the traffic has cleared." Agreed Amy.

"Why are we in such a hurry?" asked Deloris softly.

"We'll need to get through these 56 miles of mountains and down the peninsular road before it gets dark." Ernie said, as he maneuvered the small truck along the narrow mountain road. As the sky began to open up, Alan and Deloris realized they were exiting the mountains. Ernie turned south and Amy explained that they were now on the Southern Highway which runs from just west of Dangriga all the way to the border of Guatemala. She went on to explain that Dangriga is the county seat of the Stann Creek District in which Placencia is located. To pay taxes or do things such as renewing car tags or license, a trip from Placencia to Dangriga is necessary. Dangriga is located on the coast and is about 7 miles east of the Southern Highway.

Now that they were on the Southern Highway, they had traveled all the paved roads in Belize except for the Northern Highway which lead north out of Belize City to Mexico.

As they traveled for about an hour along this road, they passed through a village called Silk Grass. From the road, they could only see a couple of open air structures that appeared to be places that food was served. Amy told them that the village itself was located closer to the ocean on their left and that it was a very small village with only a few residents so basically no factors that would draw visitors to it. They saw the Maya Center with the entrance to the Cockscomb Basin Wildlife Sanctuary on their left. Amy pointed out that one of the places that processes chocolate is located here and that they should try to make time to visit because watching chocolate bars being made from start to finish was fascinating. Amy explained that Cockscomb is also known as the premier site for Jaguar preservation in the world. She told Deloris that there was a beautiful waterfall located within the Sanctuary. "I think that one is much more accessible." Amy exclaimed.

Deloris made a mental note that she wanted to visit that one as well. She certainly would love to see the process of making the chocolate bars as well. As they continued along, Amy explained that there was also a Waterfall in the Cayo area of Belize that was called the '1000-foot falls'."

"Where is Cayo?" asked Deloris?

"When we were at the market in Belmopan, we headed east, back toward the coast, if we had been going to Cayo we would have continued west on the Western Highway. It runs all the way to the Guatemalan border and passes through the twin villages of San Ignacio and Santa Helena. They are connected by this incredible bridge and by incredible I don't mean that it is an engineering marvel, I mean it is incredible that I have the nerve to drive or even ride across it." laughed Amy, "When you come back we will have to plan a trip there and we will stop at the Mennonite village of Spanish Lookout on the way. You will love it as well." she continued.

"When we come back?" laughingly asked Deloris, "We aren't even there and you are planning when we come back?"

"Of course!" stated Amy, "Everyone comes back to Placencia." she said smiling.

Deloris wondered why Amy seemed certain that they would want to come back. Alan asked Ernie, "Hey, what is this bridge that Amy is talking about? What makes it incredible?"

"Oh, it is a suspension bridge and I think it was built in like 1949 or so and it does not look like a structure you would be willing drive over in the states. That is what makes Belize so wonderful. You will do things here that you would never do in the states and it liberates you."

After a pause, Alan said, "I have heard the same thing about drugs. Are you telling me that Belize is like a drug?" "Well, I haven't heard many better descriptions" said Ernie with a raised eyebrow.

The four rode along in companionable silence, each thinking their own thoughts. To the right were the green mountains. The sunlight made them look green and richly textured. They are relatively low mountains, with the highest peak being Victoria Peak at 3688 feet. It is located in the Cockscomb Basin Wildlife Sanctuary. These mountains are unexplored to a great degree and the 'rule follower and planner' that Deloris is, found that fact ignited the spirit of adventure that lurked deep inside of her. Soon they turned left onto a dirt road made of red clay. It ran the length of the peninsula that led to Placencia. This 23-mile-long deeply rutted, pothole filled road was very rough and no matter how hard he tried, Ernie could not miss all the holes and ruts, so going was very slow. "There are plans to pave this road one day, but who knows." He explained.

The road was quite like a washboard. It was bad during the rainy season since the ruts became deeper with each rain and during dry season the ruts and potholes because cemented and dust became another problem. It took an hour and a half to drive the 23 miles to the village of Placencia. They felt as if they'd been in a washing machine. During the drive, they talked about the development that was taking place on the peninsular. The different styles of single family homes that were under construction along the way, gave rise to the independent nature of many people who come to make their new homes in Belize. It was apparent that many had plans to include this peninsular in their future. Observing these things helped ease the pain that the shockless truck inflicted on their spleens. That was in 2005 and by 2012 the road was paved. The paving of the road was met with great excitement... It was a long time coming. It had been promised for many, many years before it finally happened. It made Placencia much more accessible to the rest of Belize. Amy pointed out that many of the homes they had seen along the way did not have a common supply of water and it was necessary that they collect rainwater to use. When Deloris heard about collecting rain water to be used, her heart sank, she thought, "Do they mean we are actually going to be drinking rain water?" but did not say out loud. This trip was important to Alan and his happiness was important enough for her to suffer in any way she must, she then asked. "What about electricity?"

"Well the village has a supply, it is somewhat spotty occasionally. Belize gets most of their electricity from Mexico", replied Ernie.

Soon they were passing a part of the peninsula that was very narrow and you could see the ocean on one side and a lagoon on the other. There was a lot of 'For Sale' and 'Sold' signs on lots along the road. Real estate was going quickly and was still sometimes even bargain priced in this tropical place.

Ernie commented that this area was growing fast in large part because so many ex-pats were coming to build homes and live in this area. Deloris was struck by how much this area reminded her of the Florida Keys. Water could be seen on both sides of the road because here the peninsula is very narrow. Much of the vegetation is low growing grass and mangroves. Building lots were at a premium in the areas where the ocean and lagoon were only separated by a couple hundred feet. In these areas, the mountains could also be viewed off to the right and offered a beautiful backdrop. It seemed that the peninsula was even narrower than in the Florida Keys. In many of the places it was apparent that the mangroves had been removed to utilize most of the building lots. She knew that, as it was in Florida, this must be a matter of contention. Since the road reminded her of the Florida Keys, she could only hope that the journey to the end of the peninsula would lead them to a village that was more like Key West than the one she was imagining from the descriptions she had heard.

After just a couple of miles they passed an area that Ernie had called Maya Beach. This was certainly one of the areas that offered that spectacular view of ocean, lagoon and mountains. Soon they arrived at another small village that had a much different feel. Here the peninsula was wider and you could not see the ocean from the road. The area he had called Maya Beach, sported houses and good landscaping, nonetheless you saw very few people out and around. Here in this village, there were small groups of black natives standing along the side of the road. Children played alongside the road and often ventured into the road. Driving with care was a must in this area. Many of the people that they saw had dreadlocks and the men wore only shorts with no shirts nor shoes. Many were drinking beer and congregated in small groups, many of the groups were directly beside the road. Amy explained, this was Seine Bight and it was a Garifuna community.

The Garinagu are mix-raced descendants of West African, Central African, Island Carib, European and Arawak people. "Deloris, if we get a chance I want to bring you back to see Lola's Art." explained Amy. "Who is Lola?" asked Deloris.

"Oh, a very interesting lady who paints in a very distinctive style. You will see her work all over Placencia, especially at the Art and Soul Gallery on the sidewalk in Placencia. You may or may not like her style, however lots of people love the style and while her work is not inexpensive, many people buy it to take back home. Lots of people really love it. We will definitely try to get back so you can see her studio here and maybe meet her." continued Amy. Deloris realized that Amy was pointing out things that she really wanted to do; Deloris was beginning to wonder if insisting that they only stay one week, was as wise as it had seemed at the time they were planning the trip. She did know that the waterfalls, caves and now the local art were things she would enjoy exploring in this new and foreign land.

Ernie chimed in and said, "Alan, when you hear the "Punta Rock" that is so prevalent in Belize, remember that it is based on the Garifuna culture. My guess is that you and Deloris will say it is too loud, but it is big here in Belize and you will hear a lot of it while you are here. Another interesting thing about this place is that they said that pirates always find the best hideouts and they are the ones that found this area. The beaches here are breathtakingly beautiful! It is close to Placencia, but also a world away."

Soon they approached what Amy identified as the Placencia airstrip. The road paralleled the airstrip and made a hair-pin turn and parallel the other side of the airstrip. Ernie explained that you needed to watch for planes landing or taking off and if you saw one, you needed to stop. The airstrip was very short and the takeoff and touchdown had to occur in a short span since both ends of the airstrip were bordered by water. The planes could not have much altitude as they left or returned to the airstrip and proceeded out over the water, and sometimes at the end of the runway they were not high enough to clear the top of a vehicle where the airstrip ended and the road began. Both Alan and Deloris looked at Ernie to see if he was joking with them and since he didn't smile, they quickly realized that he was not.

"There is not even a sign that tells you that." stated the cautious Deloris.

"I know, and I have pointed that out to the airstrip employees several times. Maybe someday they will get around to it." laughed Ernie as he peered into the rear-view at Deloris with a smile.

Ernie and Amy's lifestyle in the states was elegant. They lived in an immaculately kept home where everything was perfect, but as they started through the village of Placencia, Deloris realized that the village Ernie and Amy now loved so much, was filled with disorder and a lack of modern amenities and a multitude of potholes in the road. They made their way through people walking, bicycles, and the occasional motorcycle or car. The houses were unpainted structures that were raised off the ground and did not look like they could endure a strong wind. There was trash and clutter all around the street. Naturally Deloris's first impression was, "What have I gotten myself into?" but she kept it to herself.

When they arrived at Ernie and Amy's house they were shown around. The construction was stucco on a two-story house. It was nicer than most of the village's dwellings, but nothing the Bennett's would have deemed livable in the states. The structure had a two-bedroom apartment on each level and therefore would accommodate four couples if necessary. There was one bathroom on each floor and Amy had explained that this house did not have hot water when they purchased it, but they now had hot water available. Many Belizeans do not even use hot water to bathe, it is considered a luxury to have hot water in Belize. The kitchen in the downstairs unit that the Bennett's used as their own, had no superfluous amenities. However, Deloris did spot a beautifully carved turtle fruit bowl on the simple, tiled kitchen counter. She immediately picked it up and asked Amy where she had gotten it. Amy explained that there was a store that displayed local artist work and she had purchased it there.

There will come a day in their Journey to Paradise that Deloris gets a turtle fruit bowl for herself, but it will be acquired in a typically unorthodox Belizean way. Deloris and Alan will soon adopt the phase "There is always a story". You will discover that very few things are accomplished in what you have come to believe is the typical way. Belize causes the routine to become either funny or frustrating depending on your attitude.

Amy took Deloris around and pointed out a few other items that were displayed on the walls of the home. While it in no way rivaled Amy's U.S. home, Deloris saw that Amy's eloquent taste in selecting items for display had not been lost in her journey to this strange place. To describe the house and decorations as a simple design would have been an understatement. Amy and Ernie took Alan and Deloris outside to look at the property. When walking out of the house there was a clear view of the mountains in the distance and the sunset would clearly be visible from the front porch. Amy had again picked a place with a potential to be something great if she chose to live a lifestyle closer to what she had in the U.S., Deloris's mind immediately went to the type of house she would build in this location. The possibilities were endless with this view. They then wandered to the back of the property and found it to be no less magnificent, with views through the openings of the thick mangrove and the ocean stretching out endlessly in front of them. Deloris noted that they had left most of the mangrove growth intact and knew that they understood the importance of mangroves since they too were from Florida. This must be the very best of Placencia's views, Deloris decided.

Ernie said, "Well we had better get going if we are going to eat at the Purple Space Monkey. Around here you never know how late something is going to remain open, since it is the beginning of the slow season. Grab a flashlight and a can of bug spray and we will walk. It is not far." Deloris soon learned the value of that can of bug spray. At first light and in the evening before dark, Belize, as most tropical areas do, have their share of mosquitos and sandflies, which are more commonly known as "no-see-ums". While, being from Florida prepared her for the mosquitos, she found the tiny little "no-see-ums, that left little red spots anywhere they bit, to be more annoying. Just putting on a preventative spray, seems to be the only way to defeat the irritation of being bitten at these times of the day.

While Deloris loved to walk, she had never seen Ernie walk anywhere. He always used valet parking when they went to dinner and she knew that he would drive around in a parking lot to find a spot close to a store rather than walk a hundred yards. Alan and Ernie walked ahead with Ernie pointing out where different people lived and where people fished along the way. Deloris and Amy followed while Amy pointed out different plants, flowers and views. Deloris ask Amy, "Ernie said this was the beginning of slow season. I would think that the beginning of summer would he high season." Amy explained that for some unexplainable reason that tourist choose not to come to Belize as much during the summer months. Perhaps because during these months the U.S. and Canada had their best weather or because people chose to stay home for the fear of hurricanes, resulted in this being slow season for the entire country. Anyway, the high season was from November to the end of June and then July, August, September and October were very slow in all of Belize, but especially here in Placencia.

They had walked about half a mile with several turns, one around the local soccer field, when they arrived at an open air, thatched roof restaurant named the Purple Space Monkey.

It was obvious that Ernie and Amy were regular guest, they were greeted with hugs from the owners as well as many of the customers. It was almost as if a family member had returned from a long trip. Alan and Deloris were introduced to a group of locals, several other Americans and quite a few Canadians. This place was popular and as much as it was akin to some bars and grills in the U.S. it was so different as well. There was no cookie cutter furniture designed for easy moving and cleaning, no institutional napkin holder, no mass-produced menu. It appeared that all the things used for furniture were designed and made by an individual. Amy told Deloris and Alan that this was the only place in the village with an Expresso Machine and it had a big draw in the mornings for many ex-pats and other coffee lovers. The furniture was all heavy and bulky in design. Deloris suspected that the furniture she had seen in the two restaurants they had visited was locally made just for them. It had no similarity to mass produced commercial furniture. The wood was beautiful but the design was very heavy. The decorations were cheap and almost seemed to be made to look simple. Beautiful is an understatement, but Deloris was one who could design in her head and her mind was racing. This menu offered more dishes than the first, each of them chose a different dish. Amy chose a dish called Fish Placencia and Deloris followed with a Chicken Placencia while the guys each chose a fried entrée of fish for Ernie and Chicken for Alan. The chicken and fish had been advertised as Fry Chicken and Fry Fish, so Deloris realized that this strange Kroil language must consistently use fry instead of fried as they used stew chicken instead of stewed chicken. Deloris decided that food tasted better in Belize. Exhausted, they returned home shortly after finishing their dinner and were ready for bed as soon as they were back to the house. They climbed into a bed that had a simple wooden frame and a mattress. "No box springs? We'll be sore in the morning," Alan said, but were soon fast asleep.

When the two awakened in the morning, they were surprisingly well rested and didn't feel sore at all. The place was strangely gaining favor with the skeptics. They made their way to the kitchen where Amy was making coffee that she's packed in her luggage. The hosting couple were cooking eggs and bacon. Deloris remembered the unrefrigerated eggs and asked Amy, if it was safe to eat unrefrigerated eggs.

Amy answered, "Well, when I first came to Belize I was as horrified as I assume you were, but I was told that as long as they are not refrigerated that they will have a reasonable life span. But, once you refrigerate them you have to keep them refrigerated. I accepted the Belizean theory and have constantly eaten the eggs here with no problem."

Amy pulled out the small bananas and the Mamey Fruit from the day before and sliced them, putting a piece on each plate. There was also toast being buttered and it all smelled so wonderful. The toast was served with a locally made jelly and there was a bottle of hot sauce on the table from the same producer. Deloris realized that she had seen this hot sauce on both restaurant tables that she had visited since arriving in Belize. When she asked Amy about it, she was told that the hot sauce and the jellies were made by a local woman and that it was possible to visit the place that these sauces and jellies were made. Another thing she would enjoy doing, but for now, she only wanted to enjoy this wonderful smelling breakfast and taste the curious looking Mamey and the little banana. She first tried the banana and was amazed; it tasted like an apple. She looked at Amy in amazement and told Alan that he had to try the banana. He agreed that the banana did indeed have the flavor of an apple but the consistency of a banana. When she tasted the Mamey fruit, she loved the taste. "This is wonderful!" she exclaimed. "It tastes like some of my favorite foods, pumpkin pie and candied yams combined."

"Glad you like it." answered Amy with a crooked smile.

"Belize has just been elevated one more notch in my book." Deloris proclaimed as she continued eating the strange fruits. When the dishes were washed and put away, Ernie took them out to look at the property at the very end of the peninsula. This was part of the property he had purchased with the house. While the house's location was good, this location was great. The view they were now exposed to was absolutely a breathtaking scene of the bluest water all the way to the mountains in the backdrop. The land mass itself was no more than 300 feet wide. Ernie told Alan and Deloris that they were developing condos on this property. The land was right on the water and at the very end of Placencia, a perfect location in this paradoxical village of Placencia.

Directly across the lagoon from where they were standing there was a point of land on which there was a small group of thatched huts. The lagoon was about 300 feet across and the buildings sat on land between the lagoon and the open ocean. About seven miles beyond them toward the mountains was the mainland. From that point of land across the lagoon there was a view of the mountains and the peninsula and the open ocean. "What a magnificent location, that is as well". The only drawback that Deloris could see was that the property appeared to be accessible only by boat. "That is Soul Shine" Amy answered the unasked question.

"It is beautiful and looks so serene." Deloris said.

"Yes, it caters mostly to honeymooners. They do have a restaurant there so we'll go there for dinner tonight, if you'd like.

Deloris confirmed that the only way to get to that point of land, was by boat. Amy explained that you summoned the boatman by ringing the bell and that usually someone was listening and would ferry you over in their small boat.

Even though, she did not like boats, Deloris said she would love to have dinner there this evening. If she was going to have to get into a boat, it might as well be a short ride across the lagoon as her first boat ride in Belize.

"Okay come on, we'll need to go over and let them know that we want to eat there tonight." said Amy.

Deloris ask if they needed to go now and why they would need to inform a restaurant that they were planning on coming there to eat. "Is it by reservation only", Deloris ask.

Amy smiled and said, "The season has already slowed to the point that they will only cook if someone request them to do so or if they have guest in the resort. Since we don't know if there are any guests staying there now, we had better be sure that there will be a cook there tonight. It'll be fine, we simply need to let them know." A slower and more relaxed way of life, even for business owners, here in Belize appeared to be the norm, Deloris decided. After telling Alan and Ernie of the plan, Amy and Deloris walked over to ring the bell to summon the ferry and the two guys walked back up the peninsula road toward the village. A large man, with very dark skin, an ample belly, and a bright welcoming smile, jumped into the small boat and rowed across to pick up the women.

"He has to row?" asked Deloris rhetorically as she eyed the small boat that already seemed to be filled with the large black man. They climbed into the boat and the boatman expertly rowed back across the lagoon and tied up in front of the only large building on this beautiful point of land. The building was beautiful in its simplicity. It had a thatched roof and was made of rough sawn mahogany logs. Amy introduced the boatman as Larry as he helped them out of the boat and onto the dock. A sturdy looking woman with "creamed coffee" colored skin and braids covering her head, stood at the door as the girls covered the few steps to what was obviously the main building. The woman had jet black hair, wore a calf length dress with yellow and purple flowers on it. She placed her hand up to her forehead as to block a bit of the sun and wipe the constant sweat away from her brow. "Can I help with sumtin?" she said with a thick sing-song accent. "We would like to eat here tonight. If you have a cook available." Said Amy.

She told them they would be happy to have them and inquired as to how many would be in their party.

"Dat be good, Miss. What ya want for dinner? We don't got nobody else comin."

Amy looked at Deloris and asked, "any request?"

"How about Eggplant Parmesan?" answered Deloris with a question.

Amy turned and ask, "Can you make Eggplant Parmesan for two of us, and then you can make a pork dish for our husbands."

"Dat be fine if I had an eggplant, but I got none."

Being familiar with the problem of obtaining the ingredients you need to make any meal, Amy quickly suggested that they would go to the market and see if they could find an eggplant. The woman who introduced herself as Tiffany agreed that would be fine. The closest produce stand was on the main road, so after having the boatman return them to the business side of the canal, Amy said, "We can walk or take the bikes."

Deloris looked at the potholed road and said, "I think I would be better off walking."

Amy agreed and off they went. As they walked along Deloris said, "I have not seen any golf carts here."

"I know." said Amy, "I am sure they will start coming any day now. The other beach tourist area, San Pedro at Ambergris Cay is full of them." They soon reached the market which was located just on the other side of the soccer field on the main road that ran through town. Immediately they spotted two perfectly shaped Purple eggplants. Deloris picked up one but there was a soft wet spot was on the other side. It had ruined from sitting too long. Not surprising with this heat and bright sun. She was hopeful as she lifted the other, but it too was rotten. They tried another produce seller a little further up the main road, but they had no eggplants at all. They decided that they'd have chicken parmesan and the men would have their pork dishes. They would let the cook decide how to cook the pork. Amy told Deloris that the pork was wonderful there in Belize. Deloris questioned why Amy had not suggested a beef dish, turns out that the beef in Belize is rarely good and usually very tough. Beef is not aged as it is in the states and therefore not as tender. They walked back down Sunset Pointe road along the lagoon and rang the bell for the boatman. They informed Tiffany of their trouble finding eggplants and gave her their new request for dinner. After returning to the other side, they spent the rest of the day with Alan and Ernie wandering around the village. It was notable how friendly everyone in the village was. Everyone spoke as you passed and soon Deloris realized they were greeting the Americans whether they knew Ernie and Amy or not. It was obviously a poor village. Many of the houses and buildings were covered with different colored or unpainted boards; a pink board thrown onto a faded white building, or a variety of different colored boards to patch wood that was rotted or holes that were in the buildings. Alan said, "Why do the buildings look as if they are built with scrap lumber?"

Ernie told them that is exactly what it is, that scrap lumber had been used to patch or repair the damage done when Hurricane Iris hit Placencia directly, in 2001. It was the most destructive Hurricane in Belize since Hurricane Hattie in 1961. Iris was the second strongest storm of the 2001 Hurricane season on the Atlantic side. Water swept across the peninsula devastating the houses and businesses. After the storm, the villagers gathered wood from wherever they could find it to repair the buildings. Belizean's have always had the ability to make the best of whatever situation they have to face. They can take what is available and make it work when faced with a situation that we would think would require a completely new start. On the other hand, if a part breaks they may have to throw away something that we in the states would simply order a part to fix. "You will learn that the Belizeans have a totally different perception of what one needs to survive and be happy," said Amy.

"Hurricanes are a real threat here?" asked Deloris.

"No more than they are in Florida or the East Coast in general. There hasn't been another hurricane to hit Placencia since 2001 and while it is a fear, it isn't enough to change the building code or for the people to abandon the vulnerable peninsula." added Amy as they walked past the colorful buildings.

They arrived across from Soul Shine around seven p.m. as appointed and rang the bell. The distinctly happy boatman, Larry, hurried to gather the four for dinner. Getting into the spirit of the friendly village, Deloris introduced Alan to Larry as they crossed the narrow lagoon. They arrived to find the restaurant deserted except for a waitress. She wore an all-white dress, knee length and accented it with a pink scarf wrapped around her small neck.

She seated the four in the small dining room and assured that they were comfortable before leaving. The room was beautiful. The walls were all wood and decorated with other wooden carvings. The floor was a hard mahogany and the ceiling was a beautiful design, but the best part was that the wood was not been stained and was left to age perfectly. Deloris has always loved wood and particularly wooden designs and architecturally different layouts, these always captivated her. The wooden chairs and tables were clearly handmade, the bar was another magnificently made one of a kind design. Deloris loved the idea of allowing the beautiful bar, tables, chairs, floor and ceiling to fade naturally, giving them an unusual color and rustic island appearance.

The view, looking out the large breezeway was magnificent. The ancient mountains were built by both volcanic forces as well as tectonic forces. They've been the "creator's masterpiece" in Central America for many millions of years. The sun was just touching the soft canvas of the perfect horizon. The scene was breathtaking.

Amy placed a soft hand on Deloris's shoulders and said, "That is why they named the road, Sunset Pointe. It is beautiful every day."

"I can't imagine a more beautiful place in the whole world." Deloris said with the admiration of a young child.

"This is absolutely the best place to watch the sunset in all of Placencia." said Amy softly.

"I'm glad I am experiencing it." Deloris replied as she continued to look longingly at the sunset.

The waitress returned with menus made of very small diameter bamboo with a single sheet of paper attached. Since they had ordered their meals ahead of time, Deloris was unsure why they were given menus but she was happy to have a chance to see what they served on a regular basis. She assumed the menus were simply for show. The waitress made her way around the table taking the drink orders. She did not make small talk in the same way most good U.S. waitresses would. She was efficient but almost seemed shy. Deloris, the odd one out, ordered ice water, while the others ordered rum punch. As the evening went on, the four were discussing everything imaginable about Amy and Ernie's plans for the condos. The feeling was that something of this quality and style and craftsmanship had not been done on the peninsula yet and it would be quite a challenge for it to meet Amy's standards. Deloris envied Amy this challenge. She could understand Amy's excitement, it was contagious. As the rum flowed and the friends bonded further in the excitement that this new venture entailed, the vail of candor slipped away. "The normal ways of checking a contractor's ratings and integrity simply doesn't exist down here. If you are not careful, you could be in a lot of trouble in a situation like this." exclaimed Ernie, as he held up his empty rum glass. The waitress rushed in with a new one. "You can't expect a Better Business rating here in Belize." stated Ernie in a voice slightly louder than normal, as he began to feel the rum coursing through his veins. He was always a happy drunk and would never say a cross word to anyone when he was drinking. The two men continued to enjoy their drinks and discussed the shortcomings of skilled craftsmen in Belize. Ernie told Deloris and Alan of the issues they'd had getting clear titles for the ancient property. Alan shook his head and listened to the story of the many people and agencies that were involved in simply purchasing the land for the condos. "In the states, you find land, you do a title search and you buy it! Not here, my friend! Here you have to find Harry's uncle, cousin or brother-in-law and make sure that he didn't get drunk and give it to a friend or relative or that he didn't sell it for a boat motor. But that is what makes Belize so attractive as well. Nothing's the same and it is never boring. There's always a story in Belize." Ernie quipped. "That reminds me of a story," Amy chimed in, who was also in a very happy and excited mood after 3 'Panty Rippers' (a rum drink in Belize) that she had since dinner.

"Oh, I know the one you are going to tell!" shouted Ernie with a smile, "Tell them, they won't believe this." he laughed.

"Well ..." began Amy, "There was this incredible lot on the ocean. Many years ago, a son thought that he had inherited it from his father since he was the only living relative. He set about building several cabanas and a small business on it and operated it for years, and was very successful. One day a man arrived in Placencia and claimed that he owned this lot and was ready to take possession of it. Of course, everyone laughed at him because the land had obviously passed to the rightful owner. Everyone knew that the son was entitled to his father's property and they thought the foreigner was just trying to steal the land. However, the man produced a paper signed by the father in which the father obligated the land for the purchase of a motor. The simple way the agreement was worded left no room for anything other than the fact that if the father did not pay the stranger four hundred Belizean dollars by a certain date and have a paid receipt from the stranger that the entire property would revert to the stranger. It went to court and since the son could not produce a paid receipt, the court allowed the stranger to claim the land. All attempts to pay the $400.00 BZ plus 20 years of interest were rejected by the stranger and so he was able to claim the land that would probably sell for half a million U.S. dollars today. Some of the old timers vaguely remembered that the father had been desperate for a motor so that he could continue to fish and had been able to locate a source of a motor, but no one knew any details concerning repayment. In typical Belizean style, after all the legal maneuvering was over, the son simply started dismantling his cabanas and his business and move them; however, there was nothing to be done to save the property. "As a lawyer, you can imagine how horrifying I found this from every point of view." Laughed Amy.

"Never boring, in Placencia, never boring." laughed Ernie.

"Speaking of never boring ..." said Amy to Deloris, "In the morning, I'm actually supposed to go and look at some of the newer houses that our contractor has built. I want to see as much of his work as possible since I want to use his talents to full advantage."

"How exciting! I bet you are ready to see what he's capable of doing." answered Deloris.

Amy had determined that he was the only contractor that they had talked to that seems to try to learn new styles and techniques.

"May I join you? I can't imagine anything that would be more intriguing." asked Deloris.

"Absolutely, I was going to offer. I believe the guys are going fishing so we'll meet Hans and view the houses. It'll be fun." Amy assured her guest.

"Yes, we're going out to the reef with Fred, he's our regular fishing guide and never disappoints. He lives in Independence which is located on the mainland 6 miles directly across the bay from Placencia. He grew up in Monkey River, which is a small village located on the Monkey River, south of Placencia. He knows every inch of this water from Placencia down past Monkey River. He will have us bringing home fish for dinner tomorrow that is for sure." bragged Ernie. "Alan, you will find him very interesting. He is in his fifty's but you would swear he is 25 when you see him. He has a very large family and when we are out fishing, he just knows where the fish are. Never uses a GPS or even a compass. I asked him once why he looked so young and he said because he never went to doctors. His mother always prepared any medicines he or his siblings needed from roots and herbs and he still, to this day, swears by the Noni Juice that he makes himself after he picks the fruit and ferments it."

"Have you tried this Noni juice?" laughed Alan.

"No, I would, but I can't get passed the smell. I always intended to try it when I get back to the states, because now they bottle and sell it in the states, but when I am back in the states I am always too busy to remember to buy a bottle and try it. See, there's the difference in Belize and the U.S., I would never be too busy here to try something I wanted, yet when I am in the states; I always feel that way." said Ernie as if he had just had a revelation.

Alan had noted that a variety of the locals looked like they came from different backgrounds. The skin tones varied so much. He had even heard someone refer to a waitress as the 'black girl'. The Belizean's seemed to be very aware of skin color.

Alan was curious as to whether the differences in skin tones was an issue with the Belizean.

Ernie explained that it was a mystery to him since they are very aware of each other's skin tone and often refer to a person by their color, but it doesn't seem to offend anyone. He told Alan that he was shocked by the constant referral to skin tone when they first arrived. Now he even found himself doing it from time to time. He explained that when you hear the term 'clear', that they are indicating that someone is very light or white and if you are referred to as a 'Gringo' it is with no disrespect. "It is just the way it is here. Political correctness had not reached Belize and they seem to be fine." laughed Ernie.

"I understand that Mayans make up some of the culture here as well." said Alan.

"Actually, the word is 'Maya', unless you are talking about a language or culture, then it is 'Mayan'. They have had one of the biggest impacts on the culture, as they have been here for many thousands of years." replied Ernie.

"You mean like the Mayans, I mean the Maya, from Mexico and other central and south American places?" asked Alan.

Ernie explained that the Maya people occupied a large area in Central America and to this day their influence is felt here in Belize. There are many Mayan ruins here in Belize. The top ten are Xunantunich (unan'tunit), meaning "Maiden of the Rock or Stone Woman" in Maya that is in the Cayo District near the town of San Ignacio and has the second tallest ruin in Belize, Altun Ha, which is north of Belize City, and was the site where the "Jade Head", the largest carved jade item in the Maya civilization was found. Then there is Caracol, Spanish for shell, located west of the Maya Mountains. It is difficult to reach but the main reservoir is an engineering masterpiece. There is also Cahal Pech overlooking the twin towns of San Ignacio and Santa Elena. Santa Rita, which was the site of the of ancient Maya city known as Chetumal which was the genesis of the Mestizo people when the first Europeans came to the area. Then there is Lamanai, the ruin that Deloris had visited on her "disastrous cruise trip to Belize". Lamanai, was occupied for over two millennia and has over 719 mapped structures. Several periods of Maya constructions and techniques can be observed here. Cerro Maya, meaning "Maya Hill" in Spanish, is partially underwater. It is located across from the town of Corozal. There are five temples that can be seen there. Then there is Barton Creek Cave, in Cayo. The site contains many artifacts from the Maya culture. Nim Li Punit, located in Southern Belize is the site of twenty-six stelae and in the Maya Q'eqchi' language Nim Li Punit (/nim li pu'nit/) means "the big hat". Then there is Lubaantun, meaning "Place of the Fallen Stones", located in the Toledo District in Southern Belize, which has an unusual construction style since the structures are made of stone blocks that have no mortar binding them together. These ruins have cities, pyramids and ancient monoliths with fascinating hieroglyph messages about rulers and events. The ruins are in different stages of excavation. It is amazing how much they accomplished 10,000 years ago with only stone tools. Many ancient alien theorists say that the Maya were given much of their technology from aliens who visited here. Of course, this theory is controversial so I guess it is whatever you believe about how they accomplished all of this.

Deloris was always fascinated with these ancient cultures and would to talk to me about the ancient cultures when I was young. I think that was the root of my fascination with the ancient people. I even have started to learn to read and write hieroglyphic. I really think that this visit to Belize and the trifactor of ruins, waterfalls, and caves made my usually practical aunt, let her hair down a little and decide to be adventuresome for the first time in her life. Alan didn't need anything specific, just the relaxed and wild idea of doing things differently without all the rules and limitations was enough for him to like this place very much.

"We'll have to go see at least the ruin that's in the south, but it may have to be on your next trip. Tomorrow it is fishing day, Dude. Ernie laughed as he slapped Alan on the back. Now Deloris was regretting that she had not agreed to the two weeks. She already knew that there was no possible way of doing all the things she already knew she wanted to do while in Belize. Particularly, since Amy and Ernie had several planned meetings with their contractor.

The evening carried on and the conversation was seamless, so much so, that none of them realized that their meal still hadn't arrived until Alan, who was now very hungry said. "Do you think there's a problem with our meals? How long has it been since we ordered?"

"Oh, Alan no one wears a watch in Belize. A watch here only causes tan lines!" Laughed Ernie, "When you eat out here in Belize you make sure you are not particularly hungry when you arrive at the restaurant because by the time the food arrives you will be!" Ernie again, entertained himself with new information for his guest and this time he let out a horrendous laugh.

"I just thought that since we went to the trouble of letting them know that we'd be here at seven o'clock and what we'd be ordering, that they would take that opportunity to have everything ready", said Deloris.

The experienced couple broke out into laughter, "It is just the Belizean way! They move at a different pace. The sooner you accept it the better off you will be. If anyone thinks they will change that about Belize, they are in the wrong place." Ernie said smiling and holding up his empty glass for more rum.

Alan and Deloris locked eyes and without a spoken word, had an entire conversation. Alan knew his wife came because he wanted to so badly. They were having fun, but this was very different. The culture and just the attitudes were so foreign to them both. Deloris, never a difficult person, seemed intrigued with the differences that they were discovering in the way that Belizeans lived their lives, their attitudes toward schedules or planning, and the pace of their lives. Alan relaxed and soon their food was delivered to the table. The meal was fantastic and the two kept expressing how amazing it was. They ate slowly and continued small talk about the new country they were being introduced to, and the antics of a different culture. They were soon full and tired and the subject was broached by Alan, as he stretched big and gave the impression that he was done with the evening. It was early, only eight P.M. but they were ready to go to bed. Alan insisted on paying for dinner and drinks, despite the number of drinks and the four delicious meals, the cost was far less than it would have been in any U. S. restaurant that could offer this view and as a bonus, the quality of food was excellent. The four stood at the dock and soon Larry, the boatman, appeared to take them across the lagoon. Larry rowed them across in short order. They walked the short distance to Ernie and Amy's house and said good night. Alan and Deloris made their way into their guest room and looked forward to that mattress without box springs tonight. Simplicity was becoming very appealing; such a relief from their normally hectic, rule oriented life. Here simple was appealing.

The next morning Alan and Deloris awoke early and were surprisingly refreshed. A quick shower and the two walked outside to try to catch the sunrise. After all, if the sunset was that fantastically beautiful last night, the sunrise must be spellbinding. The mangroves blocked the view of the sunrise from the house, so the two walked to the tip of the peninsula and caught the most amazing sunrise they'd ever seen. After the sun was up into the sky and the world seemed to awaken for yet another beautiful day in paradise, the couple walked back to the house. As they walked in they smelled the unmistakable aroma of eggs and bacon cooking. Deloris noticed that the bacon this morning was not the normal stripe of bacon but pieces that looked a little more like ham. They sat as Amy finished up the toast and coffee.

They told their host about the amazing sunrise and how the tranquility was enchanting. They sat at the small dining table and enjoyed a hearty breakfast. The bacon was different from what Deloris was used to. A little more like a thin piece of ham, fried crisp. She asked Amy about it and was informed that it was called butt bacon here in Belize, as opposed to belly bacon in the states. After this information and another bite, she decided that she liked it better than the sliced bacon she was used to. She realized that there were quite a few things that she enjoyed about Belize and not just the fresh foods. After breakfast, the girls cleaned up and the men went off on their fishing expedition with Fred for the day. Deloris and Amy took the truck and drove through the village and then past to meet with the contractor that Amy called Hans. She had told Deloris that he was a talented builder who was a Mennonite. He was born here in Belize, and practiced a strict Mennonite life for the first fifteen years. Then his parents had taken him to America for six years. During that time, he attended college there and then came back to Belize to live. As they drove through the village, Deloris watched each person, as they passed. She tried to guess what their lives were like. She saw a lighter skinned woman with what appeared to be a dish pan on her head, walking from place to place. It appeared that she was selling some type of food. Then she saw a young boy, of about ten years of age, who was shouting out, "Tamales." There were several people already out selling food on the potholed, village street. A large black woman wearing a black and white flower print dress and carrying a large woven basket on her head, was seemingly walking home with the items she had shopped for in one of the village's fresh vegetable stands. They continued down the pothole stricken road and up the peninsula. Deloris noted that the red clay road and the people who walked alongside the road, going from one place to the other, was not that different from South Carolina when she was a kid. She daydreamed as Amy endlessly explained her ideas for the condos. Deloris would have liked to offer her opinion, but she knew Amy well enough to know that she had already decided exactly what she wanted. Knowing her this well, she knew that she would have everything just the way that she wanted it. She envied Amy a bit. Deloris had been born with an acute eye for design and she would have loved to have the challenge that Amy was undertaking. Amy had very nice things and knew how to get exactly what she wanted. Deloris on the other hand always considered the cost first and tried to get what she wanted as long as, it was practical. Today's visit to view ideas for Amy and Ernie's new condos would tease her tastes more than she could know.

Hans was standing at the road, where the driveway was clearly new, as the two pulled up to where he was standing. There were two houses of similar exterior construction on the property. As Amy exited the car, she greeted Hans.

"Hans, how are you?" as he gave Amy a bear hug. Amy stepped out of his embrace to introduce Deloris. "Hans, this is my good friend Deloris. We live in the same town in Florida."

"Ah, it is a pleasure to meet you Deloris." Hans answered in a voice with a slight accent. Deloris had read somewhere that a German dialect was the first language of many Mennonites, however, this was not always the case. Many of the Mennonites in Belize are carpenters, engineers, and many seem to be particularly knowledgeable in agriculture. As a group, they have done well since relocating to Belize in the nineteen fifties. The things she had heard about Hans and the fact that Ernie and Amy had picked him to build their condos, made her curious about his background. She had learned that Hans was from a settlement call Spanish Lookout which is located off the Western Highway between Belmopan and Cayo. This area has two to three thousand residents. Deloris had learned that a lot of the furniture that was used in Belize was built in this area. The Mennonites are a diverse group and while many practice the old ways and do not use any modern tools, others are quite progressive and bring in the equipment and tools that allow Belize to advance in techniques.

As the three of them then walked the property and Deloris was surprised to see that the structures were wooden framed. She knew that Amy intended for the condos to be concrete block. These structures were a two-story design, small in square footage, but very well built. The lower level was the living area and kitchen. They walked into the kitchen and Deloris took a deep breath. It became apparent why they were looking at these houses. There were the most beautiful dark stained mahogany kitchen cabinets that Deloris had ever seen. It was obvious that they were individually handmade to fit in the small area and she could see that every conceivable storage space had been used for drawers or shelves or other storage areas. Without thinking Deloris blurted out "Who designed these cabinets?" Amy laughed and said, "She's hooked, Hans. The way to any woman's heart is an efficient beautiful kitchen, even if she does not use it very often."

"The owners gave me a rough idea of what type of storage they needed in the kitchen and the type of wood they wanted and I designed the cabinets for them." said Hans, "That is why I wanted Amy to see these houses. The other house has a different type of design and I wanted her to see what we could do as far as built-ins. The upstairs has built-ins for storage too." continued Hans.

They wandered through the two houses which were finished but not occupied at the time. However, with all the things that were built in, it would take very little furniture to complete the move in for the new owners. The houses had breathtaking views with lots of light and beautiful colorful tile designs that seemed to play a specific song as one looked upon them. The floors were a combination of beautiful hard woods and superbly designed tile patterns. When Deloris was finally able to quit admiring the absolute beauty of the floor, she realized that someone practical had also been involved since the deep glossy hardwood was confined to the less traveled areas while the practical tile sang its song in the traffic areas. She was impressed with the combination of beauty and practicality. As they were walking back down the stairs after viewing the second home, Deloris stopped on the stairs and look back up at the house. She said to Hans and Amy, "I didn't see any closets in either house."

"We just do shelving and don't waste square footage with what you call a closet." stated Hans.

Well, I can tell you that my Aunt Deloris loves her closets and I can just imagine what this little bit of news must have done to her.

Amy spoke up and said, "Hans, and I are going to talk about the lack of closets, before we finish designing the condos. I know the Belizean idea, that closets are a waste of square footage, but I share your opinion, Deloris, that any American woman will demand a closet."

At this point, Hans shook his head slightly. He had been dealing with American and Canadian women for fifteen years and had been able to convince most of them that closets were a waste of space. He just had not encountered women like Amy and Deloris before, who knew exactly what they wanted and would fight for it. This issue was a long way from settled in either of their minds. It was just that Deloris did not have any idea that it would ever be an issue for her.

The three drove on to another house that was built out of concrete block. While it was more practical for an area that potentially could have hurricanes and tropical storms, she certainly understood the pull to hold on to the past with the beautiful wood designs. This house had the wonderful colorful tile patterns and the beautiful wood cabinetry of the other houses and was just as intriguing in its own way. Deloris realized that Amy and Hans were discussing things that Amy wanted for the condo.

She secretly selected what she would choose if this were her project. By the time, Hans and Amy had set up a meeting for the following morning to complete the building contracts, Deloris had designed and was furnishing her dream room, from the ideas she had seen here today. She reluctantly pulled herself away. After they had bid Hans farewell and thanked him again for the wonderful tour, they drove back to the village. Both women were quiet as they rode, obviously both deep in thought about all they had seen today. Amy for the practical reasons of decisions had to be made and Deloris because this was her secret passion. Once they were back in the heart of the village, Amy pulled over near an open building with two large overhead doors of about 10 foot each.

"What is this?" ask Deloris.

"The Grocery store and hardware store." replied Amy, "It is really the only place other than a fruit stand or road vendor to get supplies." continue Amy, "There is rumor that there will soon be stores here owned by the Chinese, but for now this is Placencia's major source of supplies. The store is owned by an American man. He moved here about twenty-five years ago with his wife and Placencia is now their home. The groceries are over there on the right and this is the hardware portion here. Let's go in and let you see what is available. You should know these things for when you come back." said Amy.

Deloris realized that Amy had just assumed they would be coming back to Placencia for about the third time since they arrived. She realized that there were so many things in this new and foreign country that she wanted to see and learn about. Maybe Amy knew something that she did not yet know.

As they entered the store, Amy said "I have to pick up a new toaster so let's go upstairs first. Our toaster died this morning. I will pick up another until I can bring one down."

"Why would you bring one down if you buy one now?" asked the frugal Deloris?

"Well for a number of reasons ..." replied Amy. Amy went on to explain that the electrical current here is not as stable as we have in the states and power surges damage all electrical appliance over time so having an extra of small appliances is advisable if you are going to have renters or guest. Also, the quality of what you buy here doesn't seem as good as what you can bring and it is a lot more expensive, so it is advisable to keep an extra if you can. Amy found a toaster and although she did not have a large selection to choose from, she chose one. Deloris noted that the price was about double what she would have expected to pay in the states. After looking around a little more, seeing things from mattresses to pots and pans, the two moved down stairs where there were nuts and bolts and an array of hardware items. Amy paid for her toaster, then the two walked over to the store that had groceries.

Deloris asked, "What is needed from the grocery store?" Amy replied, "We need ingredients for a salad and bread." To complete the meal that they would make with the fish that were expected from the fishing trip. Deloris wondered why they would need bread since they had purchased it only two days ago, she soon learned that bread in Belize does not have preservatives. It is made the same way that her grandmother made bread when she was a child. It was wonderful if eaten within a day or two, but very quickly turned to stone.

"What about putting the bread in the fridge? Will that make it last longer?" ask Deloris.

"I tried that." Amy replied. She had learned, by trial and error, putting the bread in the refrigerator made it as hard as a rock. The preservatives in the states keeps it soft and retards the mold growth, but here, without those preservatives, it did not remain good but a couple of days. That is the down side of being able to eat bread that came from someone's oven this morning.

When they arrived back at the house, the men were just arriving back from their day of fishing. Alan told Deloris about the beautiful water and plentiful amounts of fish. He seemed truly in awe of the things he had seen. He told Amy and Deloris about the fact that Fred had caught fish on what he called a handline. While Deloris, didn't understand exactly why Alan would be so impressed about the way fish were caught, she could tell that he clearly was. Belizeans often have a fishing line that is "hand held" and they do not use a rod of any type. They simply net bait and attach it to the hook and are able to pull in fish with this line. No expensive rod and reels, that are considered essential by most north American fishermen, are necessary. They simply make do with what they have.

Ernie held up a couple of the biggest fish from their catch and the boat was full of very colorful fish. Deloris saw several very large barracudas among the catch. While she didn't know a great deal about fish, she knew that in Florida they would never eat large barracuda. Ernie helped Fred clean the fish with competence and efficiency while Alan watched. Before long all the fish were cleaned. Ernie filleted two large red snappers and set them aside. They then bid Fred farewell and Fred pushed off the boat with the rest of the of the fish, including the big barracudas. With a wave, he was gone. Alan ask Ernie, "Will they really eat those big barracudas". Barracudas feed on algae eating fish and the coral in the reef, which naturally contains a toxin known as ciguatera. Large barracudas have consumed great amounts of this toxin by the time they reach the size of those caught by Fred; so potentially their flesh could contain amounts of this toxin that could be harmful to humans. When eaten, it causes varying symptoms such as, mild nausea to a coma. Ernie explained, that when he first came to Placencia and realized that barracuda is the preferred fish to eat by the locals, he asked about the advisability of taking the chance. However, the locals scoffed at him and said that they had been eating barracuda all their lives and thought that Americans were being silly to be afraid to eat barracuda. Laughing, Ernie explained that there was one Canadian man who spent 6 months out of every year in

Placencia, he also loved to eat barracuda, so he had this practice of taking a small piece of the barracuda flesh and placing it on the ground, as soon as he got in with his catch. He waited until the next morning and if the ants had eaten the flesh of the barracuda, he proclaimed that catch to be eatable, if the ants did not eat it he threw out that entire fish. Ernie said he had eaten some very small barracuda and he loved it, but he made it a habit never to eat barracuda that is served in a restaurant since he never knew the size. Apparently, the locals prefer this species over all others and the bigger the better.

As they went into the house, Deloris ask Alan what was so special about a "handline". "Well you know how much money my friends and I spend on special rods and reels and the way we debate the qualities of each new product that comes out, well Fred just goes out and with a simple line and catches big fish. He makes it seem so effortless." said Alan. It was clear that he was amazed at the simplicity of catching large numbers of fish here in Belize.

"Why'd we only keep two fish? There were a lot of fish there. We could have kept some in the freezer." Alan asked Ernie as they walked into the kitchen.

"That is how it works down here, my friend. The foreigners only keep what we need for a good meal and the guide takes the rest. What he doesn't need to feed his family, he'll sell to other people for extra money. Everything here is used to define, 'Live or Die'" Ernie explained as the two beautiful red snapper fillets were popped into a hot skillet. The men continued to chat, as Amy prepared dinner. Deloris tried to help, but Amy would have none of it. With all the excitement about the ease of catching fish and the abundance of fish, Deloris had not had a chance to ask about the fact that the men had gone out in a small boat with a single motor, today. However, always the worrier, she finally had to ask the question. "How far out did you guys go today?" Ernie explained that the reef was located about 26 miles off the coast of Placencia and that it is necessary to go out to the reef and take one of the few breaks in the reef to reach the open ocean. This is where the best fishing occurred. "Ernie, I am surprised that you would venture that far out in a small boat with one single engine like that. Does the guide have a GPS or is there Sea-Tow or some other rescue source here? I have heard you say over and over that you need two or three motors on your boat in the states into order to be safe when you are fishing off Jacksonville's coast. What is the difference?" Ernie looked at her for a long moment and then began to laugh. He explained to Deloris that this is what is so strange about Belize. In the states, you tend to think in terms of safety and convenience. In fact, the guide does not have a GPS or even a compass a lot of times. A friend, if he happens to have gas is his boat, is your only hope of help if you get stranded on the ocean. Here you do things the way that Belizeans have done them for years and years and then you realize that this is what life should be like. It is operating without much of a safety net. You are just living in the moment. It is liberating and is the appeal to many of us. You will find yourself wanting to escape to this Paradise even if there is no safety net. Your point of view changes when you are in Belize and surrounded by people who take life one day at a time, use what is available and never miss what they don't have. As if to change the subject before anyone thought too much about the risk involved, Ernie took a deep breath and looked at Alan and winked. "Well dude, I think it is time that you share with the girls our biggest adventure of the day." "Okay, I will start but you jump in anytime you want," said Alan.

"Deloris, do you know what a Whale Shark is?" Alan asks. Deloris, looked puzzled and told Alan that she did not, but that if it was a

Shark she was sure he loved it. Alan explained that while a Whale Shark is a shark it is also very much like a whale. It is also the largest fish in the world. It could get up to forty-five to fifty feet long and it is cold blooded and extracts oxygen from the water. It filters its food and it eats plankton and fish eggs and small sea life like squid. "Okay, that is all very interesting, but where is this going", laughed Deloris. "Well today I had my first encounter with a Whale Shark", stated Alan.

Alan began to tell the story of their encounter with the Whale Shark. It seems that just before they were ready to leave their fishing spot outside the reef, that Fred had told both Ernie and Alan to grab their snorkel gear and get ready to jump in the water. Then he pointed out a large dark spot in the distance which was moving toward them. He instructed both men to put on their snorkel gear and slip off the boat into the water, swim a short distance from the boat and stay there. Alan was skeptical but Ernie assured him that he knew what was going on and he assured him that it would be great. They followed his directions and after swimming about 100 feet away from the boat, they saw that a massive creature was approaching them in a slow and graceful path. It was headed directly for them.

Now I can tell you that Alan must have had a lot of trust in the fact that Ernie and Fred had told him it would be great. Approaching them was a 20-foot creature with a massive head. It was grey with white spots and very pale stripes on its body. It was a magnificent creature and despite being massive, moved with unbelievable grace. The Whale Shark approached within about 10 feet and veered slightly to the right. It circled around and approached them again. It was obviously as curious about them as they were about it. Alan had the distorted impression that he could have reached out and touch the creature, but something stopped him from doing it. This was the type of adrenalin rush that Alan lived for. The creature made about 4 passes around the two men before turning away and swimming away from the reef. Alan was speechless. As they returned to the boat his mind was reeling.

As he finished telling the exciting story of his first up close and personal encounter with the Whale Shark, Deloris could see the wonder and the amazement in his eyes. "I cannot believe that you did not tell us about this as soon as you returned.", Deloris said. "Well I wanted to take my time in telling it because I am not sure I believe it really happened, even now. It was such a great experience.", said Alan.

The fact that Alan did not touch the Whale Shark is amazing because for years the divers and others who encounter the Whale Shark often did pet them. While this would seem like a harmless practice, there are those who let the "petting" stage become harassment. These are wild creatures and while we long to interact, it is best just to observe them.

The normal season to see these magnificent creatures is March, April, May and June during the days closes to the full moon. Dive shops set up a schedule for these months have boats that take divers and snorkelers out to Gladden Split where they see these creatures as they come through the Split to eat the eggs that happen during spawning. These trips are closely regulated and Placencia is known as the best place to attempt to spot these creatures.

Deloris and Alan were intrigued by Belize for different reasons. Deloris loved the idea of the ancient civilizations and the mysteries that they had left as well as the caves, waterfalls, wonderful carvings and exotic woods. Alan's intrigue was the excitement of a wild adrenalin producing adventure with the Whale Shark and the unknown adventures of the ocean. Amy could see that Belize was sneaking up on these two without either of them even knowing it.

They finished a wonderful meal of blackened Red Snapper with a green salad and garlic bread. Amy served a great red wine and the last bite was as good as the first. Deloris really enjoyed the fish and even the red wine that night. She was surprised to see that Alan had seconds because fish was not one of Alan's favorite foods. Deloris was an exceptional cook, but didn't usually cook fish. However, she knew she would duplicate this meal for him many times. As early as it was, the four were tired enough to call it a night. The simple mattress on a wooden frame was beckoning Alan and Deloris, they sighed as they crawled into the pleasantly captivating smell of sunshine, from the obvious line dried sheets. Instead of missing the softness of sheets dried in a dryer, Deloris took a deep breath of the freshness radiating from the sheets and felt the last thread of stress flow out of her body. All the tension she normally carried while she lived her life in the states had left her relaxed and happy.

The next morning the four decided to go back up the peninsula and visit the artist that Amy had told them about on their trip down. The house where the paintings were displayed was off the beaten path and they realized that only the informed would ever be able to find it. The paintings there were very unique. Deloris could see the appeal that many people found with these paintings.

When I was in Belize I was amazed at the number of Belizeans that with no training are very talented artist. I knew that the country had a large number of talented carvers and people who worked with wood, but I was astonished at the number of people who could draw and paint. It seems to be a talent that is widely possessed in this culture.

After returning to the village, they decided that Ernie and Amy would remain at their house so they could do some brainstorming about what needed to be done to complete the instructions for

Hans, so that their condos could be started. Alan and Deloris would go into the village and look for some gifts to take back. There were lots of stalls with people selling handbags, beach cover-ups, jewelry and all sorts of carvings and paintings located on the sidewalk. Deloris had seen these displays but she had not spent much time looking at the merchandise. As they walked along they talked about other Caribbean places they visited and reminisced that the people in those places seemed only interest in you, if you were buying something or they were soliciting your business for a tour. Yet, here the people seemed genuinely friendly and welcoming. They loved the atmosphere of the village. As the two were coming back down Sunset Road toward Amy and Ernie's house, they noticed a man sanding an overturned boat. Alan stopped and soon learned that the man's name was George. The boat he was busy sanding, had been damaged when it ran onto a coral reef and he was finishing his patch on it. Alan asked, "What would cause someone to run into coral?"

George laughed and said, "Well, we always try to avoid the coral, but these waters often become shallow so quickly that only the most experienced, of us, can be on the water all the time and not have an accident like this."

Alan remembered, that on their great adventure with Fred, that they would be speeding along and for no apparent reason Fred would slow the boat drastically, he realized that Fred was picking his way through coral outcroppings. This had happened without benefit of a GPS or any warning signs. Fred was one who did not even have a compass on board. Apparently, the places that Fred had navigated were not the only place in Belizean waters that the coral was dangerously close to the surface. Alan continued to talk to George, about the danger that the Belizean waters could pose for someone who did not know the waters.

Soon a woman stepped out on the porch. She had an arm load of clothes which she began to hang on a line that was strung across their front porch. George said, "This is my wife, Constance. Connie, these are the people who are visiting with Amy and Ernie." "Connie, nice to meet you.", stated Deloris.

Constance, a beautiful black woman with a smile that lit up her entire face asked, "Can I get you two some fruit juice?" It was extremely hot and muggy so both Alan and Deloris accepted her kind offer. As they waited for the juice, George, who was a light skinned man and clearly Belizean, explained that his family was part of the original group of families that had settled Placencia. He spoke with a dialect of Créole but the couple could understand him quite comfortably, although occasionally he would use a name or word that seemed out of context. George sat down on a cement block that was sitting beside the damaged boat and offered seats on his front stairs to Alan and Deloris. He then went on to entertain them with the historical story that 5 families originally settled this area that was now known as Placencia. He went into great detail about who was related to whom and the family politics that still to this day played a major role in the interaction of individuals in the village. He went on to explain that he was the only boat mechanic in the village. He said that there was another mechanic on the mainland, but he was busy with the boats there, so most of the boat repair that needed to be done in Placencia came to him. He explained that he hoped his son would join him in the business to help him some day.

Now I can tell you, that Alan would normally have been bored to tears with all this seemly mundane information. However, he sat and listened to all this information with as much interest as he would have done only if someone was sharing with him the information to complete one of his many business plans. Deloris, who would have normally acted interested, but would have been thinking about all the things she needed to be doing, found that she was hanging on to each word and thought of follow up questions she wanted to ask. George shared easily with the couple as if they were old friends who were returning from being away a long time. If was as if he was just bringing them up to date on the latest news which they craved to know.

Soon Constance joined them and handed them a glass of a sweet red juice. As Deloris took her first sip, her face showed surprise. She looked over at Constance and said, "Is this Watermelon Juice?"

Constance laughed and said "Yes, do you like it?" "Yes, it is amazing, but where do you get it", ask Deloris. "Oh, when there are watermelons in the village I buy one or two and juice them as a special treat. My family loves it." "It is very good and something I would never have thought of juicing." said Deloris.

"Do you want to buy a hotel?" George said out of the blue. Alan laughed and said, "No, why? Do you know of one for sale?"

George explained that he owned a small hotel located on the water just down the path from his house. He pointed out an opening in the land across the road as the path. He said that he and Constance had grown tired of working it, his partner and his wife had been helping them but they all really wanted to sell it; because it took up so much of their time. Deloris laughed and said, "I can understand why you want to sell a hotel, because it is a lot of work, but what makes you think that we might be in the market for a hotel?"

George looked at her in total seriousness and said, "Ms. Deloris, all Americans and Canadians are looking for good deals when they come to Placencia and this hotel is Paradise."

"This is our first trip to Belize and we are just here on vacation. We have businesses in the states that keep us both very busy. I am not even sure we would fit in here." laughed Alan.

"Oh, you fit in fine here. We have people from all over de world. No reason you do not fit in here as well." George petitioned. Nonetheless, Alan and Deloris soon departed and didn't plead their case any longer.

All their married life Alan and Deloris have taken non-conventional ideas and built that dream into a profitable business. Building businesses from ideas that no one thought would work, was not just a job to them that earned their living, but they nurtured those businesses like they were their children. I know now, that the seed was planted in both Alan and Deloris's mind that there was an adventure here. Although, if asked, neither one realized that this was anything other than an interesting hour spent with a stranger who imparted his knowledge about a strange new place. Though, the seed was planted that they could once again take an idea and against all odds, build that idea and dream into in something that no one thought possible.

They returned to Ernie and Amy's house and were told that they'd be going to a restaurant called "Teri's", if it was open that night. They both agreed and didn't dare ask why this "Teri's" would be closed on regular business day. Later that evening, around sundown, the four of them headed out walking toward the village. Soon Ernie and Amy cut to the right through a yard close to George and Constance's house. They walked down a dark road and realized that the road appeared to end ahead of them. Alan and Deloris rushed to catch up with Ernie and Amy, giving each other a worrisome glance when their hosts turned through a neighbor's back yard. They seemed confident, so Alan and Deloris followed closely. After walking between two close houses, they ran into a giant crape myrtle bush and after pushing it aside, they could see an opening to the beach and heard laughter. Soon they saw a small "over the water dock bar" with open seating and Christmas lights strung along the upper beams holding the thatched roof.

They could hear, clearly now, the sound of steel drums and calypso music being played by a small four-person band sitting in the corner of the bar. When they stepped off of the cool sand and onto the grey wooden steps leading into the bar, they realized a majority of the customers were expatriates. There were many more Americans and Canadians in Belize than Deloris had first thought. The accents were the tell-tell signs of where they were from. Everyone seemed to be drinking and enjoying the music. The leader of the band was clearly Belizean and played the part of a Central American well. He wore no shirt, but had on an open, sleeveless, blue jean jacket. His pants were short, to his mid-calf and his callused feet showed evidence of him not wearing shoes, often. His forehead shined bright from the light beaming down on him and his hair was braided into cornrows with the occasional bead thrown in for effect. A brightly colored pipe-cleaner was used to tie his hair on the ends to complete the effect. The man playing the steel drums wore a colorful shirt with a mixture of red, brown and orange that was much too big for him. He wore rose colored sunglasses and a constant smile was plastered on his face. The other two members of the band were significantly younger and it was clear that they were not near as confident as the older, more experienced members of their band. The four did a fine job of entertaining the crowd. They obviously enjoyed playing music as one picked up a home-made xylophone and the other beat roughly on a standing base. The music was something that Deloris had heard before, but never heard it played quite like this.

Again, Ernie and Amy were greeted by many people with shouts and hugs. They'd been coming to Placencia for seven and a half years now and had made some great acquaintances along the way. They introduced Alan and Deloris to one couple after another. Always giving a short description of what the people did here in Belize. Deloris soon realized that people came and stayed in Belize for a multitude of reasons. Some seemed to be involved in their own businesses, some seem to come and go often, others just seemed to be retired there. They found a table to sit near the center of the room and on the same side that the band was set up on. A short, happy Belizean woman approached their table while still shouting playful remarks at a man sitting at the bar. She hugged Amy and was soon introduced as Teri. She and her Canadian born, husband, Roger owned the bar. Deloris and Alan listened as the quips between Teri and her husband, and the other patrons in the bar displayed a feeling of friends out to enjoy the evening in an almost family-like atmosphere. From this gentle prodding and kidding it was clear that she and her husband enjoyed running a bar & restaurant. They lived only a few yards away from it and Teri was clearly an involved hostess as she waved at each person entering the place and shouted to everyone leaving. Ernie said, "This is where a lot of expats and people who live on boats full time come to hang out, so if you ever find yourself missing home, come here and it'll feel like you are back in Florida. Haw, Haw!"

Teri excused herself and went back behind the bar. Soon a waiter approached and took their drink order. The four chatted and listened to the band performing. Their drinks arrived and Ernie asked, "Can we order dinner?"

The waiter, obviously unsure if they were able to serve food tonight, went in search of Teri. As he scurried off he said, "Ummmm ... let me check wit miz Teri." Isn't this a restaurant as well as a bar?" Alan asked naively.

"Well, in Belize there is never anything written in stone and rarely planned. You could plan something, but you will never know if it'll happen until it is actually happening. Ya see, if a restaurant runs out of food, or simply decides to stop serving food, that is their prerogative." Ernie replied. "Seems like it would be bad for business." Alan rebutted with dismay. "This is Belize, Alan. Nobody makes a schedule here." Ernie schooled the greenhorn as he followed the waiter with his eyes now who was returning to their table.

As the waiter noticed Ernie's eyes following him, he displayed a big smile and quickly said, "Yes, you can have grill fish or grill chick'n and we also have vegetables and potatoes."

The four quickly decided what they would have and placed their order. The young waiter quickly walked away to tell Teri what they were having and Alan watched as the young man placed their order and returned to the bar to serve drinks.

The band began another song and in an instant, everyone jumped to their feet and began dancing and laughing. They sang and clapped along with the obliviously familiar song. Everyone seem to know the words ...

"Well, he came down on vacation, cause he like de tropical sun.

Margaritas and the music made it all seem fun

Him bought a piece of heaven on de Caribbean seas.

He's now a happy camper livin in Belize.

Dey began to build a condo, but the labor cost was high.

His girl stole de money and left him high and dry.

His land is still a mud hole where you sink to your knees.

He's just another Gringo livin in Belize.

The band was having a great time performing what was obviously one of the crowds' favorite songs and the crowd responded as if it were Elvis himself singing it. There were only two people seated at the end of the song and that was Alan and Deloris. Amy and Ernie danced and sang along, but Alan and Deloris did not feel comfort enough to join in. Deloris smiled and watched the crowd, who were now returning to their seats, laughing and talking. Ernie and Amy were smiling as they returned to their seats and Ernie shouted, "You guys should have joined in! That is what we do here. When we have fun, we have fun."

"Aw, you know me better than that, dude. I don't dance and I don't sing." Alan said with a smile.

"Alan, that is the thing about Belize. This place lets you do things that you normally wouldn't. People don't mind a person cutting up and having a good time here. In fact, it seems to be almost a requirement in order to fit in and enjoy the relaxation that this place provides."

Deloris watched the exchange and agreed with Alan that he is not a dancer. He gave her a tilted grin and then he asked Ernie, "Is that a song that this band wrote?"

Ernie looked at the band and then at Amy and the couple broke out in laughter, "No. That is a song by Jerry Jeff Walker. He spent some time here and wrote it. Everyone loves it."

"So how does everyone know it so well? Hell, they are all so animated over it."

"You will understand and appreciate that song much more after spending time a while here in Belize almost everyone here can relate to the lyrics" Ernie answered with a halfhearted smile. Alan watched as the crowd went from resembling a teen pillow fight to a calm chatty group again. He heard the words, but didn't think that the song was something to be joyful over. The poor guy in the song lost everything and his girl stole his money, his boat was stolen and wrecked … Didn't seem funny at all; to Alan.

They chatted away about this and that as they waited for their meal to arrive. It was an hour and a half later when the waiter began delivering their meals.

Time didn't seem to matter, as they enjoyed the music and the conversation at the table. Alan noticed a larger building next to Teri's on the beachfront. He asked, "What is that place there?"

Ernie and Amy looked, but said they didn't know. They explained that, other than Teri's, they weren't familiar with this area of the beach in Placencia. They only came down to the beach along here to visit Teri and Roger or to occasionally eat dinner. Ernie motioned over the waiter to refill the glasses. "What is that building there on the beach, Jose?", ask Ernie.

"I tink dat is a hotel dat George own. Paradise is de name, I tink." He answered as he retreated to fill the glasses.

Ernie explained to Alan and Deloris that there are many places here that look cheap and run down, but are active businesses. "I don't know how the hell they stay in business. If you aren't a local you don't even know that they exist." It seems that in Belize word of mouth is the primary form of advertising or getting directions, signs are few and far between. Just asking anyone where something is located is the accepted form of finding anything, from where someone lives to where a business is located. Directions are always far from being exact and you are expected to know basic landmarks, like where the Hokey Pokey boat picks up, where the water tower is located, or where a mutual acquaintance lives, in order to follow the directions, you receive. "I can see how that would be an issue. Why don't they fix it up and advertise?" ask Alan.

"Well, most people here don't have money. You can usually tell which businesses are owned by expats who have recently bought the business and which are owned by the locals by how dilapidated they are. Most expats spend money on repairs and paint, because we are used to that being a requirement to stay in business in the states. The Belizeans think only about functionality and not presentation."

As the two men chatted about the values and differences of the cultures, Deloris's mind returned to the conversation that they had with George. "Alan, I wonder if that is the hotel George was talking about." she asked. "Maybe, he did say that it was on the beach." Replied Alan.

"George? You mean the boat repairman?", questioned Amy.

"Yes, he offered to sell us his hotel today. I wonder if that is it." Deloris answered.

Amy's eyes grew wide, as she all but shouted, "Oh my god! You guys are thinking about buying a hotel here? I knew you two were hooked but I didn't expect that you would go as far as buying a hotel."

"Oh, no. We aren't buying it. We were walking this morning and met George and his wife Constance. He just asked us if we were interested in it. We told him that we know nothing about running a hotel." Deloris said. She watched Alan, as he continued to look at the building. She wondered what captivated him about it and knew that the dreamer in him would be hatching ideas of how this could be an exciting adventure. She, on the other hand, had to stay grounded, this meant that Belize was out of the question. She couldn't understand why she was beginning to fall in love with a country that was so unlike home, but she could feel it happening. They finished their meal and returned to Ernie and Amy's house.

The next morning Alan and Deloris woke before Ernie and Amy and had breakfast ready for them when they came into the kitchen. They discussed the plans for the day as they ate. Ernie and Amy would finalize the rest of the contracts and finish up a few items that they didn't get done previously with Hans. This left Alan and Deloris free to explore more of the village.

The next morning, they drove back up the rutted peninsula road turning on to the Southern Highway. The place that chocolate bars were made was a small concrete building located on the dirt road that leads to the Cockscomb Basin. After meeting the owners of the business and another group that was there to see how chocolate is made, they walked back across the Southern Highway and through an orange grove that was quite muddy at this time of year, to the place that the cacao trees grow. It was surprising that the trees looked as if they grew wild. There were no straight lines of carefully tended trees, but trees grew haphazardly in an area behind the orange grove. Chocolate was invented by the ancient Maya culture. It has long been thought to have many medicinal properties and is being used today by many to combat diverse ailments. The cacao bean, is actually a seed that grows inside a pod. The guide let them taste the pulp that surrounds the cacao seeds. These seeds are referred to as beans. The taste of this pulp was sweet and almost citrusy, nothing like chocolate. He showed them how the beans were dried and what steps were necessary before the beans could be ground into a powder. This powder then becomes what we refer to as cocoa. When they returned to the building they were allowed to participate in the hard work of grinding the beans. The cocoa nibs are placed on a Metate, which is a volcanic basalt stone, then a metlapil, handheld stone, is used to hand grind them into a soft paste. It can take 3 to 6 hours to grind the nibs to the consistency to make bars to sell, but after 20 minutes or so they had a paste that they could put into a mold and refrigerate so they could taste it. They were shown how these bars could have added flavors like mint or ginger. They also learned that the bars were made into Milk Chocolate and Dark Chocolate. In the U.S. we are familiar with chocolate bars with 10% or 12% cocoa, but here the bars are routinely 60% to 80% cocoa and this results in a very different taste, but one that Deloris found she liked even better than the chocolate at home.

Their time in Placencia had passed quickly and on their final walk before leaving Placencia, they found themselves at Teri's. Drawn there perhaps, by the hotel that they had been seen next door named, Paradise. With no words, Alan and Deloris both agreed that they wanted to see and explore this property that was named Paradise. They slowly walked over to the property and what they found was a two-story frame white and blue building. There was also a long dock out over the water. It was a perfect addition to the property. They slowly walked out to the end of the dock and looked at the sail boats that were anchored in the harbor. Despite not wanting to be on a boat, Deloris loved watching the sail boats sway in the afternoon breeze. It was a beautiful, relaxing view. After determining that there was no one around, they decided to see what they could of the hotel from the outside.

Now I am going to tell you that my Aunt and Uncle would not have gone wandering around a property without an appointment with a real estate agent in the states. However, here in Belize and particularly in Placencia, it seemed like the normal thing to do.

The hotel was perhaps thirty feet by sixty feet. Surprisingly, the hotel was positioned so that the thirty-foot side was on the ocean and therefore, the rooms did not have a view of the ocean. There was a large porch on the upper floor that looked out on that magnificent view. The front portion of the lower floor had another small screened area, but the rooms were positioned off a long hall running the length of the hotel. The screen door was open so that they could walk down the length of the hall and exit a rear screen door. It appeared there were 4 rooms on each side of the hall. The doors to the rooms were locked, but the rest of the hotel was fully accessible. They climbed the stairs leading to the upper rooms. There appeared to be another 8 rooms along this upper hall. The hall ended on the screened porch that they had seen from downstairs. As they walked out onto that porch they realized that there were several small appliances so that guest could make coffee and toast while sitting on the porch taking in that breath-takingly beautiful view.

They walked back downstairs and Alan estimated that the lot was perhaps 110 feet on the ocean. It was impossible to determine the side boundaries of the property because there were no fences. Deloris wondered aloud, why would the rooms not have been positioned along the 110-ft. side along the ocean to take advantage of this ocean view. The area beside the hotel on the north was covered in tropical trees and bushes with a path through the area. The tropical plantings virtually hid the hotel if you approached the hotel along the beach from the north. The side area did create a tropical feeling to the side yard of the hotel, but it also was the reason that people visiting Teri's would not immediately realize that there was a hotel next door. On the south side of the hotel there was a very dilapidated house on stilts that was leaning precariously. Walking around the outside of the hotel they realized that the toilets and showers were outside. They looked in the outdoor toilet room and saw that the showers were simple concrete stalls with no tile and simply had ancient shower heads on the 3 showers. Then they saw three simple stalls for the toilets. This entire building was elevated about three feet on a concrete base and the access was by a plank board ramp leading up to it. It was obvious to both Alan and Deloris that these accommodations would not be acceptable to most Americans looking for a vacation get away. The hotel was run down and needed lots of repairs. The building was simply built and only sat about forty feet from the water's edge. They were about to walk away when they were startled by a voice behind them, "So. You may want to buy it after all?" they turned quickly to see George walking toward them.

"Oh, we aren't in the market for a hotel. We just wanted to see it before we leave tomorrow and head back to the U.S." Alan answered as if he had been caught breaking in.

"Oh, dat is fine. Let me show you de place." George said as he began walking toward one of the rooms and pulled out a set of keys. A dark-skinned girl who was very thin and petite walked towards them. She was small boned and had very high cheek bones. She wore a white blouse and pencil thin black skirt that ended above her knees. Her hair was pulled up into a small tight bun on the top of her head. George introduced her as Donna, the girl who helped him run the place when they had guest there. Donna was a happy bubbly girl and Deloris guessed she would do good at greeting guest and making them feel at home. Donna told George that she was going to the office and get ready for a guest that would be arriving on the last bus tonight. She advised him that she would leave all the paper work for him and that he could meet the guest and have them sign the registration form and pay when they arrived on the 6 p.m. bus tonight. It was apparent that George would come back, meet the guest, take the money and open the room for them. It appeared to Deloris that the guest would then be left alone at the hotel that night, when George returned to his home. It was very different from what she was familiar with but seem to be perfectly normal here in Placencia.

When Donna had walked away to take care of her clerical duties, George lead them to the downstairs rooms. The rooms were very small, perhaps 10 feet by 12 feet. They were minimally furnished with only a bed and a hardwood chair which sat in the corner. The chair had a very straight back. The beds were simple platforms with very thin mattress and only sheets to cover the thin mattresses. The proud owner showed the couple around and bragged that he had showers and toilets as well, right out back with running water to them. Deloris asked, "Is there hot water to the showers?" George, looked at her as he would a naïve child and said, "There is no need for hot water, it is always warm here in Placencia." Deloris, decided to ask one more question. "George, why don't you have restrooms in each room?"

George looked at her as if she were slow and said, "They are all rest rooms. They have a bed for rest."

"Deloris smiled and realized that the terms were probably different here, "I mean a toilet and a shower in each room."

"Oh, dat is way too expensive and if de toilet backs up into the room, dat would be a bad ting."

"Yes, I understand, but aren't your guests inconvenienced when they have to leave their room to go to the shower or restroom? I mean bathroom?" She corrected herself.

"Too much money to have it in each room. Belize is mostly this way. People who come here, dey are aware."

George proceeded to tell the couple how he had built this hotel little by little, adding to it each year if the fishing had been good. He told them how he had worked late into the night doing most of the work himself and how his wife, Connie and his two sons had been here with him as he worked. It was obvious that much love and care had gone into creating this hotel. He told them that a few years ago he had taken in a partner so that they could help him operate the hotel since Connie could not do it any longer since she cared for the two sons and several other children in the neighborhood. He bragged about the fact that they had many guests who returned to Paradise to stay each year.

The couple thanked George for showing them around and said goodbye to him. Again, George asked if they were interested and they assured him that they were not, but they loved the fact that he had shared his story about how the hotel was built and that they would keep the fact that he wanted to sell it in mind and would tell anyone they knew who might be interested in buying a hotel. They returned to Ernie and Amy's house just in time to clean up for dinner.

The next morning Alan and Ernie went fishing with Fred, who explained to Alan that he was the proud father of eight children. He went on to explain that each of his children, as well as his wife shared the first letter of his name. The three men laughed about it and shared a good visit before Alan and Deloris needed to leave for the airport.

Chapter 4

After returning to their home in Florida, Deloris and Alan returned to their hectic but mundane lives of managing the Animal Hospital and their other businesses. After about six weeks or so of being home, the obvious conversation needed to be had. While sitting and having coffee one morning, Alan looked at Deloris and asked, "So what about Belize?"

"What about it, Alan?" she replied. She knew that he had been thinking about the offer of the hotel and so had she, but wouldn't admit it.

"I mean, would you like to go back?"

"Sure, I would love it. I enjoyed it much more than I originally thought I would."

The two discussed it and agreed they wanted to go back and Alan asked Deloris to call Amy and ask when they planned to return to Belize. Amy told her that it would be months before they return, but that they were welcome to stay in their house there if they'd like. Deloris agreed and told Alan about their offer. The couple made their plans and scheduled a date to return for at least two weeks on this visit.

It had been four months since they were last in Placencia, they flew into Belize City and had booked a flight to Placencia on one of the small planes that fly around Belize, almost like a bus service. Their trip to Placencia was aboard a small twelve-seater, single engine plane which allowed them the ability to see the canopy of the peninsula from the air. The emerald colors of the canopy and the beautiful surrounding ocean was enchanting and they tried to take a lot of pictures, but the plane's windows prevented the best of shots. Deloris stared at the trees and the coastline as they met in a beautiful dance. They watched as the tip of the peninsula came into view. The small village grew larger and larger until the aircraft began to descend onto the airstrip. The two were excited and returning to the village felt almost as if it were a homecoming.

That night the two went to dinner at the Barefoot Bar & Grill and enjoyed the fact that people they had met on their first trip remembered them and came up to say hello. They sat and watched as the expats interacted with the locals. Deloris looked at Alan and asked, "So what is it that captivated you about Placencia?"

"I guess it reminds me of the way things were when we were growing up. Things are so much slower here and the hustle and bustle of the life we live in Florida has made us so busy that all we do is work." He answered.

"I agree completely. I was actually very surprised that I enjoyed it as much as I did when we were here last time. It almost feels like home, when the people here remembered our names and spoke to us, it was nice." replied Deloris.

"Other than that, is there anything else that you liked about it?", asked Alan.

"I can feel something, but I can't quite put my finger on it.", she looked puzzled as she answered.

"Same for me, I guess. Can't quite put my finger on it either."

Well, I can tell you what they were feeling, but I will wait until the story reaches that point. I have been there and there is something that draws you to Placencia, like nowhere else on earth. You will learn what the mysterious captivation is soon enough.

The locals seemed all too happy to talk and share their stories. Alan soon realized that if you need to find who was selling fresh fish today or needed to find where you could get a haircut, you simply needed to ask someone and they would help you find it. In fact, they seem to take great pleasure in showing the visitors the ropes. Of course, if you bought them a beer or a meal, it was greatly appreciated as well. This practice of sharing knowledge in return for food and a few drinks is generally accepted and a way of life for many of the local Belizeans. The enjoyed bragging about the wonders of Belize. Deloris and Alan enjoyed the food that they had experienced in the village, it was different from the states, but it was very good in its own way. They commented more than once that everything tasted better here.

The missing elements were Trans-Fat, preservatives and steroids that we pump into our beef and vegetables as we grow them and process the food in the states. Most of this was truly healthy food, although a few too many items are fried and one needs to choose wisely if they want to take advantage of the healthy lifestyle that is available here. The practice of having everything fresh, which the North Americans have left behind, to produce more fruits and vegetables more quickly, or grow our beef faster and larger to inflate profit. In the U.S. producers, have gotten away from quality and focused on quantity instead.

Tess was a person that Amy had introduced Deloris too during their first visit and when they spotted her walk into Bare Foot alone, Deloris motioned her over. Alan, never the shy one to ask personal questions, soon had Tess telling them the story of why she was in Belize alone.

Tess and her husband Sandy had been vacationing in Belize for a month each year for the last six years. They loved Belize and its way of life. They were in their early forties but they had decided that they wanted to get away from the hectic life in the states while they were still young enough to enjoy life. Tess was a beautiful woman with a smile that lit up the room and her good humor was contagious. Sandy's job could be done online so he could make his living from anywhere in the world. Tess had raised their two girls and the oldest was off and on her on, the youngest child would be starting college the following year. When she was younger, Tess had been in the hospitality business and had ran a large restaurant. However, over the past few years she made jewelry from glass and shipped it all over the world. While the profits from her business were not great, they were enough to allow the couple to take time off each year and spend time together. They had been able to save a nest egg and while it was not enough to take them through their retirement years it was enough to invest in a small business in Belize. They decided that it was time to make the move to Belize. Their plan was to buy a small business that Tess and Sandy would run and they would live off those profits along with the money that Tess made from her jewelry business. They could then save all the money that Sandy made for their retirement years. They had traveled all over Belize, but last summer when they visited Placencia for the first time they knew that this was the place for them. Tess had returned to Placencia 3 months ago and started her search for just the right business. While their plan seemed so practical, Tess had learned that practicality and Belize did not always mesh. After bringing all her equipment to make the jewelry, she had learned that if she was going to sell the jewelry she made to anyone in Belize, that she needed a work permit. The alternative to selling it here in Belize, meant shipping each piece out and the cost of mailing it from Belize was extremely high. Also, the reliability of the pieces reaching its intended receiver was not a sure thing and certainly not in a guaranteed time frame. In order to obtain a work-permit she needed to fill out numerous pieces of paperwork and submit it to the government. The alternative was to remain in Belize for one year, with no more than 14 days away, and then apply for residency. The quest for residency could take several months up to a year or more. Tess knew people who had applied for work permits or residency and after 5 or 6 months were still waiting. All this had to be done without working to earn money while here in Belize. Despite, all the problems, Tess was still determined to find a way that she and Sandy could live here in Belize. She and Sandy stayed in touch via video calling and she took the opportunity to call Sandy and introduce him to Alan and Deloris. Deloris and Alan immediately bonded with this couple and determined to stay in touch. After sharing a meal Tess left to meet other friends.

The next day, after eating almost all their meals in restaurants, the two decided it would be fun to eat at their own dinner table tonight. Deloris and Alan went to the market for fresh produce, then to the grocery store to find the other things they would need. In Placencia, you needed to go to the grocery store to determine what is available before deciding exactly what you would have on your menu. The options were limited to the things that the grocers could get in Belize. Things like fresh plastic cartooned milk, frozen vegetables and you'd never see the normal candy bars on the isle, to mention a few things, so this was much different than the ideology that the American grocers have of "Many Choices".

Now I will tell you that by the time I visited Placencia there was many stores for groceries and all but one was owned by Chinese families, however when Alan and Deloris first visited, there was only one grocery store and it close at noon on Saturday and did not reopen until Monday morning. The options were limited but the simplicity of the Belizean ways was growing on Deloris and Alan quickly. They began enjoying the adventures of not being able to control each aspect of their life. They were able to find enough options for Deloris to create a very nice meal and they enjoyed dinner that evening alone.

The next morning, Alan woke up before Deloris and strolled out to the end of the dock to watch the sunrise. Alan loved fishing and diving, but he also enjoyed any activity on the water. He decided that he wanted to go fishing. Ernie had given him Fred's number before he left to come back to Placencia. He called Fred and asked if he would take him fishing for the day, Fred of course agreed. That afternoon, Fred arrived with two of his teenaged sons and the four men went fishing. Deloris wandered the village and seeing things that she hadn't seen before. Beautiful bushes and plants that seem to grow everywhere. Plants that she had to go to the nursery to buy for her yard in the states, seem to just grow wild here like the hibiscus and crotons. The variety of houses and buildings reminded her that she was in a whole new world and no longer in "Suburbia" America. The way that people lived and what they considered a necessity for their homes reminded her that this was a completely different culture. She walked down the road alone and was greeted by nearly every person that passed. It was rarely a "Hello", instead, the greeting in Belize depends upon the time of day that you see someone. If it is morning, the greeting would be "Good Morning" after noon, the greeting changes to "Good day" and at night, the greeting and goodbye from the Belizeans was always "Good night."

I can tell you that I never got use to greeting someone in the evening and saying, "Good Night" when what I meant was "Hi". We often forget that our way of doing things seems so alien to others just as their customs seem different to us. The differences allowed her to relax and realize that the things she considered vital at home, took a back seat in a place like Belize. It was a liberating feeling.

When Alan returned, they had a boatful of fish. After helping Fred and his sons clean the fish he took his appropriate share and bid Fred and his sons a good night watching as they pulled away from the dock. The sun was setting as he made his way to the house. He raised his catch to show Deloris as he approached and smiled with satisfaction. He loved to fish and he loved to brag about his catch, so she was ready to listen intently to his story today. She made a beautiful, fresh salad and garlic bread to go with the fresh fish, "So you enjoyed the fishing, but how does it compare to fishing in Florida?" she asks.

"Oh, it is nice here! You can see the bottom in a hundred feet of water. I watched so many fish so I asked Fred to set up a dive for me. I want to dive this beautiful water and explore the reef. He agreed to take me as soon as he is free. Fred does a lot of free diving. Every Belizean that I have talked to, that dives, seems to be able to free dive easily."

"You can come too. You may enjoy it." Alan said.

"You know I'm a land lover and don't care for boats much." She chuckled, it was their standing joke. Alan knew that she wouldn't go, but wanted to invite her. They enjoyed the peace and quiet with no television, no car horns honking, no police sirens blaring in the distance and no phones ringing to break the tranquil silence. This was new and welcomed to both of them.

Over the next couple of days Alan enjoyed fishing and diving the crystal-clear waters of the Caribbean with Fred. Occasionally, Fred would take other expats that were visiting Placencia. Alan learned that the type of people who visited the village were quite diverse. The thing that surprised him was that the people he met on these fishing or diving trips all had visited Placencia many times and it almost seemed like a second home for them. Deloris enjoyed walking the village and reading. Here it did not seem that it was always necessary to be doing something productive. Placencia taught her that it was alright just to relax and not always be pushing ahead. Her inner designer surfaced as she walked through the village and looked at the buildings on the different lots.

In the states, they had often purchased property, usually with an older home on it, and with Deloris's ideas for decorating and designing they would take an ordinary home and put touches on it that would allow them to turn the property for a good profit. They lived in the houses while they did this and this way of life had worked well for them.

While walking up the beach one morning, Deloris met a couple from Michigan. The three of them struck up a conversation. Soon they found themselves sitting on an old boat that was beached upside down, and the story of how Bill and Krista had come to own a hotel in Placencia, spilled out. Krista found herself needing some time away from their lifestyle in the states. She had come to Placencia alone. She had visited Placencia one other time with friends, so she knew she would feel safe in Placencia. While here, on a whim, she had looked at a hotel on the beach that was for sale. After returning home she had talked Bill into buying the hotel. A hotel that Bill had never seen. They now owned a small hotel and were running it. They employed one-part time Belizean girl, but for the most part was doing all the work themselves. They told Deloris that they were having trouble getting their work permit. They had been trying for 6 months now and here in Belize it was necessary to constantly remind the person who was handling your work permit to not forget you. However, there always seemed to be another piece of paperwork that they needed. Despite all the "red tape", Bill and Krista seemed to be happy with their life in Placencia. However, Deloris could tell that this inability to obtain a work permit was causing them a great deal of frustration. This was her first indication that worries could visit even in this seemingly worry-free village.

On one of their many walking trips up the dirt Sunset Pointe road, as they passed George's house, he was on the porch and came out to greet them. They'd been back in Placencia for several days now and hadn't stopped to say hello. "Good day, Alan and Deloris." He said loudly as he waved. "Good day!" Deloris shouted. "You guys ready to buy the hotel?" George asked quickly.

Deloris had expected that the question was coming and Alan replied, "Well, we haven't thought much about it, George." "You'd be happy here and you would enjoy being a host to a variety of different people who call Placencia a home away from home." He coaxed.

Deloris looked at Alan and then said, "Let's look at it again, George. If you will show us again, we'll be glad to look." She noticed that Alan was giving her a curious look in return.

"Okay, great! Let me get de keys" George seemed to catch another gear as he hurried into his house. Constance peeked through the door as he rushed through and then spoke to Alan and Deloris, "Good day! How are things?" "Good day! Everything is great and yourself?" Deloris replied.

"All is going good." She answered and then disappeared back into the house.

They were alone for a moment, and Alan asked quietly, "Are you seriously interested in this hotel?" Deloris leaned over a bit and whispered, "He's never going to stop asking until we look at it and after we do, we can turn him down once and for all. I figure if we go and look at it, we can tell him that we aren't interested and be done with it. Besides, it can't hurt to look at it."

"Okay, you are right. Let's check it out and then we'll break it to him afterward." Alan agreed, as visions of fishing and diving popped into his head.

In order to reach the hotel, it was necessary to walk about a block down a dirt path. There were houses up on stilts on both sides of the path. The path was about 8 feet wide and most of the houses along the way were built very closely to the path. "Is there no way to drive a vehicle to the hotel, George" Alan inquired, as they made their way to the hotel. "Vehicle? questioned Fred. Alan realized that this was a question that Fred had never contemplated, because vehicles were not a large part of his life. "Are there any guests staying at the hotel now? Ask Deloris. "No, not at de moment. It is de slow season." George answered. and then followed with a shoulder shrug.

The slow season in Placencia was the summer months, as people didn't really need to escape the weather in North America in the summer months. Visitors only poured into the village during the nasty months of winter. She remembered that they were there in June and it was slow as well, it was now October and it still seems slow. George assured them that next month, in November, people would be flocking to the village like migrating birds escaping the harsh winter months up north. He showed the two around the hotel again and pointed out things that could make the place better, as if he already knew that they were going to buy it. The question of the price was not brought up. Alan said, "It is a nice place, George. Let us discuss it and we will get back to you." Deloris looked at him as if he had fumbled a football in the big game. He simply winked at her and they said their goodbyes to George.

Before heading back to Ernie and Amy's house, they wandered down another dirt road that led to the main road. As they walked Deloris asked, "I thought you were going to turn him down gently and we would be done with this hotel idea?"

"I was going to, but then I realized that George isn't the type of person who would take a gentle let down, without him believing that we at least had discussed it seriously." Alan stopped when he noticed a couple of kids playing nearby on the soccer field. He watched as the kids played with an old soccer ball. He recognized the game they were playing as soccer. Of course, there were no uniforms, no factory-made nets and definitely none of the high-priced soccer shoes that American kids would have deemed as a necessity. His mind was drawing him back to his childhood. Growing up on military bases all over the world he remembered how it felt to get together with a group of peers and play an impromptu game. It would've been football, volleyball or baseball, not soccer, but the feeling was the same worldwide. He and his friends would also play without all the fancy accessories; watching the kids of the village, Alan felt a connection hoping that they would have the opportunity to great future; a way to make a living to raise their families and to enjoy life. He wanted every child to have an education and the exposure to opportunities, but realized that he couldn't change this new world and this culture alone. He realized that he didn't see a multitude of employment opportunities here in this small village. What he had seen was a few bank employees, a few clerks in the stores, but most of them seemed to be family members, and then there was people who sold their goods on the street. There were a few tour guides, but he couldn't help but wonder how most of the people even earned a living. Deloris noticed his brow change as he watched the kids playing. They were having fun with nothing. No cell phone, no video games in their living room, keeping their attention for hours on end. She asked, "What is it, Alan?"

He looked at her as if she had interrupted a conversation and with a surprised look he replied, "Oh, nothing. I was just watching those kids play and thinking that they don't have much of an opportunity to advance their lives over here."

"Yeah, this is a third world country. They don't have a Wal-Mart or a multitude of stores to go and buy things. In fact, even if there were stores they don't have the money to buy things that the kids in the states think are essential. They must make do with what they have here. I always knew that all I had to do was to dream and the opportunity to obtain that dream was a possibility as long as, I was willing to work hard enough to make it a reality. Here what they are lacking is the opportunity to earn a good income in order to make their dreams become a reality." She had just expressed the same thing that he had been thinking. This was the first time that they had realized what was missing, it was opportunity, for the people who live in this "Paradise". As wonderful as this country is, the future generations would face the problem of no "real" opportunity to advance into a profession, that this changing world requires, unless they were able to leave their "Paradise". Would they go away and then return with the knowledge to help Belize progress into the ever-changing world or would they simply move away and leave Placencia to be destined to remain the same as it had been for many, many years. Did everyone want Placencia to change? Its charm was in fact, that it wasn't a progressive place. What is the balance? Did anyone think that Paradise needed to change?

Earlier, while they had been walking around, they stopped and asked a local, who they met on the first visit to Placencia, where they might find a good Italian restaurant. That night, as they tried to follow the directions, they found themselves going directly through someone's back yard and hesitated, until they passed by a group of locals who told them that it was fine to take this path. Walking through people's property and right pass their open doors seemed to be an acceptable practice here. They came upon a clothesline, where freshly washed linens hung to dry in the evening air, that they had to duck under. They passed another local who asked them what they were looking for in a happy tone. After Deloris and Alan explained that they were looking for the Italian restaurant, he told them that it was just ahead. They continued; however, Deloris pulled Alan closer as she felt a bit uncomfortable passing through people's yards. After a short distance, they came upon another set of clotheslines and found a family of four seated at a picnic table enjoying their dinner. The obvious patriarch bid them "Good night" with a smile and the embarrassed couple replied, "Good night."

"Are ya lookin for de resrant?" asked the middle-aged man who was clearly a hard worker. He sat at a picnic table and his muscles were gleaming in the dim light that spilled out from the tiny building that sat close by and served as the place the family slept. There were no shoes to be seen on any of the family members, the man and his son did not have on a shirt. The mother and the younger daughter wore shorts and off the shoulder blouses. They were enjoying the ocean breeze. It was obviously cooler here than inside the small house. This stretch of land, that had an amazing view of the ocean, served as their living and dining room.

"Yes, we are trying to find the Italian Restaurant. We were told to come this way, but didn't know that it would be through so many yards." Alan explained with a soft voice.

"Dat is fine, mista. Jus keep right on goin dat way and you will find it soon." The man said with a smile.

"Okay, thank you very much." Alan expressed and the two began walking away. Deloris quickly turned and said, "Good night!" with a smile.

Before long the couple were at the restaurant and seated. Alan asked Deloris, "So what do you think about the hotel?"

She laughed and said, "In my mind I've already torn it down and built my dream home on the ocean front property."

"Sounds logical. That hotel is an eyesore as it stands. Even George said he would change everything." Laughed Alan.

Deloris made a second attempt at ordering Eggplant Parmigiana, which again was thwarted by the lack of eggplants; so, the two enjoyed their wonderful meal of Chicken Parmigiana with pasta and basil roasted potatoes as they discussed the dilapidated hotel. They were the only two guests there and had a chance to meet the owner. He was a happy man, with a delightful smile. His five-foot, five-inch frame struggled with the weight of his belly and his waddle was clearly not voluntary. His smile seemed so earnest and true as his rosy cheeks and lined forehead helped to highlight it. He explained that it was just him and his wife who ran the place, with the occasional help from a local boy named "Tattoo" during high season when the place was filled to capacity. He told them that he and his wife would return to Italy for a month so they could see their family while the season was still slow and would return just before the end of November. It was already well into October and they would only be away for a few weeks. Deloris asked, "Do y'all do that every year? I mean travel back to Italy for a few weeks for the season break?"

"Oh, we usually go for July, August, September and October, but disa year we hava niece whosa getting married so we stay here longer in hopes of earning a little more money. We will go lata to helpa with the cooking for de wedding." He spoke with an accelerated Italian accent. "So normally you'd have already been back in Italy?", ask Deloris.

"Yesa, we would hava went ina lata July." He answered with an English/Italian compilation that Deloris enjoyed. Two other families entered the restaurant and he excused himself to seat them, but insisted that they enjoy their meals before he retreated.

While the couple enjoyed the atmosphere and one another, the couple noticed that there was only one table open now and discussed between themselves how the restaurant would be better expanded and could seat more people and increase income. A short time later a group of six entered and Alan and Deloris were shocked when the owner turned them away by saying, "Ima sorry. We nota taking any more customers."

The couple quietly discussed the possible reasons that the man turned away business and decided that they must not be prepared to handle so many at once. Soon a lady approached the table and was clearly the owner's wife. She was a plump woman and had sweat beaded up on her forehead, she had been in cooking in the hot kitchen. Without asking, she refill their drinks and quickly checked on the other customers. She had salt & pepper hair that was loosely pulled back. Her smile was authentic and her pride in serving a wonderfully prepared meal was written on her face as she asked, "How was the meal?" in struggled English.

"Oh, it was magnificent!" Deloris answered quickly. "Thank you so much for a wonderful meal.", she added. "Yeah, it was really good food.", Alan agreed.

As she walked away, Deloris said to Alan, "Those people work very hard and they do such a great job."

After finishing their drinks, the two paid their check and left a hefty tip for the couple. The man said, "Oh, thatsa not necessary. Itsa way too much."

"Please accept it. The meal was great and the atmosphere was excellent. It was a pleasure to meet you.", said Alan.

"Wella okay, it wasa nica to meet you too. If you coma back ona Friday, we willa hava eggplanta for you."

Deloris smiled big and said, "Oh, thank you so much. I can't find anyone here who has it."

"We willa have it ifa you coma back ona Friday. We willa get soma froma Belmamopana and I maka sure it isa the very besta Eggplanta you ever have!", he assured her again. And then said, "Choa."

Deloris said, "Okay, we will definitely be back on Friday. Good night and thanks again." As they walked away waving, they felt special. This was truly great customer service, that was not a result of training, yet comes from pride in what they do. Deloris remembered them turning the party of six away and asked Alan, "Should we give them a time that we will be here on Friday so that we aren't turned away?"

"Nah, they will be expecting us around the same time. We will be okay.", he assured her. They walked back toward the yards that they had crossed on their journey there. They came across the picnic table that was now filled with men drinking rum and bitters, "Good Night!" The crowd of men chanted as soon as they realized the couple was there.

"Good night!" The new, more experienced couple replied.

While lying in bed that night, Alan said, "I think we may want to kick around the idea of making an offer on George's hotel." "Are you serious?" Deloris replied in a sleepy voice.

"Yeah, I mean, we love it here and it is just sitting there.", he answered as he stared at the ceiling. "Okay, let's talk about it in the morning." She answered as she fell asleep.

The following morning, sitting out on the dock and watching the perfect sunrise onto the blue Caribbean waters and picturesque sailboats in the area, they discussed buying the hotel. There was little apprehension from either side as they discussed the possibilities. Alan imagined having his own tour company, as a part of the hotel. They could offer guest diving or fishing trips and Alan could accompany them whenever he chose to do so. How wonderful that would be. It seemed that the idea of Paradise becoming their next adventure, had become an accepted fact. Was this an investment they should make? How could they do it and make it work? This wasn't a business that they knew anything about, but it was, however, typical of them to think of new investments. In the past, they would use the "ready, get set, go" theory, but not on this project. Typically, Deloris would make sure it could become a reality by formulating plans A, B, C or usually D. She would examine every possibility and have a backup plan to prevent disaster. Alan, like me, is the dreamer and always had the big picture in mind. Deloris is the pragmatist who made sure the money was available and could be moved to make things happen. This normally took months and sometime years to set the detailed plan into action. However, this idea seemed to be coming to them both without all the planning. They were seriously thinking of buying a hotel in a third world country, and they had no idea of what they would face.

In the U.S., Deloris would have insisted that they have a feasibility study done and investigate a thousand other questions before deciding if it was a good idea or not. They'd have learned how a hotel works and the market strains prior to even considering it, but here in Placencia, they jumped and then looked, it seemed. They were considering buying this hotel even though they did not know the first thing about running a hotel; not to mention, that it was a hotel that looked dilapidated and they had no idea if it was profitable when in operation or not. They realized that here in Belize, things worked quite differently. They had no idea of what the hotel was worth, what it grossed or netted yearly. They could only hope for the records, as Belizeans rarely needed that sort of thing.

With the lack of knowledge and ignorance of profit and loss or even general business practices in this country, they were considering buying this hotel in Placencia, Belize, Central America … Can you believe that? I will tell you, that doesn't sound like my aunt and uncle at all. When I heard about it, I thought to myself, "There's no way. Someone has the story confused." But it was true! They were thinking about buying a hotel in a place that I had never even heard of and I realized that they don't stop once they have an idea. That is what I admire so much about them. They have a plan and then make it happen. Anyway… Deloris, always the realist, asked what he thought the price would be. Alan replied, "I'd only offer property value, because the hotel has no value to us. It will actually cost us money to remove it and build something that we would want to operate."

Because of their background in buying property in the states and flipping it for a profit, just buying property would not have been so strange, but this was a business that they were buying and running a business requires living in the same place, at least for a while, in order to get it up and going. They had never even contemplated buying a property without knowing the asking price from the beginning, so "Go! Ready, Get Set!" in this situation was what they were doing. They spent hours throwing around ideas and discussing possibilities well into that night. Now you see, the results of, "what happens when you are inflicted with "Tropical Fever"". Certainly, Aunt Deloris and Uncle Alan were in the grips of this mythical disease. They had contracted the disease on their very first visit and now the disease was a full-blown case. At least that is my explanation of such uncharacteristic behavior.

The next morning, they decided to go out for breakfast and headed up Sunset Pointe Road to find a restaurant for breakfast. As they were walking past the soccer field, they noticed a place with a few people sitting at tables eating. They walked in and there were only five tables, surrounded by a chain linked fence. It was obviously a place frequented by locals. They found a table and sat down. After placing their order, they listened in on the conversation taking place, which it seemed everyone in the restaurant was participating in. They inferred that the owner, was the local Justice of the Peace, and everyone was discussing a document that he had been requested to witness. When he delivered their meal, he introduced himself as Mr. Perry and informed them that he was indeed the Justice of the Peace for the village. He was also the local repairman for anything refrigerated and also owned a building next to his restaurant where he rented rooms. Alan asked him, "Do you know anything about the hotel on the beach that George is trying to sell?"

"Oh, yea, dat is a nice place. George is tired of running it and needs to sell it." The dark Belizean man assured. He wore a cotton shirt and brown pants. His shoes were a dark leather sandal and appeared to be very worn.

"Why does he need to sell it so badly?" Asked Deloris.

"Oh, dat because he owes too much money to de bank." Deloris was shocked to realize that apparently everyone's personal business seemed to be fair game for discussion by the entire village. No one else seemed to think this was strange.

"So, is there really a need for another hotel here in the village?" asked Alan.

"Well, de people here is fine wit what is here, but I talk to more and more of de tourists dat come here who want air conditioners and a private bathroom in de room."

It was clear that he wasn't a fan of the tourists who asked for so much, needing air conditioning in their rooms, above all, why would anyone in the world need a private bathroom? Deloris and Alan assumed that the JP (Justice of the Peace) would tell tourists, if they needed all those things, they didn't need to be in Belize. Air conditioning was a rarity in Belize and many people in Belize had never even felt its cooling seduction. A private bathroom was also another rarity and many people didn't even have one in their homes. The ol' out-house was still very much in effect there. Locals came and went in the restaurant and the conversations changed to whatever was on their minds. Alan and Deloris thanked Mr. Perry for the information and a great breakfast and finished their meal.

They decided to see if they could find George and inquire about the price of the hotel. When they arrived in George's yard, he was busy sanding on the boat that he had been working on for a while now. He greeted them warmly with, "Good day, my friends!" as he sat the sanding block down and rushed over to them.

"George, we were wandering if you had a price in mind for selling the hotel?" Alan said as he shook George's hand.

"Oh, I will have to ask my business partner and get back to you." He answered with a big smile, seeing that they were indeed interested.

They asked a few questions, such as, if an appraisal had been done on the property? George looked at them with confusion. It was apparent that an appraisal was not something that he was familiar with at all. "George, I will only be willing to pay the land value. The hotel doesn't do me any good as it is."

"I know we need to sell it for a particular amount, but I will have to get with my business partner and get back to ya about exactly what that number is." George retorted.

"Okay, we will be at Ernie and Amy's house. You know where that is?" Alan asked.

"Oh, yes. Everyone knows where dat is, Mista Alan."

"Okay, we'll be there this evening. Just come by and let us know when you have a figure."

"Okay den. I will let my partner know that you will only pay land value and that was what was offad to avoid de confusion." George agreed.

That evening, while waiting on George and his partner's response, Alan and Deloris discussed an acceptable offer and the amount they could come up with from their available assets. They decided that if the price was acceptable, they'd tear down the current hotel and build a lodge that could host groups for fishing or diving. Now let me point out again that this was so atypical of my aunt and uncle. Here they were offering to buy a piece of property in a foreign country that they had no idea what the comparable land had sold for or any idea of what it would cost to tear down the current structure, or the cost to rebuild the new structure. The idea of bringing groups, of divers and fishermen, over to stay in this hotel seemed to have come to them both, but they had no idea if the idea was financially feasible or not. For some couples, this may not seem strange, but I just want to impress on you from what you have learned in the first part of this book about this couple, how truly different this was from anything they had ever done before. This book is a tribute to their actions that day and to the actions of many other people they came to know during their upcoming adventure and how often this phenomenon occurs in the foreign land of Belize.

When George arrived, he had another man with him. He introduced the man as his business partner, Ron. Ron was a young man with black hair and piercing blue eyes. A Belizean with a wide smile and a very professional manner. George informed them that Ron also owned a large bar on the peninsula. After some small talk and introductions George excused himself, as he had other things to do, and the other three sat and discussed the property. Deloris and Alan thought it was strange that George left while they discussed price, but assumed that it was what Ron wanted. The price that Ron had in mind was exactly what the couple had assumed earlier in the day. Alan asked about the title and if there was a mortgage or lienholder on the title. Ron explained that there was a mortgage, but a clear title could be obtained without issue from mortgage holder, which was the bank. Alan and Deloris gave one another a look of agreement, and Alan agreed that they would buy the hotel at the asking price. He asked about a contract, but was assured that there was no need for a contract as long as he had their word that they'd buy it. Alan agreed and was quite surprised when Ron agreed to sell the Belizean corporation that held the hotel license and the dock permit, as they could then use them for the new hotel on the property.

With the offer of the hotel license and dock permit, the couple realized that they really knew nothing about how things worked here. In the states, they were knowledgeable about what permits or license were needed, but here they were at a total loss. They'd have to learn, if they were to run a business here in Belize. They assumed that all the rules would be neatly written and could be obtained by simply asking, were they in for the shock of their lives. Rules and the way things are done are a moving target in Belize and often money is the only way to get someone to commit to telling you exactly what you needed and helping you acquire it. They would soon begin to learn this lesson.

When Ron left, Alan looked at Deloris with excited, wide eyes and said, "I can't believe we just did that!" "Yeah, but I didn't think it would be that easy. We just agreed to buy a hotel in Belize, Central America!"

"I can't either. Do you think we are losing our minds?" inquired Deloris. "No, I think it is great. We are on another new adventure", laughed Alan.

Deloris laughed and said, "Yes, it is great! We would never have done that so quickly in the states, so sporadic and off the cuff like that. But I'm glad that we did and it feels really good to be so impulsive." She quipped.

Chapter 5

The night before they returned to the states they ran into Tess and told her of their agreement to purchase the hotel. She was so excited for them. She still had not found the perfect business to buy for her and Sandy. Deloris told her the story about Bill and Krista and suggested that she go talk to them. Tess did not think she had met them, but knew where their hotel was located. Deloris suggested that they may want partners or know of other opportunities in the village. In Deloris's one conversation with them, Krista seemed to know about everything that was going on in the village and Deloris had already learned that the best source of information in this village was to ask someone who kept up with the local happenings.

They had agreed to purchase a hotel on their second visit to Placencia and now they were returning to the states. It was days before the fast-paced pressure of the modern world subsided and they finally were caught up on all pressing matters that had piled up while they were away. They were finally able to seriously discuss their plans and make arrangements to purchase the hotel. Their plan, at this point, was to tear down the current hotel. In rebuilding the possibilities were endless, but the one that seemed to have come unbidden to both of them, without any discussion was to build a lodge with the plan of bringing people in to dive or fish. These would be small groups and they would accompany each group and serve as host and hostess to these groups. They decided that the hotel would not be opened when they were not there. They would have people in the village to come in when they were bringing in a group and operate the lodge. This seemed to fit perfectly with the work ethic that they had observed in Belize. Many of the locals seemed to like jobs that did not require year-round dedication. They decided that going to different dive shops and fishing shops and to groups that were abundant for people who loved these activities would generate enough groups each year to support the lodge. They would use the lodge as their second home, when they did not have a group going down and they wanted to get away. This way they could maintain their companies in the states, while also experiencing Belize when they wanted. They would still be able to visit Belize and even make a profit with their new property. They began contacting dive clubs and fishing clubs in Florida. They were bombarded with the same questions from everyone, "When will it be ready? How many people can you accommodate?" etc. They had decided that 12 people would be the absolute maximum that they would take at any one time. They assured everyone that it would be ready for the next season, which gave them almost a year for their project to be completed. The lodge would have only 6 suites and then they would have a suite of their own. Since it was now November, surely a year was plenty of time to get the new lodge open. However, they'd soon learn that things in Belize would go very differently than they planned. They had now done the math and discussed the rates that they'd have to charge to be profitable. This would be very different, because they would be offering people a chance to be personally escorted to Belize and hosted as if they were visiting friends. Deloris wanted to make these trips feel like she felt when Ernie and Amy brought them to Placencia. She wanted to introduce their guests to the magic of Belize, while enjoying diving or fishing that they loved. She wanted everyone to fall in love with Placencia the way she had. She wanted them to feel the stress fall away and all the details that they had thought were paramount when they were in the states become small and insignificant while they were in the magical place of Placencia.

Once they had arranged for the money to buy the property, they focused again on the operation of their businesses in the states. They were very busy, so, it was not surprising that it took them some time to realize, that it had been three months since agreeing to purchase the hotel, and they had not heard anything from Ron or George. Deloris looked and couldn't find an email from either of the men, but could find one for the hotel, so she sent an email to them there. She asked about the progress and asked to be updated. It was more than a week before she received a reply from Ron. He explained that since there had never been a title on the property, everything had to be submitted to Belmopan where the title and land office was located and that they should hear something back within sixty days. When Deloris checked back sixty days later, the answer remained the same. It had been five months since they thought they had agreed to purchase a hotel, still no change in progress. Finally, after seven months of waiting, they received the long-awaited email from Ron stating that the attorney had the title in hand and would be contacting them directly. They still had no instructions for an exchange of money. Deloris was excited and couldn't wait to get started on this new adventure. They booked their flight to Belize City, assuming that they could get some other things done while they were there waiting on the closing appointment. Deloris made arrangements to have her bank transfer the purchase price to an escrow account once she was at the closing and had the necessary information. She remembered that the hotel handled booking flights from Belize City to Placencia, so she sent an email asking Donna, the employee that they had met previously, to book a flight for them to Placencia and gave her the date and time of arrival of their international flight. She assumed Donna would handle this for them and they would handle the reimbursement at the closing. They had no details of how the accounts would be transferred and no opportunity for a great lawyer they knew and trusted to review the documents.

This was so uncharacteristic of Deloris, that had I known this at the time, I would have been very worried about her. She did not do things like this. She always checked and rechecked every detail.

They flew into Belize City and with Phil's assistance, made their way to their connecting flight. They exchanged greetings with Phil. He knew all about their purchase of the hotel and was excited for them. She remembered that the hotel normally booked their flight with Maya Island Air. If Deloris had not been infected with "tropical fever" concerning all things Belizean, she would have confirmed her flight information, at least once prior to their trip. She told the Maya Island Air employee at the counter that they were supposed to fly to Placencia and had a flight scheduled. The dark Belizean woman flipped through a reservations book and then said, "We have no reservation for you to Placencia today."

"I'm confused. I asked Donna to book us a flight to Placencia today."

"Okay, maybe I should check with Tropic Air. Maybe she booked us with them", said Deloris. Since the counters were side by side one short conversation confirmed that Tropic Air did not have a reservation for them either. "Dat not a problem. We can get you on de flight." Said the Maya Island Air employee.

"Okay, that would be great. Thank you." Deloris replied and pondered again why Donna wouldn't have made the reservation. They flew into Placencia and took a cab to their new business. The cab was an old vehicle that was obviously not in the best mechanical condition; however, the driver negotiated the many ruts to main street, then turned and continued down to Amy and Ernie's house and waited for them while they unloaded their luggage and then took them back to the path that led to the hotel.

As they were making their way down the narrow path toward the hotel, Deloris tried to think of all the reasons that would have prevented Donna from making their reservation. She had been hoping that they could retain the employees at the hotel, but such an oversight was not acceptable. When they arrived at their new business, they walked into the office and was greeted by Donna. Deloris immediately asked, "Did you not book us a flight on Maya into Placencia today? I sent an email requesting that you do so."

"Oh, yes mum, I made dos rezavation." The girl answered with a large smile.

"I see, did you put them under Alan's name, or mine?"

The employee looked at her with a tilted head and replied, "Oh, neither. I didn't know your names. I jus tol dem dat it for de new owna of de hotel." To Donna that seemed to explain the mix up and she simply stood there nodding her head, as if, to prove that she had done as ask. With that issue resolved, the two retreated to Ernie and Amy's house. They began walking the few blocks to the house and discussed the booking confusion. It was a mistake that would never had occurred in the states, but here, in Central America, it may be a common occurrence that they'd insure wouldn't happen to any of their guest. The burden of the busy world they had left behind in Jacksonville seemed to fade away with each step. They were able to chalk it up to the nature of being in a new place and learning their ways. They weren't used to being in a small enough place that people would understand who they were because they had bought, or were buying a hotel. They discussed the way that

Donna had explained the issue made sense, if they were to use the Belizean mindset. The clerk who had taken the reservation at the airline was probably still waiting on someone to ask for the reservations in that manner. Again, they chuckled about it and carried on.

The next couple of days, they spent making plans. They discussed that maybe they would need someone who was experienced to supervise the hotel staff. They agreed that if they could get someone like Tess to just keep an eye on what was going on when they were not there, it would be helpful. They became engrossed with the perceptions of the people who lived there and were soon understanding a bit more of how they thought. Deloris compared the village to a large family. Everyone assumed that everyone else understood relationships and knew everything about the lives of each other.

The couple did not have a cell phone that they could use in Belize, but they knew that George was well aware of where they were staying. They assume that George would simply come tell them when the attorney was ready to close on the purchase, hours turned into days as they waited for someone to contact them. When they passed George's house no one seemed to be around. They began to wonder if there was another hold up in the process, as those were becoming common, in this beautiful country that they were coming to know. After another two days, Ron appeared at their door one morning and told them they needed to be at the attorney's office in Belize City at ten A.M. the next morning. Without a second thought, they packed a bag and planned to immediately fly to Belize City so they would be there bright and early in the morning. They needed a ride to the airstrip. Deloris volunteered to walk up to the main road and try to find a taxi to take them. As she headed up to the main road to locate a taxi, she thought to herself that in the states, Alan would have insisted that she stay behind while he walked up the road. He would not have wanted her to walk alone looking for a taxi. It was obvious he felt that she was safe to walk up to the main road alone. This was uncharacteristic of him, but that is yet another example that shows how differently he viewed Placencia. It was a tight net community where everyone knew everything that happened and everyone watched out for one another. Again, Deloris compared the village to a large family in her mind.

As she reached the main road, she spotted two vehicles that she assumed were taxis. She approached the vehicles as the two drivers were visiting. She told them that she and her husband needed a ride to the airstrip today and would need someone to pick them up from the airstrip the next day. One of the men said that wouldn't be a problem and opened the side door for her to get in. She climbed in and they arrived at the house to pick up Alan. As they drove through the village, Alan ask the driver about how long he had lived in Placencia, and learn he was born and raised there. Alan shared with the driver that his perception of Placencia had changed since his first visit when he saw only poverty and dilapidated homes that had been partially wrecked from the last big hurricane and the lack of maintenance; but now he realized that there were so many more things about Belize and Placencia that are hidden during a simple visit to the village. He now viewed it as a relaxed and happy culture of people, who weren't held to such strict standards, much different than in the U.S. There schedules had to be kept, standards must be met and everything had to be in order. He wondered if one way was better than the other; however, his contemplation came to an abrupt halt as they arrived at the airstrip. He looked up to see the door of the building close to the door of the van and said, "Thank you!"

The driver turned in his seat and asked, "Why you come to de airstrip at dis time of day, sa?"

"So, we can go to Belize City. We have an appointment there in the morning." Alan said as he handed the man money.

"Well, sa you know dat de is nobody here right?" The driver stated with a curious look.

"Are you serious?" Alan asked.

"Yes sa, did ya not know dat?"

"No, we don't have a schedule of the flights, but we assumed the flight would leave soon to Belize City."

"No, sa. Not till fo clock.", the driver explained. It seemed that the last morning flight had left at 10 a.m. and since it was now only 11 a.m. there were no flights out until 4:30 so the employees didn't come back until 4 p.m.

Now, the question became if they returned to the house and waited or waited someplace else. Handing them a crude business card, proclaiming that in addition to a taxi driver, he also did tours, he said. "Nex time ya need a flight, call me and I handle it far ya. Why don I take you on a tour de village while ya wait on de plane? If ya plan on livin in Placencia de tings ya should know."

Alan and Deloris agreed and off they went. The van that they were in would be forced to be parked in the U.S. because no one would inspect it or title it. The exhaust was missing a few components, probably from the rough roads, the window was missing from the rear passenger side and a blue tarp taped across the window prevented the rain from coming in. The driver drove around and shortly pulled into an upscale resort and turned off the engine. The building was beautiful faded hardwood with a large veranda running the length of the front of the building. He faced the couple and said, "My name is Kevin and I am pleased to show you the very best of Placencia. Ya have ta buy a drink to see what I came to show ya, but it werth it." he said in his thick Belizean accent. Alan thought this was a bit of a strange way to begin a tour, but many things seemed strange to him in this place. Deloris found that her breath was almost taken away as they walked into the open-air restaurant. The polished mahogany wooden floors were straight out of a magazine. The beautiful floor glistened in the midday light with a shine that one couldn't possibly describe. She felt guilty to even step onto the work of art. The waiter quickly came and escorted them to a table and seated them. The chair hugged her body like a long-lost relative as she slipped into it. They were a split stained Mahogany wood, built into a barrel shape and were as beautiful as the floor. She knew that, after hearing of Amy's experience of furniture shopping in Belize, that one could have anything built; she'd find out who made these chairs. The tables in the restaurant were decorated with carvings and there were indigenous plants and birds of paradise sitting on each table. They were enhanced by the beauty of the manicured landscape, that they could see from the table at which they sat.

The beauty captivated her and she was falling in love with Belize and its people, over and over again, with every new sense that was piqued by her sight, sound and touch of this beautiful place. After the waiter had taken their drink order, Kevin told Deloris, "You mus see de rezroom."

Deloris tilted her head and inspected the taxi driver for a grin, but there was none. He noticed her expression and clarified by saying, "It is de very most beautiful ting you will eva see."

Deloris slowly rose from her seat and walked over to the hallway and into restroom. Her breath came quicker, as she was stunned by the beauty that the large room held. It was all wood, but with the same detailed polish of the dining area. The room was laden with the finest fixtures and proclaimed an unexplainably pleasant fragrance of tropical flowers. She walked over to the sink and looked for the handle to wash her hands, but didn't find one. After a little investigating, she found a foot pedal that operated the water.

After returning to the hallway, she began to laugh and she shook her head in disbelief. As she took her comfortable seat again, Kevin informed her that he'd had as much trouble finding the foot pedal as she had, on his first visit here. She told Alan all about how amazing she thought this place was and she remarked about how different her outlook was here in paradise now that she had visited more than once. Kevin shook his head in agreement and explained that many people only look at the poor aspect of a country like Belize, but fail to see the rich cultural aspect of it or the fact that with money you could take the simple things that Belizeans can create and make them beautiful. He explained that when people see the boarded-up windows, mixed color paint on buildings and a half-finished fence; that is their lasting impression and never open themselves to the truth of the people. Belize has such a rich history and has been secluded from the world so well that when people think of Belize, they relate it to Guatemala, Honduras or Mexico, but Belize has much more history than one could imagine. All one has to do, is look around and learn the history and attempt to understand why the culture has developed as it has. Deloris understood what Kevin was talking about, as she and Alan were the people that he had mentioned when they first visited. Now, however, it seemed that they had discovered that the Belizean culture and attitude was something that could teach them to appreciate a slower paced life as well. Belize would never be changed by outside forces. They had to take the best parts of this lifestyle and adapt it to the lifestyle they wanted to live in Belize. After leaving the restaurant they were driven back to a parking place that was easily accessible to the famous sidewalk in Placencia. Running along the beach and parallel with the main road there is a narrow side walk that extends from the beachfront at the end of the main street back up the peninsula toward the airport. They walked along the side walk and Kevin pointed out shops, homes, plants and trees. Although; Deloris had walked this sidewalk many times, she was now seeing it through Kevin's eyes and it came alive with meaning for her. He pointed out the property that the Belizean had lost to the stranger when his father had traded property for a boat motor. This was a well know and often repeated story, a part of the lore, of Placencia. Kevin pointed out property that locals owned that were prime pieces of beachfront property and how families wanted to hold on to the property but many were selling to foreigners in hopes of being able to find a better life for their families. He pointed out where Ms. Louise lived and ask Deloris if she and Alan had met Ms. Louise yet. When they said no, he laughed and said that they should try to meet her as soon as possible since she was a powerful force in this village. It would be a while before Ms. Louise came into their lives, but she became beloved by them both.

When they got back to the airstrip they booked a flight to Belize City and found that they had to choose between the municipal airport and the International airport. They were told that it was cheaper to go to the municipal and that it was closer to downtown, so imagine how surprised they were when the first stop in Belize City was the International airport and they had to continue on the get to the municipal. Deloris, being the curious one to why they would charge more to go the International airport, when that was their first stop, asked a local that was traveling on that flight and was told that since foreigners normally go to the International they are charged more so that it is cheaper for Belizeans to use the airline, she was told this without a hint of concern. When they landed at the municipal airport, they were invited by many cabs for a ride. They picked a driver who was less aggressive than the others, but seemed more experienced. They explained to the driver that they needed a hotel as close to the address that they showed him, as possible. The drive through Belize City required nerves of steel; since the streets were very narrow and cars were parked all along the side of the street. The rules of the road seem to be who had the strongest nerves, or the least to lose went first. People on bicycles seem to come out of nowhere and weaved in and out of traffic. How they avoided being hit, was a miracle. The buildings were constructed of old, unpainted concrete. They were close together and most open in the front to the street. Ghetto, probably should not be used to explain Belize City but the word did come to mind. This was rush hour so their progress often came to a standstill. They finally arrived at a gated property and the driver explained, that there was an excellent restaurant inside the hotel and they could eat dinner safely, "As peaceful as most parts of Belize are, Belize City can be very dangerous if you are caught in the wrong place." The driver continued to school the visitors. His accent was almost completely gone as he spoke.

Deloris asked, "Can I ask you why you don't have the same accent as the majority, of the Belizeans, we've met?"

"I grew up in the states and learned to speak clear English in school. Most people here speak Kroil (Creole) and that affects their English. Kroil is a slang, shorten version of English", he explained with a smile.

Alan thanked the driver and gave a good tip for the information. They were met at the gate by a bell boy and were escorted inside. They were required to show their passports for the first time, other than at immigration at the airport, when they flew into Belize. Deloris would soon learn that this was one of the things that a hotel is required to keep on record. They were buying a hotel and she'd need to learn all the government regulations related to operating one. Her adventure in trying to learn these regulations was to be a slow and challenging process.

After a short elevator ride, they were at their room. Looking out of their window at the beach, Alan asked, if after she unpacked, if she'd like to go to the beach and look around with him. She agreed and the two walked the boardwalk that ran along the beachfront. The water was much choppier than it was on the ocean in Placencia. There weren't many people on the boardwalk. There really wasn't much of a beach. Rocks lines the shore and there were limited patches of sand among the rocks. The beaches in Placencia were far better than they were here in Belize City. As they walked back inside, Alan noticed that the hotel had a casino tucked away in the corner. They decided to go in and stood behind four people who seemed to be Belizeans. The door man required each of the locals to show that they had $300.00 B.Z. with them before entering. Having heard the door man, Alan took out $300.00 U.S. to show the man. As they approached the door, Alan held up the money. The door man waved away his money and assured him that it wasn't necessary for him to show that he had money, as all Americans have money, but the Belizeans needed to do so. This bothered Alan, at some level; although, he could imagine how they would justify it. The two held their incredulity until they were inside and then giggled quietly to one another saying how rude and politicly incorrect this rule was for the Belizeans. Deloris said to Alan, "I can't wait to tell this story to our friends in the states. All Americans have money. Ha!"

Alan played the slot machines while Deloris walked around and inspected the décor of the place. Alan soon realized that the machines here weren't designed to pay out often like the ones in the states were and became quickly bored. Deloris wanted to go upstairs and freshen up before dinner. She reached the elevator and pressed the button and waited. After several minutes, the elevator was clearly not working. She walked out to the receptionist's desk and asked if there was an issue with the elevator. The clerk looked up at the elevator and said, "No, mum, it is broken." And calmly went back to reading her magazine. Deloris was insulted by the young lady's carefree demeanor about the elevator when a guest was standing in front of her, "It was working a couple of hours ago when we checked in.", she said calmly to the inattentive girl.

"Yez, but it not workin now." The girl said without looking up from her article.

"So, I need to take the stairs to the fourth floor?" Deloris asked, rhetorically, trying to remain calm. She despised anyone giving bad customer service. It was a pet peeve of hers, regardless of whether it affected her or not.

"Least you not on de tenth floor." The clerk laughed, still not looking up.

Deloris walked back to where Alan was now looking at paintings on the wall in the hotel's large lobby and explained the elevator mishap to him. He never looked away from the paintings and said, "Okay. Well, no sense in hiking up the stairs more than once. Let's eat dinner and then we'll climb them together."

Deloris was shocked! If this were to happen in the states, he would have been outraged at the staff's attitude toward the problem. He would have criticized them for allowing something like this to continue without prompt attention or at least a proper apology for inconveniencing guest. This was a more relaxed attitude. It was an attitude that surprised Deloris. It was not a great feat to climb the stairs, but that the young lady didn't seem concerned at all about inconveniencing guest. She even joked about the fact that they only needed to climb four floors instead of ten. The lack of customer service training was apparent.

They enjoyed their meal and then climbed the eighty steps to their floor. As they reached their floor, they joked about being out of shape to one another, "You'd better get in shape, Alan if you are going to survive in Belize.", she poked.

"You had better start walking again regularly.", he wheezed. They laughed aloud and stopped for a break before opening their room's door. That night, before drifting off to sleep, Deloris thought about how remarkably different Alan was in this country. Something had taken over him and it was a beautiful change. He surely hadn't noticed it himself, but she had witnessed it on several occasions. She hadn't seen him this excited in a very long time; not since he had bought the Hummer, had he been so optimistic and happy about anything. His bout with cancer had seemed to rob him of many things, yet, when this journey began, his energy and joy seemed to return in an instant. He had a newfound youthful like, dreamer's enthusiasm about this new business. As if, in an instant, he realized that life is quite precious and he must seize every moment and live life to the fullest; after all, the next time that the great accountant came calling, he may have to pay the ultimate tax for life. Alan felt as if he had cheated death in some way when he thought of all that had happened. He had seen the silent killer that he had to fight, but only in the radiated photos taken by the doctor. However, he seemed to have won that battle and Deloris had seen the changes in him and today she noticed an even bigger adventurous look in his eyes.

She had been trying for years to accomplish what Belize had accomplished in only a few visits. Even the next morning when there was no hot water, it was all taken in stride.

After her shower, they gathered their things and headed to check out. After walking down, the four flights of stairs, they arrived just in time to hear the "ding" of the elevator. They turned to one another and burst out into laughter. The people exiting the elevator watched the couple giggling and avoided coming too close. Heeding the cab drivers advise they ate their breakfast in the hotel before heading to the attorney's office. "You know, Placencia has much nicer views and the people are also much nicer there.", Alan offered.

After finishing their meal and walking out, Alan asked one taxi driver the cost of taking them to the attorney's address. The driver explained that it was only a couple of blocks up the road and then two streets over. With that information they decided to walk, since they were going to be early anyway. He tipped the driver for the information and the headed out along a wide sidewalk that ran parallel with the ocean. They walked for about two blocks. This street was four lanes wide and by far the nicest road that they had seen since being in Belize. The town was to their right and there were buildings that were four or five stories tall. However, intermingled with those building, were still wooden houses, raised on stilts, where families lived. There were street vendors selling breakfast tacos along this wide avenue. The directions the man had given them, instructed them to cross the avenue and cut through an alley as a short cut, to get to the street on which the Attorney's office was located. When they entered the alley, it was cluttered with broken bottles and trash. They remembered that Belize City had a reputation for being a dangerous place and even though they had been treated well here, they decided that this alley wasn't the best plan of action. Why poke the bear if it isn't awake? They returned to the wide avenue to look for a cross street that look less threatening. While the auto traffic was not nearly as heavy, as it would be in the states, there was still a lot of cars traveling this road. It was obvious that while Placencia was limited in the number of people who owned a vehicle, Belize City was different.

The fact that they had decided to avoid the alley, added several blocks to their walk. They spotted a cross street and although there were no signs, they decided that this should take them in the direction that they needed to go. As they walked this cross street, the auto traffic was now bumper to bumper and moving at a slow pace since this was another very narrow street and again they noticed that cars stopped and parked at odd angles while a passenger got in or out of the vehicle. There were no traffic lights and it was a mystery as to the order, in which, the cars proceeded through intersections. Although they had not followed the directions they had been given, they felt confident that this turn should take them in the right direction. As they walked down the cross street they spotted the exit of the alley that they had refused to take earlier; they looked to the right of the alley and the attorney's office was the building bordering it. Now it made perfect sense as to why the alley was a short cut, but it still had seemed wiser to stay on an open street, the area was very run down. Many of the buildings were concrete but they were unpainted. A few had glass front windows but most were just wide openings. Many wares were displayed on the street adding to the crowding on the narrow sidewalk. This street was crowded with people. They entered the building that housed the attorney's office and realized that there wasn't an elevator, but instead, a wide and rather steep flight of stairs that extended to all four floors.

They entered the attorney's office. Ron and George were already there waiting. Ron explained that he had gone to Ernie and Amy's house that morning to give them a ride, but they weren't there. Alan said, "Oh, we flew up yesterday and stayed at a hotel nearby. We walked here just now, it wasn't far."

Ron and George, both looked puzzled and shocked, stating in tune, "You walked here?"

"Yes, it seemed silly to take a taxi only a few blocks." Alan said, as if he were in trouble.

"You cannot do dat!" George expressed loudly.

"We just thought it was easier to walk.", Alan explained again.

"No American should walk in Belize City. It is too dangerous for de Americans here!", George almost shouted.

"Okay, we won't walk again, George. We are here now and didn't realize how dangerous it was.", Alan calmed him. He and Deloris took their scolding again from the two men who explained that Americans were targeted here in Belize City because all Americans had the reputation of having money.

After their scolding, they were introduced to the men's attorney and then they were handed a large stack of papers. They looked over the papers as the three other men chatted seamlessly in the background and the couple seemed to be required to sign almost all of them; the attorney then walked over and took the stack.

He straightened the stack by pounding them onto the desk. The attorney then said, "I assume dat you have already paid de ownas of de hotel?"

"I have not been given the banking information yet, so we haven't made the transfer yet, but I am ready to make the call to my bank whenever they are ready at their bank to receive it.", Deloris said cheerfully. The three Belizeans in the room seemed surprised that she did not have the check in hand. In this day of digital transfers, Deloris had assumed that transferring the money digitally would be the preferred method of making the payment. Of course, if they had told her to bring a check, she would have done so - another example of Belizeans and foreigners not communicating complete information in advance. One should never assume that things are done the same way in Belize as they are at home. "I can make the call right now. My bank is expecting my call. The money will go into the attorney's account right away." Deloris explained quickly.

"Why would you put de money into my account?", the attorney asked curiously.

Knowing that there was an outstanding mortgage to be satisfied, she said, "We assumed that the money needed to be deposited into an escrow account for distribution.", she said.

The attorney explained that the money would be directly deposited into Ron's account and the bank would take their fees and then the remaining balance would be released to Ron.

"Okay, that is fine as well. Just give me your account information, Ron and I will have it deposited into your account."

Ron and George stared at one another for a moment and the attorney interrupted their gaze by saying, "De Central Bank of Belize will neva allow dat much money to be deposit witout an explination."

"But it is for the purchase of the hotel, so shouldn't the bank allow the funds to be transferred without issue." Again, Deloris was assuming the same logic that would be used at home would apply here in Belize.

Ron and the attorney whispered back and forth for a moment as Alan and Deloris looked on in anticipation, then the attorney said, "Okay den, put de money in him account den. We will hol de papas until de funds clear."

Deloris and Alan still assuming that Ron should be able to immediately verify the funds in his account, agreed. The call to the bank was made and the funds transferred. When she had gotten a confirmation number, their business was concluded. She made a mental note that she'd need to learn all of these business and financial shortcomings if they were to do business in Belize. It was so very foreign from the business tactics and ethics in the states. Seeing that her idea to transfer the funds digitally, involved some government agency calling the Central Bank, made the men uncomfortable. This, in turn, showed her that she had a lot to learn.

That first business transaction was the first of many that they would find confusing. The next thing that she learned was that when you went to a government office, it was routinely required that you fill out the information with one clerk and then go to a totally different clerk, and sometimes even to a different building, to pay the money for the permit or license or tax that you were trying to obtain. Convenience to the person doing business was never considered. The plan seemed to be that to separate the paperwork from the money, was the Belizean way of being sure that the government received all the money that came into the office. They could match the paperwork with the total fees that were paid to be sure that all the money was accounted for, it often required standing in several long lines. Dealing with government employees is complained about all over the world, but combine the usual problems with the slow pace of life in Belize and you are in for a situation that requires the patience of a saint to accomplish the simplest of tasks that involve the government. The sooner you accept that, this is the way it is in Belize, the happier you will be, trying to change it would be futile.

When they left the attorney's office, Ron insisted that they let him give them a ride to the airport and again reminded them that Americans should never walk alone in Belize City. As they waited for their flight to be called, they discussed the new venture. They technically owned a hotel in Central America now. They didn't yet have papers to prove it and their money for the purchase was in cyberspace being scrutinized by something called the Central Bank of Belize, but they owned a hotel in Central America. They had so much to learn and that in fact was becoming all too clear to them.

After returning to the village, they decided that they should take this opportunity to visit some of the places that they had heard about but never taken the time to see. They contacted Kevin and ask him if he was able to take them to the Mayan ruins that they had heard about in Southern Belize. He was available and agreed to drive them.

Tonight, they decided they would try a new place to eat. They had spotted a restaurant located on a cemented walk way that ran from the main road over to the sidewalk. It was called the Pickled Parrot. They made their way to the strangely name restaurant. It was an open air thatched roof bar and restaurant. It was owned by an American couple and that night they enjoyed a pizza. While not Belizean, it was a pleasant reminder of home.

The next morning, they left the village very early in Kevin's cab so that they could see the ruins at Nim Li Punit and Lubaantun in one day. Because it was necessary to go all the way back up the peninsula on the rutted road and then take the Southern Highway south on the mainland, it took about 2 and one-half hours to get to the ruins. They visited Nim Li Punit first and employed one of the guides on the site to show them around and tell them about the ruins. Kevin was not knowledgeable about all the history of the site and he suggested that they would learn more, if they had one of the guides who specialized in the ruins to show them around. The guide was very knowledgeable and showed them the artifacts on display and explained the history of the discovery and excavation of the ruins. It is an ongoing project. He pointed out that the longest stela in Belize was located at this site. He explained how the script on the stela is read. Once they had climbed up to the site they found themselves in a beautiful spot overlooking the Toledo plains. They spent a couple of hours listening to all the stories that the guide had to tell them and looking at the mysteries of the remaining structures. Deloris decided that someday she would come here and spend the whole day just wandering around this site. The guide suggested that since they wanted to see Lubaantun today that he would accompany them the short distance and show them that site as well. Time was a factor so they decided to leave Nim Li Punit and head to Lubaantun. It was lunch time so they decided to stop at a local café that was known to serve a buffet and was very popular. Walking the pathway up to the restaurant they walked through a garden that was filled with Hibiscus, Bougainvillea, Birds of Paradise and several other tropical flowers. The tropical flowers filled the air with their beautiful fragrance. It was at this restaurant that Deloris was introduced to a vegetable called Callaloo. She almost didn't try it because they referred to it as Belizean Spinach.

She does not like spinach so she was reluctant. However, the owners encouraged her to try it and it became her favorite vegetable. It was more like the turnip greens that she had grown up loving. However, the favor was better. There was also pork and chicken, rice, beans, beans and rice, as well as another vegetable known as the Heart of Palms that was very good. The owners of the restaurant personally welcomed them when they entered and took care of their every need. They were served a locally made ice cream as a desert. The visit to the café and visiting with the owners was not just a stop to eat, but another opportunity to get to know the people of Belize since the owners were open and knowledgeable. They shared their experiences freely. Reluctantly, they left the restaurant and headed the short distance to Lubaantun. Lubaantun has serval large pyramids and is the biggest of the ruins in Southern Belize. It was once a ceremonial center between 700 through 900 AD. There was so much to learn and they realized that trying to see both of the ruins in one day was a little too opportunistic. They learned that another smaller ruin, Uxbenka, was also in the same area as well as many waterfalls that Deloris immediately wanted to visit. Before heading back, Kevin drove them to the town of Punta Gorda. Punta Gorda is located right on the coast and the beaches are covered in rocks. It is not a tourist area and most of the stores focus on the needs of the locals. It seems so different from Placencia. It was hard to explain the difference. The landscape was hilly and it seemed more commercial even though it is a small town. They left Punta Gorda and headed for the village of San Antonio, that is located very close to the Guatemalan border. The small village of San Antonio is located atop sloping hills and has tangled vegetation growing in abundance. There they saw a Catholic Church built of limestone, that was taken from the nearby ruin sites, before these sites were heavily protected. The story is that the large stones were carried by the Maya in the area. This small village has electricity, a telephone system and central water. This is not true of many of the other villages in the area. Kevin explained, that they were now in the Toledo District of Belize, these Districts are similar to states or providences in North America. It was soon time that they begin the journey back to Placencia so they could reach the village before dark. None of them wanted to be on the rutted, potholed Peninsula road in the dark. There wasn't any lighting along the road, only moonlight and the lights on the van to keep them from being in total darkness.

They visited their hotel every day, but it was only a few days before they had to returned to Florida. They were waiting on the notification, that the Central Bank had cleared the money. It took more than two weeks after signing the closing papers before they received the phone call telling them that Central Bank had cleared the money and released it into Ron's account. Ron told them that they could pick up the newly formed Land Certificate and other ownership papers, as well as the keys from the attorney's office whenever they liked.

Although they had just returned to the states and had business to attend to there, they felt it would be best to hurry back to Belize to begin the process of owning a business in the beautiful village of Placencia.

Deloris sent an email to Tess to tell her about the purchase being complete and asking about how her search for a business was going. She learned that Tess had indeed met with Bill and Krista and the three had decided that she would come into the business with them. Bill and Krista would then be free to go the states to visit the grandchild when they wanted, as well as, Tess and Sandy would be able to visit their children back in the states on a regular basis too. The three had worked together for 4 more months trying to get work permits. After 7 months of being away from Sandy and with the seemingly endless paperwork that the Belize Government seemed to want, no progress had been made so Tess had given up and returned to her home in the states. Deloris was sad to hear this because she had been looking forward to visiting with her when she returned to Placencia. She assured Tess they would stay in touch. Deloris was curious to see how the quest for a work permit was coming along for Bill and Krista, surely the red tape would not defeat this couple. Ron assured Alan and Deloris that because of the large number of Belizeans that they would hire, obtaining a work permit for them would not be a problem. He said that Bill and Krista were having trouble, despite their financial investment in the country, because they employed only one-part time person.

Chapter 6

They booked their flight back to Belize within a week and made arrangement to stay in Ernie and Amy's house for a few days. Ernie and Amy agreed to meet them there. Amy wanted to see the furniture she was having made and told Deloris they would make a trip to Cayo, so she would have a chance to see the furniture that is made in Belize. The night that Ernie and Amy arrived they had dinner, again, at the Purple Space Monkey. The couple laughed and talked about what all had happened in the months since they had first had dinner here. It seemed almost unbelievable.

Since Ernie and Alan wanted to go fishing with Fred the next day, Amy and Deloris decided to make the trip to Cayo without them. Very early the next morning, Deloris came into the kitchen to find Amy already had coffee made and was ready to leave for their trip. Amy handed her a cup with a sealed lid on it and then picked up a long item in a green sheath from the counter top. Deloris couldn't quite make out what it was. Amy explained that they needed to get on the road as quickly as possible, because it was a four-hour drive and to have time to look around and be back in the village by nightfall, they needed to get going. Deloris and Amy walked out and climbed into the small Nissan pick-up truck. As they were turning onto the main street, Deloris remembered the large green sheath that Amy had placed on the back seat and asked, "What is that?"

"Oh, that is my machete." Amy said and sipped on her coffee. "Why would you carry a machete in the truck?" ask Deloris.

"It is for protection. You never know what's going to happen on the road. Better to be prepared than to not be." Amy stated calmly as she took another sipped of her coffee.

Deloris, for the first time, thought that this might not be a normal furniture shopping experience. She would be much more observant this trip. It now seemed normal to have to endure the series of potholes and the washboard like road for the twenty-six miles to get off the peninsula and onto the mainland road. The small truck shook violently when they crossed the ruts and jerked sharply when Amy tried to avoid the large potholes. Now Deloris understood how shocks in a vehicle did not stand a chance of lasting. Deloris found herself holding onto the dashboard, the seat, the armrest, or anything else available when the truck jerked and bounced as it traveled the rough road. It was an hour and a half later before they reached the mainland's paved, two-lane road, where they were able to make up some time. About thirty minutes later, Amy said, "We will be stopping at the only service station and rest room between Placencia and Belmopan, so we can use the restroom if we need to and we'll grab some breakfast there as well." When they arrived at the service station, which was located just after they had turned on to the Hummingbird Highway, Deloris was surprised when Amy asked, "Do you have a dollar coin?" as she dug through her purse.

"No, why do you need a coin? I have paper money."

"Well, that paper money is two dollars and to use the restroom, we need to pay that lady sitting by the door one dollar. She sits there all day and collects money."

"Are you kidding?" Deloris asked with a smile.

"Got em!" Amy said sharply, pulling two Belizean dollar coins from her purse. Deloris realized that she was not kidding. Amy went first and then Deloris was up. She soon found that paying the lady to use the restroom was not buying any special amenities. The door didn't quite close and couldn't be locked. There was no soap to wash her hands and there was a large window at eye level facing the store. Normal conveniences hadn't reached Belize's convenience stores yet. After washing her hands with only water, she looked for a paper towel to dry her hands, but found none. She exited the restroom wiping her hands onto her pants to dry them. Amy was waiting and motioned for her to join her in the store. They entered the gas station where they found a glass case with offerings of Johnny Cakes of different varieties. Although she could see the small flat biscuit like sandwiches, she asked, "What is a Johnny Cake?"

"A Johnny cake was originally called a Journey Cake because it was often made for one to take with them. They are made from flour, shortening, baking powder, sugar and the important ingredient is coconut milk. However, you will find that everything from Johnny cakes to rice is made with coconut milk here in Belize. The story is that they were created before refrigeration. The Loggers would take them out in the jungle to work, since they lasted for several days, hence the name "Journey Cakes" because they were prepared for the logger's journey to cut Mahogany.", said Amy.

"They are the best! My favorite is the one with ham and cheese." Amy continued and picked one up. Deloris followed suit and they both grabbed a juice as well. Johnny Cakes are split open and filled with such things as cheese spread and a very thin piece of ham or with refried beans. They paid for their breakfast and soon were back on the road. Deloris opened her Johnny Cake that was wrapped in a sort of waxed paper and took a bite. It looked a little like a failed biscuit but was quite good.

"They are best when cooked in a traditional hearth, but these were probably cooked in an oven. When they are hot, you can cut them in half and slather butter all over them and they are so good," Amy mumbled now with her mouth full of the tasty treat. As she finished that bite, she asked Deloris, "Have you tried the Fry Jack yet?"

"Yes, Alan and I both loved them.", Deloris stated. It would be hard to imagine them being very healthy, since it is deep fried flour dough, like what is used to make tortillas. In all their travels in the Caribbean, they had never seen fry jacks offered in any other Caribbean county that we've visited.

"My favorite is the 'Stuffed Fry Jack" with eggs, bacon and cheese inside them. I don't like the beans in them; however, I'm only going to allow myself one per visit since I can imagine the calorie count in one of those." Deloris laughed.

Shortly before they entered the mountains, they found that the road ahead was blocked. Cars were stopping and then turning right to exit the roadway. The cars seemed to be going directly through an orange grove. There was a policeman detouring traffic and he had his patrol truck parked sideways at the bridge entrance. Amy eased up to the policeman and asked, "Is the bridge out?"

"Yes, de bridge is unsafe fa you to cross. You must cross at de riva down below." He answered.

Deloris looked at the policeman and then at the cars disappearing through the trees and waited for Amy and the policeman to share a laugh at a joke being pulled on her, but the laugh never came. Amy simply put the truck in reverse, backed up to where the other cars were entering the orange grove. They pulled into the tall grass and followed the tire tracks until they caught up with the last car that had gone before them. Deloris could see the three cars were waiting on a small truck to cross the river. She relaxed a bit, until she watched the vehicle disappear out of sight. The next truck went and then the small car in front of them drove down the bank.

The bank was steep and each car disappeared out of sight, then reappeared on the other side. As Amy creeped up to the edge of the bank, Deloris grabbed the dash and dug her fingers deep into it. The front of truck dropped down suddenly as Amy eased forward. Amy was steering with her right hand but holding on to the arm rest with her left hand. They eased through the shallow water and then the truck almost became vertical as they climbed the other side. Deloris' eyes were closed tightly and she had both feet on the dash while holding on tightly to the headrest of her own seat by the time they reach to top of the other bank. Amy laughed out loud and Deloris opened her eyes to realize that they were safe again. She slowly let go of the seat and then placed her feet back onto the floorboard. She straightened her shirt and sat upright, Deloris breathed a deep sigh of relief and didn't say anything until they were back on pavement on the other side of the bridge. Then she asks, "Do you think they will have it fixed by the time we come back this way?"

"Yeah, they usually get these things fixed pretty quickly. The bridge will probably be opened by the time we come back, only because the policeman doesn't want to have to stand out there all day."

"Can't they just detour traffic around it?"

"Deloris, this is Belize. There are no other roads that go east and west here. This is the only one. Welcome to traveling in Belize." She laughed.

Deloris thought to herself, "I can't believe that we just did that. I can't wait to tell Alan about this." Amy quickly passed all three vehicles in front of them. "So, this is the Hummingbird Highway? This is where all the one lane bridges are located?" ask Deloris rhetorically. Just then, Deloris saw four beautifully colored macaws fly across the road directly in front of them. "Does that happen often?" Deloris asks. Amy told her that it was not unusually to see parrots and macaws or any of the tropical birds while traveling the Hummingbird Highway since this was all jungle along this highway. The mountains were low and they were covered with dense forest. They were not that many miles away from the beach, but this was the landscape that Deloris loved. From the looks of it, much of this particular area had not been explored. There were very few roads leading up into the mountains and almost no sign of it being inhabited.

They drove on to the capital city of Belmopan. Deloris asks Amy if there were no furniture makers in Belmopan and was told that there was only one and they made wicker furniture that was used mostly on porches and patios. Amy said that they'd stop there on the way back, if they had time. They drove passed the capital city of Belmopan and about an hour later, after crossing the suspension bridge called the "Hawkesworth Bridge" that spans the Macal River, they arrived in the town of San Ignacio. The Hawkesworth Bridge was the suspension bridge that Ernie had told them about on their first trip to Placencia. Now Deloris understood what Ernie meant. It was large but rattled and clanged as they crossed. Other than the road that circled the town, the rest of the streets seemed to be designed for one-way traffic. Everyone seemed to know which direction to go, and yet there weren't any signs to direct the uninformed. San Ignacio was built in hill country and was steep in many areas. They arrived at a place that looked nothing like a furniture store and parked the Nissan truck on the steep hill out front. As they walked into the store, it looked more like a general store than a furniture store. There were pots, pans, plates and miscellaneous things all around. Amy told the clerk that they were there to meet Elisa to look at furniture. The clerk informed them that Elisa had not come into work yet, but they were welcome to go upstairs and look around. After walking up a flight of stairs, they arrived in a very hot, dim area that was filled to the brim with very elaborate English style furniture. Most was made of dark mahogany wood. There were bedroom sets, dining room sets with richly upholstered chairs and very ornate china cabinets. The seating that was there was either very formal or was "clam style" chairs that looked suitable for someone under one hundred pounds.

Most of the dark mahogany furniture was quite ornate and was obviously turned on a lathe, but there were much more extravagant designs carved by hand. This furniture was first class. It was formal furniture with rolls, whirls and cut to fit perfectly. It was a lost art that people hadn't been able to appreciate in the states for many years. While all the furniture was beautiful, it wasn't quite what Deloris had in mind for their future business. Their business would be on the beach and having fishermen and divers dragging their wet equipment through the lobby, simply wouldn't work with such nice furniture. It was just not practical for her needs. Deloris looked in despair, as she thought to herself, "Drove four hours to get here, not to mention having risked my life forging a river and shaking my spleen lose on the bumpy road and the furniture isn't even what I need." She loved looking at all the beautiful things, things that she'd never seen before, but she was shopping to be practical, not to furnish a mansion. Amy had called ahead and told Elisa that they were coming, but people in Belize aren't the schedule or appointment type. Elisa finally arrived and greeted Amy, warmly. Amy explained to Elisa that Deloris had just bought a hotel in Placencia and that she was looking for furniture to furnish it. Elisa expressed to Deloris, that if there wasn't anything she was looking for in the showroom, that she could bring a picture and she'd have it built for her. Deloris asked about how long it would take to build a piece of furniture but Elisa explained that each piece was different, and it depended very much on what type of wood one chose and the style. She said if they already had the wood and it was cured, it would only take about six to seven weeks per piece. If the wood had to be dried and cured, it could take as long as three months per piece. Deloris couldn't imagine furnishing their entire hotel with things that would take several months for each piece to be made. She decided that she'd have their apartment furnished in this manner, but not the guest's quarters. She would talk to the contractor, whoever they hired, to build the new structure and at least the beds for the rooms, then they could sort out the other needs when she had time. She had no idea how long it would take to tear down the hotel and build their new building, but had an idea of it taking a few months. She took Elisa's card and Elisa again told Deloris that if she would email her a picture, she could have anything built that she liked. She showed Deloris several different types of wood that she could choose from. Mahogany is the national tree of Belize and is used widely for furniture, but there are woods such as Zericote, Jobillo, Poison Wood, Grenadillo and Black cabbage bark that are also used widely and she showed Deloris pictures of beautiful cabinetry that she had made for different clients. The samples of all the different wood were displayed by being inserted into a table top of a small round table that sat in one corner of the showroom. The woods were all beautiful, but Elisa explained that some were harder wood than others and therefore better for certain pieces of furniture. She also pointed out the woods that were the most plentiful and which ones would take longer to get. Elisa told her that as soon as she received a picture that she would be able to quote her a rate and give her an approximate time it would take to complete the piece. Upon completion, they would deliver it to Placencia. Elisa asked Amy if she would like to go over and see the progress of her furniture at the factory.

"Yes, that is another reason that we have come today." Amy answered excitedly.

They climbed into the truck and followed Elisa to a building several blocks away from the store and Deloris realized that this must be the factory that was mentioned upstairs. They parked on a narrow, one-way street and then walked a short distance to what appeared to be a house with a large fenced in yard. The "Factory" was in fact three men working with hand tools on various pieces of furniture. The smell of saw dust and stain lingered in the air as they walked into the yard. Deloris was already fascinated with the wooden furniture she had seen in Belize, but to watch the masters at work was a treat. The Mahogany wood was beautiful and there was an array of different cuts and sizes. They used Mahogany there like the people in the states used Pine wood. There were several beautiful chairs, tables and a beautiful bed being built in that area. The different hues of wood were being used to make creations of unimaginable beauty. The smell and sights took Deloris back to a time when she was a child as she remembered watching her grandfather build a quilt chest.

Amy's furniture was in different stages of progress. There were several chaise lounges, chairs for their veranda, a beautiful carved dining room table and a beautiful bed. Each piece was designed with an array of different colored wood and laid together as if they grew that way. Deloris realized that she nor Alan would be comfortable in the chairs that she saw because padding did not seem to be in any of the chairs.

Amy was obviously pleased with the progress of the furniture and told Elisa that she was so excited to see it finished. They made plans for Elisa to send Amy an email when everything was two weeks away from completion. After some chit-chat, Amy rushed Deloris to the gate and told Elisa, "I want to take her to Xunantuniach after we grab some lunch." Amy apologized for rushing but explained that they had to be off the peninsula road before dark. She said while she felt safe traveling in Belize she did not want to drive that dark road after dark.

Elisa laughed and said that she fully understood that no one wanted to be on that road in the dark, and agreed that Deloris should at least see the ruins of Xunantuniach while she was this close.

After they were back in the truck, Deloris asked Amy about the chaise lounges and Amy explained she had seen a picture of them in a magazine in the U.S. and simply emailed them to Elisa. Deloris couldn't help but ask, "So how much is it costing to have them made here?"

Amy explained that the ones she saw in the magazine were priced at two thousand U.S. dollars each, but Elisa priced them at seven hundred and fifty each. It was cheaper to have them made here and she was saving money since she did not have the cost of shipping them to Belize. Amy went on to explain it also takes a special permit to get furniture into the country."

"Why would you need a special permit to ship furniture into Belize?" Deloris asked curiously.

"If you ship any wooden items into Belize, you need a special permit because that wood doesn't come from Belize. They don't want any cross contamination and honestly, it is because tax on imports is a source of revenue for the government.", said Amy.

"So how do I get a copy of the rules and regulations?", asks Deloris.

Amy tilted her head and laughed, "You can't, it would appear that there are different rules for each one of the agents that check shipments. You just learn by trial and error here. If there was a book of rules in existence, it wouldn't mean that the rules would stay the same one day to another."

Deloris sighed and came to the instant conclusion that it would be an interesting journey completing the tear down and rebuilding of the hotel and getting their new business into an operational status if the rules were going to be made up as they went along. She turned her focus to their destination and asked, "What is Xunantuniach?"

"Oh, it is an ancient Mayan ruin here in the Cayo district. It sits on top of a ridge above the Mopan River and you can see the Guatemalan border from the top, which is only about a half mile away. Xunantuniach means "Stone Woman" in the Mayan language and is the current name. The original name is still unknown, but it is a beautiful place, you will fall in love with it.", she explained as they traversed onward. "Oh, it sounds beautiful already.", said Deloris.

They had gone a couple of miles outside of San Ignacio when Amy turned right onto a dirt road that led up to a large building that looked like a house. Amy told Deloris that this is where they'd have lunch today. They were seated on the large veranda and it was a beautiful day outside. The hills in the area were laid out as if they were sculpted by the creator himself. The tropics always offered a broad spectrum of different colors mixed with many shades of green of the canopy above and below as the hills dove and rose again to reach the bluest sky one could imagine. The mountains seemed to rise out of nowhere and continue forever. The moment of admiration of the scenery was broken by the waitress's voice, "What can I get ya to drink?" They turned to see a beautiful young black Belizean girl who had a soft voice.

"I will have a Red Fanta and the Garnaches." Amy answered quickly.

They had their lunch and Deloris discovered that Garnaches were small, round, flat corn disk with refried beans, a sprinkling of cheese and a few chopped onions on them. They were served at room temperature and she decided that they were not her favorite food, but now she would know what they were. She had often heard vendors on the road in Placencia offering them for sale.

The two women got back into the Nissan and were off again. They drove a few miles and Amy pulled off the road. Deloris noticed the sides of the road were lined with tables of wooden items. They got out and walked by several tables. The tables were filled with carvings from a variety of the Belize's indigenous trees and there were numerous items made of slate. These craftsmen had used pieces of slate to make a variety of items, but Deloris found the pieces of slate that had carvings of the Maya calendar too appealing not to buy. These pieces were designed to be displayed by being hung. She purchased the piece as Amy wandered ahead. A young Belizean boy, who appeared to be about sixteen, ran up to Amy and threw his arms around her waist. "Why did you not call me, miz Amy?" He shouted as he squeezed tightly.

"I just got the idea of coming by to see if you could give us a quick tour, Kendu. I didn't know if you would be available, but I wanted to stop and say hello to you and introduce you to my friend, Deloris." Amy said with a large smile on her face.

"Deloris and her husband just bought the hotel, Paradise, in Placencia." Amy explained. Kendu released his embrace on Amy and offered his hand to Deloris as she approached. "Deloris, this is my friend Kendu. He is a guide for the ruins here at Xunantuniach.", Amy said, introducing the two of them. Kendu had dark skin and stood about 5 foot tall, but he was fine-boned. He had dark piercing eyes and a smile that was wide, white and welcoming. Although, he appeared very young, he was close to 19 and had finished his schooling here in Belize and longed to go to the U.S. to continue his education. He had a wide knowledge of the ancient Maya culture and wanted to become an archeologist. However, this would require a lot of money and a sponsor, if he was to be able to obtain this dream.

After shaking Deloris' hand, he looked back at Amy and asked, "How much time ya have?"

"We have to be on the road in no more than thirty minutes." "Den come, let us take de ferry across, so we can show Miz Deloris what her is missing." Kendu urged the two ladies.

"Okay, we will just go across, but should we walk, or bring the truck?" Amy asked.

"It pretty muddy, so I would bring de truck, Miz Amy." He answered with a serious, all business looks on his brow. The three got into the truck and pulled down to the river bank. Deloris could see an old, flat, wooden ferry pulled up to the river's edge. She began looking for her handprints from their earlier trek and then asked, "Are we really going to drive this truck onto that thing?"

Kendu offered her reassurance as he replied, "Oh dat is no problem, Miz. Dey have much bigga truck on dis ting all de time and no problem."

Amy listened to the exchange, but never said a word as she eased the two front tires onto the wooden ferry. Deloris watched the water pour onto the ferry's flat, wooden surface and she began to grasp tighter now. The ferry recovered after the next set of tires were securely on it and then stayed on top of the water as the weight was balanced now. Deloris watched as the ferry began to move gently. She watched as a large, thick rope that was tied to the ferry rose out of the water. She looked on the other side to find three large, black men tugging on the rope and soon the ferry was well on its way to the other side. She smiled after realizing that she had yet again escaped death, or at least wet clothes. "Ha! A real life "Rope Ferry" I have heard of these, but have never seen one.", said Deloris.

"Yes, Miz. Dis one very old. But it safe." Kendu assured her as she looked at the young boy.

"Okay, I hope so. Is this the Mopan River?" She asked as she stared down the river through her passenger window. "Yes, the Mopan Riva." He answered.

After reaching the other side Amy drove the Nissan off the ferry onto the muddy river bank. In front of them was a hill that lead up to a plateau. They drove up the muddy slopping hill and when they broke the plain at the top, Deloris was amazed. There was a large parking lot that seemed to appear out of nowhere, surrounded by perfectly manicured grass of the greenest color. She was captivated as her eyes found the seventeen-hundred-year-old ruins of Xunantuniach. Here in front of her was a picture of history, perfectly preserved by nature and she couldn't imagine it when it was new. Her mind drifted away to dreams of when the ancient Maya people had finished building it and were hurrying around the courtyard in their daily chores. She could picture a beautiful Mayan Princess, with long, flowing, black hair carrying a purple Gardenia bulb and placing the short stem behind her ear before climbing the steps.

The vision was interrupted by Kendo's voice, as he explained that if they were to take a tour, they would pay at the small shack near the parking lot and then join a group; or they could wonder around the ruins on their own to check it out. She smiled as he said, "But de smartez peoples hire me to take dem on de tour an show dem around."

They entered the ruins site and saw the famed El Castillo with the magnificent carvings near the top. While the core of the site only occupies about a square mile there are 26 temples and palaces. It would have been hard not to be impressed by the magnificent of this place. There were steps leading up to the tops of the structures and Deloris was immediately aware that the length of the stair treads was short. Looking at the sleeping shelves, she also realized that these structures had been built for a race of people who were considerably shorter than people were today. When one realizes that these structures were built without the help of modern technology it is impossible not to be in awe.

Deloris immediately knew that she and Alan had to come back to Xunantuniach when there was time to spend and explore the area completely, so she asks Kendu for a card. He quickly reached into his pocket and produced a makeshift card with his name and a phone number on it, "You can call me on dis numba, Miz Deloris."

It was time for the trip back across the river on the ferry. They got back into the Nissan and were soon dropping Kendu off on the other side, then off to Belmopan again on the Western Highway. Deloris decided that although, she hadn't liked the unmarked, one-way streets of San Ignacio, she very much enjoyed the rolling hills and Mayan ruins that awaited her return. Amy enjoyed her friend's excitement and explained that when she returned that she should also plan on seeing Cahe'l Pech which is close by. Amy explained that Cahe'l Pech is smaller, but in 1988 they discovered 10 mounds and there are 34 structures and five plain stelae at the site.

They were able to stop at the shop that makes rattan furniture in Belmopan and here Deloris saw comfortable chairs with cushions that could be used both indoors and outdoors. At least now she knew she could get a comfortable chair in Belize. They were not as exotic looking as the handsome wooden furniture but they did have cushions.

After Belmopan, the drive in the mountains was uneventful until they found themselves in the middle of the mountains and behind a slow-moving, large Semi truck, filled with oranges. Amy pulled to the left to pass, but realized that there was another one in front of that one. The large trucks struggled up the long, steep hills and were averaging ten miles an hour or so. Deloris watched intently, as she knew that Amy would eventually grow impatient and pass the trucks. Amy explained that this happened often in the mountains. There was no room for the trucks to pull over, even if they had been so inclined. Passing two large semis on this curvy road was too dangerous. However, at this pace it was going to be hard to make it back before dark.

Are you beginning to see a pattern here with my Aunt Deloris? She worries about worrying, but that is who she is, folks. Now back to the ladies' journey home...

After several miles of a slow-paced drive, they came to a plateau and the trucks turned into a side road and the traffic, that was now backed up for a mile or more, passed. Soon they crossed the one-lane bridge that they were forced to detour around earlier in the day and it was back open to traffic. Deloris relaxed as she found the bridge in operation. In the U.S. repairs would not have been approved so quickly and several agencies would have been involved before traffic would have been allowed back onto a bridge, so Deloris was relieved as they made it across the bridge without dropping into the water below. As they came near the end of the mountains, Amy said, "Keep your eyes peeled for the sleeping giant."

Deloris asked, "What is that?"

"It is an outcropping of rock that resembles a giant lying on his back. Look to your left and you will see it up ahead."

After a few miles, Deloris found the slumbering giant, just as Amy had said. The rocks looked just like the silhouette of a huge man lying on his back. The nose, mouth and eyebrows were as clear as a painter could paint a shadow to look. "It really does look like a sleeping giant, Amy!" Deloris said with excitement and wished only for a moment and a camera to capture it. "Is there anything to do if you were to hike up there?", she asked.

"There is a cave up there called Saint Herman's and people go cave tubing up there a lot. You and Alan should plan a trip up there as well sometime." Amy urged.

Before long, they were back at the service station and decided that they should stop and use the restroom before they tackled the bumpy road to Placencia. After the restroom break and two more dollars given to the toilet lady, Amy filled the Nissan with gasoline and then they were off again. They turned right onto the Southern Highway and soon passed the Jaguar Preserve and the Mayan Center.

Soon they were turning onto the peninsula road and as they came to the place where they would normally turn south, Amy explained that they were running late and she thought they'd take a short cut through the banana plantation. She explained that there was only one bad spot and it was the bridge. Deloris' mind raced when Amy spoke those words. What kind of bridge would be given the label 'Bad' by Amy, if she hadn't thought that the others were bad?

Soon they were surrounded by banana trees and Deloris was reassured as she looked into the back seat to find the machete was still there and close by. She began to think about the many instances that they may need such a weapon to defend themselves.

Amy slowed to a crawl. Amy explained that she was lining up to be sure that they hit the bridge just right. The small truck accelerate forward. Deloris grabbed the back of the seat's headrest. The sound from the tires of the truck changed for a moment. The "Bad Bridge" they had just crossed was simply two long boards that spanned a small creek and were no bigger than railroad crossties. Amy had to hit those boards exactly right to prevent spilling them into the creek below, but she had done so without issue. Deloris sighed and sat up straight into the seat. She thought, "There is no way that Alan is going to believe this story, but you can bet he is going to hear it." The day was over now and they were safely back on the road and soon back in the village. She climbed out of the truck and realized that her knees were shaking. She wasn't sure if she had ever had more adventures in one day any time in her life, but was sure that Belize would offer her more opportunities to make that distinction later.

Chapter 7

The building, the business, and the land that they had purchased was referred to as "Paradise" by the people in the village, and Deloris and Alan found themselves referring to the Hotel as Paradise when they talked about what their plans were. After a brief trip, back to the states, they felt the need to return to Placencia and get started on the plans for Paradise. They felt they needed to be in Placencia to make the final plans, for the future of Paradise. They flew into Belize City and after a short layover, they flew into Placencia on Maya Island Air's small turbo prop plane. It was an eight-seater plane and you definitely want to sit at the rear of the plane so that you can have a decent seat. Anyone over 4-foot-tall must duck or receive a bump to the head. The middle seats are for very small people and not comfortable in the least. After the plane landed, they felt the prop shutter and then go full throttle again. The plane eased up to the area to unload passengers and luggage, then came to a jolting halt. This hadn't bothered Deloris and Alan though, they were excited to be back in Placencia and get started. They deplaned and waited on their bags to unloaded. Deloris waived vigorously in the direction of the parking area beside the terminal building. It was Kevin, their taxi driver friend. He rushed over and shook Alan's hand, then gave Deloris a bear hug. He gathered their bags and while having a short chat about the weather, he placed the bags into the taxi and closed the door. Kevin opened their door for them and asked, "To de hotel, mista Alan?"

"Yes, Kevin. We officially own it now and it is time to get started."

"Dat is very good!" He said and put the taxi in gear as he climbed in himself.

The arrived at the head of the path leading to the hotel and Kevin insisted on carrying their luggage down the path to the office. He went into the office and placed their luggage inside, when he came out of the office he found the two of them quietly staring at the building. He asked, "Every ting okay?"

"Yes, we are okay, just taking it all in." Alan answered. What had they done?

As they walked into the office, Donna stood quickly and greeted her new bosses with a wide smile and immediately hugged Deloris and thought about hugging Alan but decided that a handshake would be more comfortable for him. There was only one painting on the wall and it was of a small sailboat on the water. The walls were bare and the designer in Deloris was awakened when she thought of all that she'd do to decorate their new business when it was finally built. Alan watched as her nose wrinkled as if she had bitten into a lemon, "Don't look so sour. We'll fix it. This is all going away, remember?" He said, interrupting her dream state.

She smiled and replied, "We have a lot of work ahead of us, Alan."

"That is what we already knew. Look around you ... we own a hotel in Belize, Central America, Paradise, nonetheless! I think we should keep the name Paradise. It seems to fit this place, don't ya think?" he asks. "Yes, I think that is a good name for this place." She liked his enthusiasm.

Alan was generally an unemotional person and often seemed distant and gruff to the untrained eye. Deloris could tell his mood with one look after all the years of marriage. She often felt the need to explain to others that he wasn't angry, he just seemed that way. But here, in Placencia, he didn't seem his gruff, distant self, he wasn't rushed, disappointed or angry about anything. He seemed to be honestly content and other than his optimism, and readiness to get started on this new adventure, he seemed to not have a care in the world. "It seemed that nothing, nor no one could upset him here in Paradise," she thought as she remembered the elevator and the freezing cold water at the casino they had stayed at in Belize City. He had laughed at both and to show that much joy for Uncle Alan was kind of a big deal. I remember once when I was a young man, Uncle Alan and I watched someone put a fake saddle with a toy cowboy on a big dog and the dog ran like crazy to get it off. I laughed until my side hurt, then when I looked at Uncle Alan, he didn't even smile. The strong silent type he was. The new laughter and carefree side of him was very welcomed. Their friends in the U.S. still didn't believe that they had bought a hotel in Belize after only visiting a few times. Why would they believe that they had done something that was so out of character for this couple who was normally so detail oriented and had such business minds. What possessed the normally conservative couple to jump into the purchase of a business that they knew nothing about? What indeed! She felt it all at once and realized that she and Alan were under some sort of spell, some incantation of freethinking that they had never known before. She believed, that she remembered when it happened; when she and Alan were sitting on the dock, on their first visit and waiting for the sunrise. As soon as that huge orange sphere broke the plane of the horizon, they were then the grateful captives of this place called Belize. They were struck with the enchanting, mysterious and seemingly secret spell, but what was it? What had such power to overtake such a superfluously strict pair? I'll tell ya this much ... I bet people have been falling under this spell since the

Maya days. I bet Nim La' Punit's chieftain was so struck in three-fifteen B.C. that he found himself ordering the construction of his megalithic structure on the same day that he found the place. Can you imagine how powerful such a spell is? I couldn't. I was nowhere even close when Deloris told me about it. I assumed that they were simply getting older and looking to retire in a beautiful place and Placencia fit the bill. Deloris, being the eternal hopeless romantic, felt that she must name this phenomenon and she'd do just that by calling it "tropical fever". It is a fever that makes normally cautious people throw caution to the wind and do things that they normally wouldn't under any circumstances and even thought that those actions were careless and ridiculous for people to make, that was it! That is all that it took. They were infected with Tropical Fever and a cure, as much as they didn't want to search for it, did not seem to exist. They had already realized that they didn't want to find the cure and would let this seemingly invasive parasite continue its course. The two were now in a whole new world and loved the idea of being on a journey such as this, with the destination's secret withheld for now.

Despite the compulsiveness, in which, this purchase had been made, they had decided that the practical plan was to maintain the business as a hotel on this location until all the plans for the new building were complete since they had Donna's reassurance that everything was under control. The two focused on all that they needed to accomplish to get started on their new business. They needed to apply for the obviously hard to obtain, work permit, open a new checking account for the hotel, honor the booked rooms already in place and paid to the previous owners, and see what other bookings that they had to honor that had not yet been paid. They needed to visit with contractors to discuss the best way to handle the demolition and construction, in order to get the new structure, they needed. All this was necessary before they could open their dive and/or fishing resort. It had taken 9 months from the time they agreed to buy the hotel and when it was finally closed. It was now June and they knew that being opened by the start of the season in November would be impossible. However, they hope to be operational during the peak months of the season. They'd get the estimates and as soon as possible they'd begin construction. They needed to review the books for the hotel's financials and how the books were being kept up to this point. They had bought the property and were ready to get started. They had decided that Alan would be the one to spend the most time in Placencia and Deloris would focus on keeping the U.S. businesses operating until they could finish construction and get a good manager for Paradise. Deloris would visit often to help with the decisions on construction.

They decided that a trip to Belmopan and Belize City was necessary. They would go to Belmopan to get a better copy of the certificate of incorporation. The one that the attorney had given them was a dull copy of a copy and barely legible. They had opened a personal bank account on their trip to Placencia when they closed the purchase, so they knew how particular the bank was about having original, legible copies of documents. This time they had brought the long list of documents required to open a business account and hoped that they had all the documents it would take. After much discussion, the decision to purchase a vehicle to drive while here in Belize was made. Rental cars were very expensive and not always dependable. They arranged for Kevin to drive them to the car dealership in Belize City that Amy and Ernie had used. At the dealership, they were greeted by a short, thin Belizean man who hardly acted as if he was excited to be at work. Alan opened the door on a maroon colored Nissan four-door and glanced inside. Deloris followed suit and they sat in the seats to get a feel for the vehicle. After looking at the options that the truck had, they walked around the lot and looked at several others. The salesman seemed uninterested and asked when they'd be buying a vehicle.

Alan, didn't make eye contact and answered, "We'll buy one today."

"Today, sa?" The question was annunciated in disbelief.

"Yes, we bought a hotel in Placencia and we will need a dependable vehicle. We are here now, so we will buy one today." Alan answered as he opened the door on a blue truck this time.

The demeanor of the salesman changed drastically when he realized that he could actually sell a vehicle to the couple and he began describing each vehicle in detail as they made their way around the lot looking at them. They finally found the one that they liked and told the man, "We'll take this one," After some negotiating and paperwork, they now owned a new truck. They shook hands with the salesman and the manager and drove back to Belmopan to get the copy of the certificate. On the drive back to Belmopan, they talked about the fact that they had made the offer to buy Paradise on their second trip to Placencia and that second trip had been only 4 months after the original visit. Now just about a year after their first visit to Belize they actually owned a hotel and now a vehicle in a country that they hardly knew existed a year ago. After reaching Belmopan, they realized that the truck's gas tank was very near empty. This wouldn't be an issue in the states because of the all too familiar convenience stores on every other street corner. Here, on the other hand, gas stations were a rarity and they had only seen one in Belmopan that they could remember. They headed to the only station they knew of and filled up with gas.

After fueling up, they went to the building that they were told housed the government offices for business registration. They were surprised to find the door locked; and even more surprised when a loud buzz and then a click was heard. They were buzzed in the door and after walking through, entered a large open room. They were two of only six people in the lobby and approached the counter and asked for a better copy of the Certificate of Registration of the corporation that they had brought. They provided the barely legible copy that they had, to the clerk. The clerk took the copy. As she proceeded to her desk, Deloris could see that the logs and journals were an indication that they still did everything by hand in Belize. There were no fancy desktop computers on her desk, no copy machine staring out from a distant wall and no telephones in sight. The clerk disappeared through a door and when she returned, she had a copy of the certificate and after Deloris looked at it, she explained to the lady that they already had this poorly, hand copied page and that was what she had provided to get the original. She explained that they needed a good copy of the original to show the bank. After a long, undecipherable conversation between two women, one looked firmly at her and said, "We only have de copy. No original papas."

Deloris said, "But we'll need the original to give the bank. Where do we get that from?"

One girl replied, "Ya will have ta get dat from de attorney. We only have de copy here."

"This is the one that we got from the attorney." Deloris said calmly.

"Den I guess dat de one ya need." Replied one of the girls, then both girls walked away and disappeared behind the door again.

Deloris and Alan stood there, as if waiting for them to return, but both soon realized that the meeting was over. They walked outside to the new truck and Alan, placing a limp hand up to his chest and puckering his lips said, "Den da's what we gat.", with a chuckle. Deloris, seeing his impersonation of the official, could not hold in the uncontrollable outburst of laughter. Alan joined in and the two soon wiped tears of laughter away from their eyes and climbed into the Nissan.

Alan suggested that, so the trip to Belmopan wouldn't be a total waste of time, that they go by the hardware store and see what they had to offer. They knew that they'd need to have some idea of the types of things that were easily available here. Deloris agreed and they soon arrived at the hardware store. The store was an open front building with large overhead doors and a loading dock near the front entrance. They walked in and then looked around, finding everything from towels to ceramic tile, doors, vanities and light fixtures. There was not a large variety of anything. They assumed that the contractor would have a source for much better variety. Alan knew from their many previous projects that she would want to compared paint colors offered to tile and draperies before making a decision on the design and color scheme that she wanted. He listened inattentively and nodded occasionally, knowing that whatever she chose was fine with him. As they continued to browse, Deloris realized that she'd probably have to use what was available when designing and decorating their new business. She wasn't discouraged though. She would figure out a great design and it would flow like a waterfall. As they were ready to leave, they stopped at the counter and grabbed a cold drink before leaving. After paying and the clerk opening the drinks, the man looked past them and asked, "Are you driving dat truck? Are you on your way to Placencia?"

Alan, still holding the bottle to his lips, looked puzzled at the man and then at Deloris. "How did you know that we are from Placencia?"

"Because you are not from here. I assume you are from Placencia. I seen de new truck you must have jus bought."

Alan turned and looked at the truck and said, "Oh, yes, we just bought the hotel named Paradise on the beach there in Placencia."

The clerk became a bit excitable and asked, "Do ya mind takin some tile back to Placencia wit ya for de home owner?"

Of course, the couple, wanting to be helpful agreed to carry it back with them.

The clerk continued, "De home owner who bought dis tile does not have a way to get it to Placencia. Dey in de U.S. and would be back soon. I have been waiting for someone from Placencia to carry it back and here ya are."

One of the store employees loaded ten boxes of tile into the bed of their truck, which dropped the rear end a little. Alan waited until the man was finished and asked, "Where are we supposed to take it?"

"It will go to de blue and yellow house on de road to Placencia."

"We are relatively new to Placencia and don't know which house that would be." Alan explained.

"Dat not a problem. Jus watch for de blue and yellow house. Dat be de one. No problem."

Deloris chimed in saying, "But I thought that the owners were back in the states?"

"Yes, mum, dey are, but dey will be someone der to take de tile from you. Jus watch for de house and if you have any problem you call Ralph.

"Ralph?" Alan asked puzzled and thought "please don't tell me that I should know who Ralph is."

"Ralph be de one helping dis American build de house." He explained. He quickly wrote a telephone number on a piece of paper and after thanking them, disappeared into the store quickly to help a customer who had driven up and walked in.

The couple stared at the empty doorway now and then climbed into their truck for the journey to find a blue and yellow house to drop tile to a guy named Ralph who they had never met before. After driving away, Deloris said, "Alan, they don't know us from Adam. They don't know where we live and they just gave us ten boxes of valuable tile to drop off at a blue and yellow house that we have no idea where it is." He raised his eyebrows and said, "Strange ways in Belize." That seemed to say, all that needed to be said.

After turning onto the Peninsula road to Placencia, they began to search for a blue and yellow house so that they could be rid of the expensive tile. They soon found a blue house with yellow trim. They stopped and knocked on the door, but there was no answer. Not sure that this was the correct house, they drove onward and found another house that was almost the same as the one they had stopped at. "I think we should head on into Placencia and give this Ralph fella a call so we don't drop this tile off at the wrong place." Deloris agreed and they continued to the hotel.

They called Ralph and he agreed to come to the hotel and pick up the tile. When he arrived, Alan and Deloris were surprised to find that he was an American. He explained that he had been living in Placencia for the past twenty years and he worked mostly for Americans who built houses there. He would oversee the progress and make sure that the construction was done right. He grinned and said, "Without supervision, the light switch will be down to turn the light on, or an electric plug will be installed upside down. You guys ever need anything, I am always around. Since you guys have bought the hotel, you will be wanting to make some changes, I'm sure."

"How'd you know we had bought the hotel?" Alan asked curiously.

"It is a small village, there isn't much that goes on that you don't hear about a few times a day. You guys are the new "Gringos" in Placencia and everyone knows that you've bought Paradise. He explained that their purchase had been "shush" for a while.

The three giggled at the name "Gringo" and all understood the meaning. Deloris took the opportunity to ask, "What do you do for healthcare here in Placencia?"

"There's a doctor who lives here. If you need him, you go to his house. If he's not home, you go look for him.", he answered.

Deloris looked at the man and waited for a smile, but one never came. He was serious. She thought to herself that this place was so much like the early years as she was growing up. Slow paced, everyone knew everyone and there was never a lack of chatter about the newest news to be heard. This seemed to be a relaxing pace of life to her, at this time in her life. She and Alan would be in for many surprises. They have only had a taste so far.

Chapter 8

Alan and Deloris realized that having a beach front property was a blessing in itself. They discussed how the rooms should be situated and how they could get the best views for the majority of the rooms. They discussed where the dining room would be and where the office and lobby should be located. They knew that they'd need to keep the hotel operational until all the reservations already taken were fulfilled, but they planned to begin the demolition and rebuild into their dream lodge as soon as the last of the reservations had been honored. Since the property was located in the middle of residential properties, "Family Zone", is what the locals called it; they wanted the least amount of disruptions possible for the families in the area. They had walked the property and decided what trees they could save in the construction and expansion process and which trees wouldn't survive the construction. George came over to the hotel and asked the couple if they had a few minutes to talk. This was the first time that they had seen George since the purchase of the hotel. He seemed strangely uncomfortable and clearly had something on his mind. Alan suggested that they retreat to a structure on the beach that offered seating for the three of them.

George began by saying, "I have heard a strange ruma dat you are planning to tear down de hotel."

Alan and Deloris both looked at George and then at each another as if, to decide who would explain it to him; Deloris decided that

Alan won the coin toss, "Well, George, we feel that tearing down the current hotel and rebuilding a completely new building, would be the best way to give Placencia a beautiful new lodge. The lodge that we have in mind will draw a lot of people to the village and help everyone because the guest will spend money while they are in Placencia. We love the property and want to make it a place that you and your family will be proud of."

George lowered his eyes as if he was shamed in some way. He began to tell the story of how he had worked countless hours driving each nail by hand, cutting each board with a hand saw, hanging each door tirelessly. He emphasized how his wife, Constance, would cry because he would work so many hours building the hotel. He extolled each property of the wood that he had chosen and the care he took while matching each board. He recalled that he had almost no help at all while building it and that is why the building of the current hotel took several years. His sacrifice was selfless; this was the message that he felt the couple needed to know. He made sure that they knew that there was little money to begin with and how he was forced to take the proceeds from the hotel each year and make improvements. He even pointed where one year's improvements stopped and the next years began. He brought to their attention how the little hotel had survived Hurricane Iris and how quickly he had gotten it back to operational order. His stories were clearly meant to inform the new owners of how much love, pride and dedication he had put into the hotel. Deloris and Alan had heard many of these stories when he originally showed them the hotel, but this time, it clearly was not a sales pitch. No, this was a cry of love for the hotel that he had spent so much time, energy and love on.

Deloris spoke softly, "What would you like us to do, George?"

Suddenly the look of despair faded away and hope gathered on his brow, "Miz Amy tol me dat you are a great creator of decoration and dat you may keep de hotel and jus decorate it. She say dat you can make it beautiful."

She looked at Alan, who was now staring out at the aqua-blue water of the bay and realized that he had left it to her to discuss this with George. She answered, "George, it would cost a fortune to get this hotel where we need it. I'm not even sure that there is a contractor in Placencia that can remodel the current hotel into what we need."

George smiled big and said, "Sure der is! Belizeans can do anyting. You jus have to tell dem what you want." "I understand that, but, George ..." She was interrupted by George.

"I knew you were good people! You part of de family now. Thank you for saving de hotel. It will mean a lot to de people of de village." And with that, George stood, shook their hands and excused himself. After George retreated with a big smile on his face, Alan and Deloris looked at one another and Alan cracked a smile, "Well."

It was late in the day and Deloris did what she often did when she had to process an issue, such as this one, she decided to wait until morning to come to a conclusion and Alan agreed that it was best to not jump to make a decision as well. She seemed to see things much clearer at first light and that time of the day was her absolute favorite time. She calls this her "Scarlet O'Hare" way of dealing with things and it often worked out for the best.

That night they chose a quiet restaurant on the beach for dinner and they laughed about George's childish way of trying to make them feel guilty enough to keep the hotel and remodel it. They knew that they had a decision to make and pondered what they'd do with George's desperate request of saving the hotel. They enjoyed the restaurant and Deloris loved the gentle sound of the water overtaking the sand of the beach. This was an orchestra that had played the same beautiful piece since the beginning of time and to this very day, it is one of the most beautiful sounds she can imagine hearing. However, tonight, it seemed to be playing for their ears only and it helped them to be still and listen. They observed the other people dining in the restaurant as they dined. One couple sat quietly, not speaking to one another much at all; other couples were on their laptops and the beauty of this place was somehow lost to them because they were so captured by the bright light of their electronic screens. She and Alan enjoyed their meal and chatted intermittently about their plans here, as well as their businesses in the states, that they didn't want to neglect in the process.

The next morning, Deloris had coffee on the beach and pondered George's request to keep the hotel and remodel it. After a bit, Alan joined her and she said, "I think that this decision is a simple one. We can choose to be the intrusive Americans to the village, or a part of the family, like George said."

"I know you are right. But we also know that leaving the structure and remodeling it will cost much more, and you won't have the perfect place that I know you have your heart set on."

"Yes, you are right, but even though I know that you wouldn't shy away from a battle to be able to do what you want, with our property, I also know that we want to fit in here. A fight wouldn't particularly bother you, I've seen you stand up for this sort of thing many times; however, it all boils down to what will benefit us in the long run. Do we save money by demolishing the hotel and starting over the way that we want to, or do we spend the extra money and show the village and George that we do care about them and what they care about?"

The decision was made and not discussed again. Of course, what she had said made sense and it only seemed logical, for the long run, to keep the current hotel and build around it. They wanted to be a part of the family of Placencia Village.

Chapter 9

Now that the decision to keep the hotel was made, they needed to meet with a contractor to get bids and discuss what could be done to accommodate both keeping the hotel and having the beautiful lodge of which they dreamed. It was finally time to shake off the tropical fever and deal with the new adventure of remodeling with contractors in Belize, Central America. Deloris arranged for Hans to give them an estimate on the remodel at his first available time. Hans arrived, looked around and inspected the property and building. He frowned at the hotel, but was clearly impressed with the location. He told the couple that he hadn't been here since the old bar had closed. There had been an old bar called "Tentacles" located over the water at this location many years ago. It never reopened after Hurricane Iris. They asked him to tell them about the bar. He told them that it used to sit out at the end of the dock, over the water. He said that it was a great place that all of the locals frequented and it was clear to the couple that he held fond memories of this property. There seemed to be no place for the three of them to sit and have a work space to sketch out ideas so Alan said, "Well, why don't we walk through the place and get an idea of what we'd like to do, then we can go next door and have a drink and discuss it?"

Hans looked over and appraising at each area and its location in relation to the beachfront. He looked for the road to access it with an experienced eye as well. After they'd retreated next door to have a drink, Hans asked the most important questions that a contractor could ask, "Okay, so what do you want to do with the hotel, and when does it need to be finished?"

Alan looked over at Deloris and knew that this is where she'd direct the project. He had already told her what he needed so that she would include that in the design. She'd worry about the details and he need only worry about having enough funds to obtain their goal. The couple decided years ago that if one was to worry about something, the other wouldn't worry about it and would focus on something else. There was no reason for the both of them to lose sleep. This adage is what has made them such a productive team over the years. They shared common goals and ideals about projects and that made for few arguments. Deloris and Alan both realized that, after knowing one another so long, that if one wanted something, it must be important so the other would make it happen.

Deloris explained her original plans to Hans, but explained that their decision to remodel instead of rebuilding came from the pressure George had placed on them. She wanted to build six luxury suites, with a bathroom and a kitchenette in each of them. Hans looked at Deloris and then at Alan expectantly, as if he were waiting for her to realize the error in their decision. Deloris looked at him and said, "Hans, I know that you are Mennonite and are only in Placencia part time, but you are Belizean as well. Do we really have a choice if we are to fit in here?"

Hans smiled softly and with an agreeable tone replied, "I understand. We will have a very big job ahead of us then. First of all, I cannot take on a project this size unless I can find a subcontractor experienced in remodeling. I do well when building from scratch, but if we intend to be proud of this hotel when we are finished, it will take someone experienced in combining remodeling and rebuilding. That takes talent, to combine the old with the new and not have it look like that is what you've done."

"Is there anyone in Placencia that you trust to do this kind of remodeling job?" Deloris asked. "No, not in Placencia, but I do know two men who live in a small village between Belmopan and Dangriga, who would be perfect for this type of project. ", he explained.

After being assured that Hans knew that they were trustworthy and very experienced, Deloris felt more hopeful.

"You will just need to tell us what you want to keep and what we'll get rid of, we'll handle the rest.", said Hans.

"Since it is lunchtime, why don't we have some lunch while we are here? That'll give me some time to mull over the options for the remodel." Deloris suggested, the men agreed. "Okay, Hans, I know what I want to do and can picture it in my head, but I cannot draw it on paper well enough to make sense of it. I can't draw a straight line to save my life! I will tell you and you can draw it.", said Deloris.

Hans agreed to transfer his interpretation of what she described to him onto paper and reached across the thick, wooden table and grabbed two napkins, He laid them out flat onto the table, took pencil in hand and said, "Shoot!"

Deloris leaned sideways and looked under the table, causing Alan and Hans to raise a curious eyebrow. She sat back up straight and asked excitedly, "Do you have a tape measure with you?"

Hans seemed to relax after her reason for peering under the table was revealed and then reached to his side and pulled out a twenty-five-foot length tape measure to show that he did indeed have one. He offered it to her and she quickly took it and walked over to Paradise. She roughly measured, the distance between the existing structure to the property lines, or what she had been shown to be the property lines. She soon finished and returned. When she arrived back at the table, she told Hans that she wanted to build a new addition from the edge of the current building to the edge of their property, which was about twenty feet. She wanted to have two rooms on the beachfront, on the upper level, with a new office below them. Then on ground level, beside the other structure, she wanted to build four other rooms. This would give them six more rooms to the hotel and a nice, big, new office with a lobby. Hans didn't look happy, but saved his comments. "What is it? You don't like that idea?", ask Deloris.

Hans frowned and said, "Well, aren't you going to have a restaurant and bar?"

Alan spoke up and said, "We really do need a restaurant and bar. You can't bring Americans to a third world country and not insure them that you can provide them food and drink while they are visiting."

"There are plenty of nice restaurants and bars nearby that our guests can visit, we'll just have to encourage them to go and visit them while they are here." Deloris protested. She knew immediately that Hans and Alan were right, but knew she would have to give up rooms to accommodate the restaurant. She agreed that a restaurant and bar would be good for business. She even agreed with Alan's point about providing their guests with a safe, clean place to drink and enjoy cutting loose in Placencia. After a few moments of silence and the men thinking of ways to convince her, she let them know that she agreed that a nice restaurant and bar would be good for business and continued, "But can I still have my two ocean-front rooms above the restaurant?" The two men excitedly said, "Yes, of course you can!"

The three laughed for a moment and then Hans began to scratch a few lines onto the napkin in front of him. "I hate to further ruin your plans, but you two will want an apartment, a place to live while you are here, or at least I would.", said Hans.

Alan shook his head and said, "That does make sense."

Hans nodded and added, "Also, you will be looking to sell in three or four years, so a good selling point would be a functioning kitchen in the owner's apartment."

Alan puckered his mouth in a peculiar way and said, "Sell? Why in the world would we sell Paradise?"

The three of them laughed at his animated question and the subject was dropped. Hans stood up from the table and said, "Excuse me, I'm going to check something.", and he walked over to their property. He disappeared behind the hotel and reappeared shortly. Returning to the table, he said, "We are close to the property line on that side and that is where I will need to put in a septic tank system. We are out of room over there, but I can build a laundry room and storage room over the septic system, then you will have a nice laundry room and storage room to use as well."

Deloris studied the drawing and realized that adding a third room across the back on the beach side would be ill proportioned and wouldn't work. She curved her lips and said, "You are going to tell me that I can only have two ocean-front rooms and a two-room owner's suite, aren't you?" "No, you can have a three-room owner's suite, you can have a second bedroom." Hans answered. "Why have a second bedroom?" Alan asked curiously.

"So that your grandkids can have a room when they visit." Hans assumed.

"We don't have grandkids." Alan said quickly.

"Well, I'm sure you will one day, then you will have a room for them." Hans said, trying to sell the building of a guest room in the owner's suite.

Alan said, "You have to have kids before you can have grandkids. We never had any kids."

"No kids?!" Hans shouted his question. His culture prided itself on having many children per family.

Deloris quietly answered, "No. No kids. We never really had time for kids." Their answers made Hans look at them in disbelief, he couldn't imagine not having any kids to carry on his name and his work after he was gone. Nevertheless, he went back to drawing on the napkin and although a rough sketch, they soon had a plan. Deloris looked over the plans as Hans described each line and was pleased with their drawing so far. She was still disappointed about the loss of the other rooms that she'd wanted, but decided that they'd make the best of the existing rooms with a major overhaul and remodel.

She told Hans that it would take her a couple of days to decide what would needed to be done to the rooms that were already there and Hans said, "That is fine. It will take me a couple of days to contact the brothers to make sure that they are able to take on the project." They all agreed to meet at the hotel in four days to discuss any changes and their plan going forward.

After Hans had left, Alan said, "You do realize that if we have a restaurant and bar that we'll need a full kitchen as well, right?" "Yes, that makes sense.", said Deloris.

"Well, that means that you will have to give up some of your downstairs rooms as well."

"Well crud! Let's do anther walk through and call it a day. I need to process all of this.", she said, disappointed.

That night, they decided to try a new restaurant. As they sat down at the table, Deloris said, "You know, I have yet to have a bad meal in Placencia."

"They are often slow, but you are right, never a bad meal.", Alan agreed.

"I think the food is better for us here as well. I always seem to lose weight when we are here, even though I eat more.", she laughed.

"Maybe it is the lack of preservatives in the food here. Ya know, in the U.S., we preserve everything to lengthen the shelf life of a product. Most of the food in the states is genetically modified organisms, the famed GMO and don't even get me started on the damn steroids they inject into everything to make it bigger and better.", Alan snapped as if he were schooling congress.

They enjoyed their meal and continued to discuss the design of the new hotel. Before they realized it, they were being greeted by people that they had spoken to only once or twice in the village. An older woman approached and said, "George told us that you two were good people and were going to keep the hotel that he had spent so much time on and just remodel it. What a grand notion that is on your part." She spoke with a perfect British accent, as she applauded the couple. She appeared to be Belizean, but certainly didn't sound like it.

Deloris said, "Thank you. We want to respect his hard work." Then paused and straightened in her chair, "If you don't mind me asking, where are you from?", she continued.

The older woman smiled and said, "I am from here in Placencia, but I grew up in England, Westminster, to be exact. My father was British and my mother was Belizean. I had the best of both worlds.", she explained. The three visited for a while, then the lady excused herself with a handshake and then disappeared. The couple realized at that moment that they had been narcissistic in their assumption that the majority of the people who visited Belize were from the United States or Canada. Many people from other countries and cultures must frequent here as well.

Over the next few days, Deloris went over the property with a fine-toothed comb and inspected, made notes and imagined what the hotel would look like. Hans returned and the three again met and retired to the restaurant next door to discuss the options and plans. Hans asked if the reformation of the hotel was ready to begin and was pleased to hear that in only a couple of weeks the last of the reservations would have been fulfilled and they would be ready to proceed. He informed them that the brothers were on board, "I have great news, Jose and Jose are ready to go and can start when we are ready to proceed."

"Jose and Jose?" Alan asked to ensure that he had heard correctly.

"Yeah, they are twins and I can't tell them apart, so I just call them both Jose. One speaks English and the other doesn't, but that is the only difference in the two." Hans explained.

Normally this would have alerted the couple that they were in for an adventure, but their normal, caution and forethought seemed to leave them as they both simply smiled in agreeance with the contractor's situation. This happened a lot here in Belize. It appeared to deepen with each breath of the tropical air. Hans produced a laptop from the bag that he had brought and shared a rough floor plan with them for the remodel. While it was better than the original two napkins, it was still difficult to imagine for Deloris. However, she still noticed that there was a seven-foot gap upstairs between the rooms and their apartment. She asked, "Why is this gap there and why can't we use this area for another room by stealing a few feet from either side?"

Hans answered in a complicated technical explanation concerning construction techniques that she didn't understand, but she caught the words "weight distribution" and "load bearing walls" so she assumed that it was designed that way because it had to be. She excused herself mentally and began imagining how she'd decorate the unused space. It may not serve a purpose, but that didn't mean that it had to look bad.

The conversation of possibilities continued as Alan asked, "Can you build me a building over the water so that I can have a tackle and dive shop, or maybe a spa?"

Hans looked at the building from a distance and said, "If the building there now is structurally sound and the dock is in good shape, other than some cosmetic repairs, that wouldn't be an issue at all."

Alan smiled, as he looked out at the dock and the small building there now, then looked at Hans and asked the big question, "Okay, so what are we looking at as far as cost, Hans?"

"Well, since we are remodeling, instead of building new, I can't set an exact price, because we don't know what we will run into when we tear into the structure. However, what I can do is take this project on at a "cost-plus labor" basis.", Hans said with an understanding tone.

The couple understood why he couldn't quote an exact price because of the things that he could run into when remodeling and the uncertainties that could arise. Knowing this didn't help the anxiety of not knowing the exact amount of capital they would need to complete the project. Deloris, the planner, craved these exact numbers, but she realized they were not to be. In the U.S. she would have run numbers and had a plan A, B, C and D and would have known where the capital was to come from for each of these scenarios. However, on this day, she only saw the dream of making Paradise into their own beautiful dive and fishing lodge where people would come and fall in love with Belize.

Hans was willing and did, offer a guess of what he felt would be close to the cost and since that number was close to what they had assumed the remodel and completion of the hotel would cost, they agreed that they would proceed based on that figure until it had to change. They established a loose contract and decided when the payments would be made to Hans. They discussed the exact date when all the guest would be gone and when the construction would begin. They told Hans that Donna would be there throughout the remodel and that they could answer any questions he may have through email; as they needed to get back to their businesses in the states. He would simply need to convey any questions or issues to Donna and she'd email them and they'd get back to him as soon as they could. They were scheduled to return to Florida in a couple of days and were satisfied with the plan moving forward. It appeared that just about everything was settled and they agreed to return about six weeks after construction had begun to discuss any changes that needed to be made. They thanked Hans for all his effort up to this point and then said goodbye.

On the plane ride home, Deloris asked Alan, "Explain the seven-foot gap upstairs to me and why it couldn't be changed to make another room for our guests."

He looked up from his diving magazine and answered, "I have no idea. Hans said that it couldn't be moved because it was a load bearing wall and needed to be there for the weight of the roof."

Deloris was a bit shocked that he said he didn't know, "But you seemed to agree with Hans about the space. So, I thought you understood what he was saying."

Alan laughed, "Nope, not a clue. But he does this for a living and if he says that it can't be changed, then it can't be changed."

Deloris laughed and opened her in-flight magazine. After some thought, she looked up from the magazine and said, "Alan, we don't have a solid contract and short of a few notes on a napkin and a rough sketch on a computer, we don't really have a design approved. We'd never do this type of project in the states without a binding contract and approved blueprints. What do you think about that?"

Alan, folded his dive magazine and looked at her, "I guess dat is de tropical feva!" As he laughed and stole his wife's magazine from her hand in a playful manner.

Deloris couldn't hold back her laughter and leaned her head back onto the seat back. She hoped that this "Tropical Fever" was not terminal. It was an intoxicating freedom from her normally cautious idealism, but she realized that it could become very expensive if not balanced with reality at some point.

Chapter 10

After a couple of weeks at home, Deloris received an email from Donna, explaining that Hans was requesting that one of them be present when the surveyor came and examined the property to set the exact boundaries. She also wrote that Hans said that he could handle it, but would feel better if one of them were present.

Alan decided that he'd go down and handle it and would stay a few days in one of the rooms of the hotel. Hans was waiting at the hotel when Alan arrived and told him that the surveyor would be there the next morning to get started. He said that the surveyors would be coming in from Dangriga and he was told that they should be there around nine, or nine-thirty.

Alan came out of his room around seven o'clock the next morning to eat breakfast in town and noticed that quite a few people were gathering near the hotel. It was as if a village meeting had been called for the community to cast a vote on a subject. Alan walked up the beach, past the pier and had breakfast at "The Shack", which is right on the beach and always seems to have a good breeze. It was one of Deloris's favorite places for breakfast. She loved their banana pancakes. Magda, a striking woman, with olive skin and beautiful black hair, owned "The Shack". She was a long-time resident of Placencia. She greeted Alan and ask about Deloris. He explained that he had come down alone because they would be surveying the property today and Hans had requested his presence. Magda laughed and said she would love to be there to see this. Alan was taken back by this comment. Why would surveying property be a spectator sport? Magda suggested that if Alan had a problem that he go find Ms. Louise and talk to her about it. This was the second time that someone had suggested that he should meet this Ms. Louise. Being a little uncomfortable that there may be some underlying drama of which he was unaware, he attempted to change the subject by asking Magda about the seaweed shakes that she sold.

Several people that he had met had crooned the praises of these seaweed shakes. She suggested that she prepare one for him with his breakfast, but he declined. She explained that she purchased seaweed from locals who collected it for her. She then dried it and when she was ready to use it, she boiled it and it formed a gelatin that she used in the shakes. She assured him that they were not only good, but she told him about all the medicinal properties contained in these shakes. As he returned to the hotel, he noticed that even more people had gathered now. They all seemed to quiet as he approached. Looking around he realized that most of the people were members of the two families living on both sides of the hotel. One of the families was George's family. Of course, there also seem to be other locals who made it their business to be involved in anything unusual that was going on in the village. Alan muddled his way through the crowd and into the office of his hotel to see two men standing there holding a long pole and a sight glass on a pedestal. Donna stood and said with her thick Kroil accent, "Mista Alan, des are de survayas dat mista Hans said wus comin."

Alan offered his hand and introduced himself to both men. Hans, choose that moment to make his entrance and he greeted the two surveyors warmly. They all exited the office walking to one corner of the property where the surveyors had pulled away sand in one area. One surveyor began by setting up the tri-pod above the spot that had the sand pulled away from it, revealing what looked like a large nail buried deep. The other surveyor then walked to the other rear corner of the property and quickly located another nail, that they called "surveyor's pins", which marked the boundary line. They walked back along the proposed property line, to locate the third pin on the beachfront, the normally calm demeanor of George's mother, who was the matriarch of the family, on the south side of Alan's new property changed. She leaned her head out of the window and shouted at the surveyor, "Ya teef! Ya steelin my prapaty!" Then she said, a number of things that were incomprehensible to Alan and he was glad at this point that he didn't speak Kroil. Apparently, being kind and neighborly didn't extend to determining property lines and boundaries. The surveyors continued their work, as if they couldn't hear the frantic woman accusing them of corruption and worse. A roar was now rising from the crowd. There were numerous arguments arising between members of the crowd, including one between George and one of his brothers. Alan walked over to George, who was standing around the original pin that the surveyor had located in the beginning. The men were arguing over their father's wishes, that he had made known, when he gave this property to two of his sons. It seems he had told one son one thing, and the other another, at least this was the case in their memories. Neither could be certain what his real wishes were. Driving a concrete stake into the sand, the surveyors continued working and one of the surveyors was writing numbers in his small book.

The insults became more personal towards the surveyor and again, Alan was shocked that the normally tranquil attitude of the Belizeans had changed. When they arrived at the beach front another argument ensured because a "Survey Pin" could not be located, but both brothers agreed that the property boundary was at the coconut tree that had been blown down during Hurricane

Iris. Now I am going to tell you, that this beach is lined with coconut trees and probably has been for hundreds of years. They argued loudly about exactly where that coconut tree had been. There was a stump of a cocoanut tree visible and George's brother insisted that this was the coconut tree in question, but George insisted that the coconut tree that established the boundary was buried several feet south of the visible stump. When the argument seemed to slow a little, Alan asked gently, "Why are you two arguing over a coconut tree that is not here?"

The two men stopped as if a bolt of lightning had hit nearby. After a moment of staring at Alan, one brother explained that there had been two coconut trees there and that a hurricane had uprooted them both, but those two trees were the ones that they were arguing over. They decided that the only way to settle the argument about which invisible tree was the correct one was to go and get a third brother.

Soon the third brother came and after a short, heated debate, the proper ghost tree was named as the one to be used to mark the property boundary. Now the side boundary was established on the south and everyone now seemed to be happy with the lines that were established on that side except for Alan, who now noticed that the property line passed smack dab through the middle of an existing concrete cistern that had been built on the side of the hotel. As he walked over to the cistern, he and Hans visited about replacing it with a new, rubber holding tank, which would be totally on the hotel's property. As they finished discussing it, a lot of yelling and arguing erupted. One brother switched from English to Kroil so that Alan couldn't understand him, but it appeared that the family had built the concrete cistern many years ago so that it could be used by the whole family if needed. The water for Placencia was supplied by mountain runoff and was piped to the peninsula by a six-mile pipeline under the lagoon. The water was then stored in an elevated storage tank, near the airstrip. It could then be pumped out to the village. That storage tank was large but in cases of disaster like Hurricane Iris, you could never have enough water. The family recognized that this small piece of their history had been sold to a gringo from the United States and they weren't willing to sacrifice the security that this giant tank, when filled, provided to their family, even if this meant that they'd have to share it with a gringo, since if they made an issue of it he would simply remove it.

Alan told Hans that he'd let him work out the necessary logistics of allowing the family to use the cistern and leave it where it was, but they'd discuss it when tempers were less flared. The property lines on this side were now marked and everyone could see what belonged to the gringo.

George to prove his point, hurried home and returned with a shovel. He began to dig and soon he announced that he had located the root system of the long-departed tree. Now the surveyors could use this mark as the boundary to establish the beachfront property line. George was again proven correct since the beachfront measurement now matched when they located the existing "surveyor's pin on the other side of the beachfront.

Before anyone could breathe a sigh of relief, the matriarch, on the other side started to scream and degrade all who were involved in establishing the property line. The paternal heads of both families were now gone but as the new matriarchs of their families, these women were very protective of keeping what is their family's rightful possession. When the sons received the property, the females didn't have rights to land at all, but if the wife of a son were widowed, then it was her responsibility to maintain ownership until she passed. At that point, she was to leave it to a male member of the family to continue passing it on. The screaming women may not own the property, but they would surely defend it for their sons or grandson, as long as they were alive. After all, this was valuable beach-front property that everyone wanted. The matriarch of this side had not objected to the rear boundary since it was much shorter than the beachfront measurement.

Alan felt confident that the beachfront measurement was correct after locating the ghost coconut tree, but he was shocked to see that what he assumed would be a ninety-degree turn away from the ocean was now looking to be a sharply angled line away from the ocean to meet the rear boundary. He knew that Deloris had wanted her precious ocean-front rooms in that area and an angled boundary would cause the loss of valuable square footage in those rooms. She had already sacrificed many of her ideas, the greatest being choosing to remodel portions of the hotel instead of building an all new structure. Now the news of telling her that the rooms she had designed wouldn't fit because of the abrupt property line change, she'd be disappointed for sure. Alan found it hard to believe the embittered reaction from the normally docile locals. When asked, the surveyor calmly stated, "Large parcels of land were originally given to the patriarch of a family and then he would divide it between his sons by way a landmark, such as a tree, or post, marking his son's portion of land. This often-let people believe that they own other people's property, causing issues."

The surveyor and his helper were gathering their tools when Alan asked, "Do you guys have to go through this mess every time that you survey a property?"

The surveyor finished placing his elevation marker in its sheath and flung it over his shoulder and then looked at Alan and said, "Only in Placencia! The families here had the handshake mentality and nothing was ever documented when land was transferred to another person. They always misremember, or never really knew what land was theirs, or where the boundaries are, so they try every time to gain a bit more land. Other places in Belize are a bit more up to speed where land lines are concerned."

Chapter 11

That night after calling Deloris and telling her the events of the day, Alan decided to go a little café on the sidewalk. It bothered him that there had been so much animosity today over something that should have been cut and dry since there should have been paperwork that could be used to establish boundaries. As he sat, looking out at the dark ocean, waiting to place his order, he wondered if there would be lasting effects. The waiter approached and just as he did, an elegant, older Belizean lady entered with a younger girl at her side. The waiter rushed away from his table and greeted the ladies with a big smile and hug. He addressed the older lady as, Ms. Louise. So here was the influential woman that he had been encouraged to meet. They were seated at a table beside him. The waiter took their drink order before returning to Alan. Alan placed his drink order and as the waiter retreated, Ms. Louise looked over at him and ask if he was the American that had purchased the hotel from George. "Yes, how did you know", ask Alan. "There is not much that goes on in this village that I don't know about", retorted Ms. Louise. She asked Alan if he would like to join them since he was alone. As he moved over to their table, the girl accompanying Ms. Louise introduced herself as Janie and told him that she had previously worked at Paradise. It appeared that Janie was like a daughter to this "icon" of Placencia. Alan learned that the two were out tonight to celebrate Ms. Louise's birthday. Ms. Louise ask Alan if he could guess her age. With some trepidation, Alan replied that she looked in be in her early fifties, only fudging by about ten years. Ms. Louise's face brighten and Alan could immediately tell that his answer pleased her. She asks him why he was in Placencia alone, since she had heard that he was married. Alan explained that his wife had to stay back in the states to keep their businesses there going. A look of disapproval covered her face, but despite that, she remained quiet, although it was known that she almost always voiced her opinions regardless of the consequences. Janie, spoke up at this point and told Alan that Ms. Louise had taken her in when she was quite young, but that actually a great number of young girls in Placencia considered Ms. Louise to be a mother figure to them. Ms. Louise told Alan that she had gone to the states to work when she was in her late twenties. With education and hard work, she had become a legal secretary in Chicago and after 20 years in the states she had returned to her beloved Placencia where she had been born and raised. When she returned to Belize she had worked for a man that went on to become Prime Minister of Belize, then she had run a well-known hotel in Placencia. "It was more like "ruled" the hotel", laughed Janie. "All of us in my age group have work for Ms. Louise at one time or another. She was not only our boss but our mentor as well. She did her best to make sure we behaved ourselves", laughed Janie. Ms. Louise, an absolutely stunning beauty in her youth, wanted the young girls in Placencia to know that they could do anything they wanted, that it just required hard work. She did not hold her tongue at all when it came to educate young girls the proper way to conduct themselves. She had become the most influential woman in Placencia. She was also a Senior Justice of the Peace. She told Alan that if he needed help getting the hotel up and running to feel free to let her know and she would help. After a wonderful dinner and very interesting conversation, Alan returned to the hotel and settled in for the night.

The next morning Alan noticed that there was a lot of activity at the house one over from George's mother's house. It appeared that they were decorating for some sort of get-to- together. Donna told Alan that there was to be a wedding there tonight. That evening just as Alan was getting ready to go out and look for some dinner, he met Ms. Louise coming down the path to the hotel. Surprised, he asks her where she was headed and she told him that she had come to take him to the wedding with her. Alan laughed and said he appreciated the thought, but he did not know the bride nor groom and really didn't have anything to wear to a wedding with him, besides he was on his way out to eat. Ms. Louise would not take any excuse and said that since the wedding was on the beach it would be necessary for her to walk through the sand to get there and she needed to hold his arm so that she would not fall. Since Alan could not think of a way to politely refuse, he agreed to accompany her. She assured Alan that he need not worry about eating because there would be plenty of food at the wedding. She held tightly to his arm as they walked the short distance down the beach and joined the happy crowd. As soon as they started to mingle with the crowd, people started to greet Ms. Louise. She promptly dropped Alan's arm and took his hand and pulled him over to a small group of people. She introduced them one by one, then looking at the group, announced in a voice, just a little louder than necessary, that Alan was the new owner of Paradise and her new boyfriend. Alan's mouth fell open. He did not know what to say. She continued to drag him from group to group and he tried to laugh, in just the right places, with each introduction so that the people would know that this was a joke. He wasn't at all sure that he had succeeded. As soon as he could get Ms. Louise out of earshot of the crowd, he said in what he hoped sounded like a joking way, "I am not sure how my wife will feel about you introducing me as your boyfriend." He knew that Ms. Louise was a force to be reckoned with but despite that, he could not put Deloris in an embarrassing situation. Ms. Louise only smiled and ask, "When is your wife coming back to Placencia? I will talk to her. It will be alright. I have a husband that lives in the states as well. They won't mind".

That night Alan called Deloris and told her all about Ms. Louise. Deloris could not contain her laughter. She had heard about Ms. Louise's reputation and couldn't wait to meet this interesting woman.

With the property lines now being established, the last pre-booked guest had departed and real demolition and remodel could be started. The old portion of the hotel would be remodeled and the addition of the restaurant, three oceanfront rooms and their apartment would be beginning. Donna would come in each day for a few hours and be their liaison while the construction was being done. Han's had estimated that the job could be completed in about 8 months. Alan was satisfied that all was well so he was ready to return home.

A year had passed since their first visit to Placencia and during that year Deloris' mother Mary had come to live with them since her health was not as good as it once was. She had always been a strong presence in Deloris' life. She was the perfect Mother, she always wanted to know exactly what was going on in their lives but never offer advise unless asked. The bond between Alan and Mary was also strong. In fact, it was at his insistence she came to live with them. When it appeared that she would need to be in a wheelchair most of the time, the decision was made to move from their "dream home" on the island to a condo that was designed to accommodate wheel chair access. Here there was an elevator to come up to the third-floor location but no stairs in the condo and there was 3000 square feet of wheelchair accessible space, which gave the three of them ample space. One evening Alan, Deloris, and Mary were sitting on their screened patio at their condo. The patio overlooked the marina on the intracoastal waterway. Alan was admiring the pricey yachts moored in the marina, while Deloris and Mary discussed the current political situation in the U.S.

The conversation turned again to Alan's experience during the survey and then on to his meeting of Ms. Louise. Both Deloris and Mary laughed because they could just imagine Alan's reaction to these situations. Both Alan and Deloris loved telling Mary about their adventures in Placencia. I suspect that Mary thought they were enhancing these stories just as Deloris had thought Amy had been. Mary had no desire to accompany them to Belize, but she loved hearing the tales and sharing the excitement of their journey.

It was apparent that Deloris had something on her mind that she was pondering. She is known for that, by the way. Never truly relaxing and always thinking, planning and discovering new ways to handle business. She finally revealed what was on her mind, "You know ... Donna probably has never even seen a home like ours. I'm sure that she has no idea how Americans live. We live the way most of our guest live. How can we expect her to give our guests the type of service and treatment that we, as Americans, have come to want and expect, if she's never even seen the U.S.?"

"But we aren't trying to create America in Belize. ", said Alan. "Oh, I agree completely, but I want our guest to have air conditioning in the bedroom, crisp clean sheets and good service. I want our guest to enjoy the best of Belize without sacrificing the small amenities like hot water", Deloris laughed.

"The Belizeans that work for us need to know the minimum that Americans expect." When Alan didn't speak, she continued, "But you know that I'm the world's worst teacher and I know that I will have trouble explaining this concept to Donna. Right now, we rely on her to teach others, but she truly doesn't know what the guests will expect. How can she teach the others if she doesn't even know?"

Uncle Alan, knowing that there was a point to this rambling said, "Okay ... So, what are you suggesting?"

Alan is a man of fewer words than Deloris. "I think that we need to bring her to the states with us for a short visit. Did you know that she's only been as far as Belize City and that was only a handful of times? She once went over the border into Guatemala to buy clothes, but that is not anything like the U.S. She's never even been to Mexico?", said Deloris.

She probably doesn't have a passport much less a visa." Alan said. "We can help her get a passport and visa." It can't be hard", replied the still naïve and ever positive Deloris.

The next trip to Placencia came quickly. Donna did indeed have a passport as many Belizeans do, because they use them to travel for shopping into Guatemala or Mexico. However, it would be necessary to get her a Visa, in order to visit the states. Donna arranged an appointment with the Belize Immigration Department in Dangriga and the American Embassy in Belmopan. It would cost several hundred dollars, which was not refundable if the Visa was denied, to complete the application for the visa to visit. Donna obtained a list of the documentation that she would need to obtain the proper paperwork for the visit. Some of the documentation she'd need would be a background report, a doctor's physical examination and a report from the Belizean authorities showing that she did not owe the country of Belize any taxes. To accomplish these goals, first they needed to obtain some of the documentation from the capital of the District, so the three of them took a day to trip to Dangriga. In order to reach the capital of the Stann Creek district it is necessary to travel up the Peninsula road, back up to the Hummingbird Highway and then head toward the sea. Located at the junction of the Stann Creek River and the coast of the Caribbean, Dangriga is a town with a definite Garifuna flavor. Its population is approximately 12,000. The land is low and flat and the town has a somewhat tumbledown look. The word tidy would never be used to describe the town or the area in general. To obtain these documents, it was necessary to request the documentation in one building, then travel to a different building to pay. Then after an appropriate wait you could return to the first building and with the receipt they would then release the documents. Of course, to Alan and Deloris, this was an inefficient waste of time; however, they had already learned that in Belize, their suggestions and observations were better kept to themselves. They were able to obtain all the necessary documentation in one journey to Dangriga. They had been warned by experienced Belizeans that they would be lucky to get this done with one try. When the appointment date to apply for the Visa at the American Embassy in Belmopan arrived, the three left very early in the morning for the trip to Belmopan.

Deloris was surprised to see how strict the security was to enter the embassy. An x-ray scanner and a machine that x-rayed anything that you were bringing into the area, was located inside the neat and clean concrete building that was the entrance to the Embassy grounds. After going through this security check, they found 15 or 20 people who appeared to be Belizeans waiting in the waiting area. The area looked like many government offices in the U.S. The waiting area accommodated about 15 people comfortably, so many of the people waiting wandered outside to sit on the concrete benches that lined the manicured lawn that covered the ground inside the Embassy border fence. A little piece of America right here in Belize. The three found seats in the lobby, after several minutes, they noticed that each person waiting had a numbered piece of paper from a roll that was displayed close to the entrance door. Deloris took a numbered ticket from the apparatus. After waiting about an hour and a half, their number was finally called. The three of them followed a clerk down a hall, past several doors leading from the lobby and was finally asked to take a seat in what appeared to be an interview room. The room was decorated with the standard American plain wooden desk, wooden straight back chairs, the U.S. flag and red carpeted floors. The official seated at the desks quizzed Donna, as well as Alan and Deloris. Their primary concern was would she return to Belize after her temporary visa expired. Deloris assured the officials that Donna had two small children and was buying a home in Placencia. The officials inquired about her two children and learned that they'd be staying with Donna's mother while she was away. After these bits of information, the officials seemed to relax a little. Deloris stressed that this visit was simply to acquaint Donna with American ways so that she could better serve the guests at the hotel. Deloris had brought the round-trip tickets showing that Alan and Donna had return flights to Belize after the ten-day stay. The official closed the file and told them that Donna would need to return in a week to see if her visa was approved or rejected. After exciting the Embassy, Deloris scoffed and lamented to her traveling companions, "Seemed that a phone call would be much easier than driving all the way back to Belmopan to check."

Donna tilted her head and with a quizzical look said, "But dat is not de way tings are done here in Belize, Miz D."

"Then let me ask you this, Donna ... How would you have been able to do these things if we were not here to drive you?" retorted Deloris.

"I would have take de bus from Placencia and rode it to Belmopan. Afta taking care of all dis, if der was a bus returning to Placencia dat day, I would have taken it back. If der was not a bus returning, I would have find a place to stay and catch de bus in de mornin to return to Placencia."

"But there is no way that you could have ridden the bus here today in time to make the appointment."

"No, I would have came yestaday and found a place to stay, den I would take a taxi to de embassy."

"That sounds very expensive and time consuming.", said Deloris.

"Yes, it is. But dat is why it is very hard for a Belizean to get a visa. Dey make it so hard dat we never try it more dan once. If dey are denied, all dat money is lost." Donna calmly stated.

She continued, "Even de airfare to de U.S. is more dan most Belizeans make in several monts. Most people here make less than forty Belize dollars a day. If de plane ticket cost a thousand Belize, it is so very hard to save dat much and dat make it not wort it."

A two week visit to the U.S would easily cost more than the average, employed Belizean makes in a whole year. Without the assistance of visiting Americans, the dream to see America would not come true for most Belizeans. Deloris decided that it was time to change the subject. It was uncomfortable to hear that Belizean's opportunities were so limited.

The weekend brought the Art Festival to Placencia. Deloris spend the morning walking the sidewalk where artist from all over Belize came to show their creations. At one of the booths, Deloris spotted a fruit bowl that was carved like an iguana. It was similar to the Turtle Fruit Bowl that Deloris had admired on Amy's counter on her first visit. They planned to put a small gift shop in the hotel lobby and Deloris knew that if she had these items for sale, her guest would love them. She talked with the craftsman and ordered five fruit bowls carved like the Iguana and five fruits bowls carved with a Turtle. The craftsman told her he would bring them back to Placencia when he finished them.

The week passed before they could return to Belmopan to learn whether or not Donna's Visa had been granted. They were told over and over by experienced people that it was very unusual that Alan and Deloris had been allowed into the interview room with Donna at the Embassy. The consensus was that the visa would not be granted. Most people believed that the visa would be denied for fear that Donna would become an employee in the Unites States. Often, people who have overstayed their visas take jobs at lower wages just to have a job. Of course, this had nothing to do with them wanting to take Donna to the U.S., but it was the way a request such as this could be perceived.

The day came for them to return to Belmopan and when they arrived, they were surprised to find that the visa had been approved and Donna could stay in the U.S. for up to six months.

For the trip to America, they called their old taxi driver friend, Kevin to have him drive them to the airstrip. Donna and Kevin had a lengthy conversation in Kroil that neither of the Alan nor Deloris could understand on the drive to the airstrip. Donna's voice was excited and they could only guess the anticipate adventures that Donna was telling Kevin that she hoped for. After Kevin finished his exchange he turned to Alan and Deloris and said "I explained to Donna dat dis is a chance dat many people from Belize neva have. I tol her dat she mus be good and respectful to you and de miss."

The three flew out of the Placencia airstrip towards Belize International Airport. Donna was clearly excited. She told Deloris that she had never even been on a small plane and that this would be her first time to ever fly. Deloris told her that she would be fine and that she needed only to buckle up and enjoy the ride to the big plane that came next. Donna acted like a pro and did a great job on the small 'Puddle Jumper' that flew them from Placencia to Belize City. When they boarded the next flight, it was clear that Donna had never imagined a plane so large. She kept looking at Deloris for guidance and when she finally had taken her seat, she read every word of the safety briefing card. After the plane was loaded, the flight attendant's voice startled Donna when the speaker above her sounded. It was clear that she was intrigued by the whole ordeal, as she was the only one truly listening to the oral safety presentation that others ignored so blatantly. She watched as the stewardess click and tighten the seatbelt model. She looked down at hers to insured that she was in compliance. As the oxygen mask demonstration began, she asked Deloris, "Where is my mask? I don't find it to learn."

Deloris laughed, but honestly couldn't find which panel it would fall from. She assured Donna that a mask would fall if she needed it and as long as, she knew how to put the mask on, she would be fine. As the large turbines of the massive jet revved up, Donna stared out at the tarmac and watched it pass by her small window. When they were ready to take off, the engines peaked and the thrust forced her back into the seat. They were soon off the ground and reaching cruising altitude in no time. Deloris explained that she could use the restroom now that they had turned off the sign. Donna was excited to use the restroom and upon returning told Deloris all about her surprise when she flushed the toilet. She was also quite surprised when the stewardess came by with the drink cart and refused at first. Deloris explained that the drinks were free and she should have a Coke or something that she liked. Donna agreed to a Coke and enjoyed it slowly. Deloris enjoyed watching her experience this for the first time and although they weren't close, she was proud that she could be the one to give Donna this experience.

After landing in Miami International, they exited the plane and began the long walk to immigration. The expression from Donna was that of a new fish in a huge aquarium. Her eyes searched from side to side and as far as she could look ahead, then she turned and looked at the other side of the long, wide hallway in the terminal. People of every color and nationality were hurrying about their business of catching the steel birds to go somewhere. She watched as some people walked fast, others ran and a few of the people muddled along, as if they weren't in a hurry at all. Her eyes found things that she'd never seen or even heard of before, such as the endless maze of connecting hallways, the bright and shiny clean concession stands offering new and exotic foods that she had never experienced, the arrival and departure displays hanging from ceiling. She followed Alan and Deloris as they made their way to their connecting terminal. Suddenly she was confronted with the escalator going to the next level, where the immigration department was for U.S. customs. Alan and Deloris didn't give much thought to the escalators as they mounted them, without realizing that Donna had held back. They heard Donna shout, "De steps are moving! De steps are moving!"

Deloris turned quickly to see their guest walking backwards trying to get off the escalator and holding on, as if she was riding with Amy furniture shopping and crossing a river. This of course, caused a traffic jam on the escalator. One man tried to calm her as he told her that the steps moved up to the next level. She wasn't buying it, as she forced her way passed two people and the man trying to help. A TSA agent was the next in line and calmly told her that it was okay, to just hold on and he'd help her get to the top. She complied with the man in uniform and soon they were on the next level. Deloris, scolding herself for not realizing that the escalators would alarm Donna, took her arm and moved her to the side gently as the other, clearly perturbed passengers looked on. Imagine how seeing something like this must feel after only seeing concrete or wooden steps that certainly did not move, your whole life. She watched as the people scoffed at her fear of the new machine and felt a bit embarrassed as she leaned over to Deloris and said, "I have seen an elevator once, but neva moving steps." Donna was in for an education over the few days.

As they reached the immigration area, Deloris noticed that there was quite a long line. She told Alan to go ahead and get a place in line and she'd join them after a restroom break. She asked Donna if she needed to use the restroom and the two entered the large restroom. After a few minutes, she heard the toilet flush and then she heard Donna gasp loudly, followed by some undecipherable mumbling. Deloris asked, through the partition, "Are you okay?" "Who flush de toilet?", asks a panicked Donna. "What do you mean?", quizzed Deloris. "De toilet ... I did not flush it. Someone else flush it.", said Donna.

"Oh, that is an automatic flushing toilet. It uses a sensor and flushes when needed." Deloris explained as she opened her stall door to find three women entertained by Donna's excitement. When Donna opened her door, Deloris, washing her hands, smiled and said, "This is much different than Belize, isn't it?"

Donna, a bit jetlagged, nodded her head in agreement and attempted to wash her hands. She found the soap fine, but looked for the handle to turn on the water. Deloris showed her that placing her hands under the water outlet turned the water on and she washed the soap off.

They caught up with Alan, who was still a long way from the front of the line. Deloris explained to Donna that she'd need to go through a different line, since one set of lines was for American citizens and the other lines were for people who did not hold a U.S. passport. She assured her that they'd wait on her on the other side. She told Donna to not be nervous, answer the agent's questions honestly and to smile, then she pointed to the line that Donna needed to be in. They finally passed through the line and attempted to wait on their foreign guest on the other side; however, an immigration and customs agent promptly told them that they'd need to move along. She tried to explain to the agent that they had a guest from Belize and that they needed to wait for her; nonetheless, the agent insisted that they move down to the baggage claim area and wait there. Deloris' appeals had no effect on the agent and he again told them to move along. They slowly made their way to the escalator to the baggage claim area and reluctantly mounted it, continuously searching for their guest.

Alan told her that he'd gather the luggage and for her to wait on Donna at the bottom of the escalator. After what seemed an hour, Donna could finally be spotted on the escalator. This time she was managing the escalator like she had been on them all her life. Deloris searched her face for panic, but found none. She waited until Donna reached the bottom and then asked, "What took so long?"

"You tol me to be honest to de man, so I tol him all about my trip so far and how de steps move and de toilet flush, even when ya not ready. He was very nice to me."

Deloris, grinned a bit and imagined what the immigration official must be thinking. She asked, "You weren't worried about being lost? What would you have done if I had not been waiting for you at the bottom of the escalator?"

"If I taut I was lost I would have ask someone where Mista Alan and Miz Deloris was and de would have tol me. People are nice here, like in de village, right?"

Deloris couldn't help but think that ignorance is bliss. Soon they were boarding their flight from Miami to Jacksonville. Donna had a hard time understanding why they had to stand in yet another line and board yet another plane to get to Alan's and Deloris' home, but after a lengthy conversation about how big Florida was and that it was easier to fly than to drive, Donna calmed and they were soon on the flight.

When they arrived in Jacksonville, they collected their luggage and Alan called the parking garage giving them the identifying information so that they could have their vehicle out and ready for them. Shortly, a bus arrived and the three boarded. Donna leaned over and whispered, "Dey send a whole bus jus for you? You mus be important people here, Miz D."

Deloris explained that the bus goes to many places and picks up many people, but they were the only ones going to that particular parking garage at this time, so they were the only ones on the bus. She assured Donna that the bus driver didn't know them, or care who they were. Donna tried to make sense of it and couldn't understand all the extra room on the bus. In Belize, there were never any empty seats on a bus and, in fact, people would pile on so heavily that many were standing in the aisle to ride the bus. She said, "But dey send a whole bus jus for you. Dat make you important." Deloris simply smiled at the repeated conversation.

When they arrived at the parking garage, the infamous, prized, yellow Hummer H2 was sitting in the lot waiting for them. Donna paused as they exited the bus. She was clearly awe struck as she watched Alan open the rear door on the large, luxury truck for the driver to begin placing the luggage inside. The driver, noticing Donna rapt expression asked, "Is everything okay, Miss?" Donna turned and looked at him and said, "I have neva seen one of dez."

After the three of them climbed into the Hummer, Donna sat very still as she felt the thick, black leather underneath her. She looked around inside the beautiful truck and said, "I feel like a queen in dis ting!"

They soon arrived at the condo that they had purchased soon after beginning the hotel build and pulled into the gate, where the gate guard greeted them with a smile. As they parked in their numbered spot, Donna asked, "What level you live on?" "We are on the third floor, Alan answered as he gathered the luggage from the back of the Hummer. Donna was clearly distraught by this and asked, "We have to carry all dis up tree flight of stairs?"

Deloris gathered her bag and answered, "No, we have an elevator here."

Donna's surprise was clear as she asked, "Jus for you, Miz D?"

"Oh, no. There are eighteen condos that share it. Everyone who lives here uses it.", Deloris answered as she showed her the way. As they climbed into the elevator, Donna held on tight and soon they were on the third floor. They walked to their door, but Donna stopped at the door before entering. She looked at Deloris with a quick glance inside and asked, "How many people live here?" Alan answered, "Just three of us. Deloris' mother lives here with us."

Donna entered the door and then turned in circles admiring the large, beautiful condominium. She finally spoke and said, "De whole village can fit in here."

After Donna's shock had passed, Deloris showed her to her room, which had its own full bathroom. Donna quietly ask, "You all have to come in dis room to get to the bathroom?"

Deloris tilted her head a little and realized that Donna thought that they all used the bathroom in the room in which, she would be sleeping. Deloris explained that each bedroom had its own restroom and that she'd be the only one using that particular one, which pleased her very much.

That night in bed, Deloris asked Alan, "Does Donna make you feel badly about how we live in this country?"

Alan stared up at the ceiling and answered, "Not badly, but it does make me aware of how many differences there are in how we live here and the way most Belizeans live."

They lay there in silence for a while, then he turned on his side to face his wife and asked, "Do you think we would be crazy, giving all of this up, building onto an old hotel in a third world country and trying to make a life in a country that doesn't have any of this?"

"Well, I'm not sure that we are giving all of this up, we are trying to make a life for ourselves in Belize and hang on to all this as well. As long as, Mother is alive you know that I cannot be gone for too long and there is no one to do our jobs at the Animal Hospital either. I think our plan for finishing the hotel and taking small groups down for a week or two and then returning, will work. I believe we can make enough money to run the hotel and we will have our vacations paid for and the cost will only be that we have to play host and hostess to each of our groups. I think it will be fun."

Deloris is a very early riser and we, in the family, call Aunt Deloris "Bubbly" in the morning. If you aren't quite awake, it is like watching dogs race around a coffee table, because she is able to tell you all the ideas that fill her head and expects you to follow her line of thinking as quickly as she does. This is when she loves to talk about plans, for the future and express new ideas. The following morning, before Alan was quite awake, she started to talk about the logistic of how their plan for the hotel would work. She could envision the two of them taking long weekend trips to neighboring states and visiting dive shops and fishing shops and persuading the owners or managers to put together a group to bring to Paradise. There would be incentives so that owners of the shops would get to enjoy the trip at a very reduced cost. They knew that dive clubs and fishing clubs, put these trips together for their members on a routine basis, so they just had to go to these clubs and convince the group that they could come to Belize and participate in their favorite activities. It would be fun soliciting the different shops and groups and showing them all that there was to do in Belize. They knew that getting employees who would want to work a few weeks a month would not be a problem. They would have the employees prepare the hotel for the group's arrival, staff the hotel while the guest were there and then the staff would clean the hotel and be off until the next group's arrival. It seemed that this was a near perfect solutions so that they could travel to Belize often and yet keep their businesses and homes in the states. Perhaps some of the people who traveled there would fall in love with Belize as they had. She did know that this was an exciting adventure that they had undertaken.

Deloris decided that it would have to be later in the day before Alan was really ready to discuss their plans in detail so she went into the kitchen to make coffee and as she did so, she heard her mother, who I refer to as "Grandma Mary", arriving home from visiting relatives in South Carolina. She had chosen to visit with her grandson while Alan and Deloris were gone this time. Mary came into the kitchen and after greeting each other, they walked out onto the patio to have their coffee and watch the sunrise. Mary knew they were bringing Donna back with them, and ask questions about how Donna had liked the journey so far. Deloris glanced inside to find Donna awake and wandering about the condo. She beckoned her and introduced her to Mary. Donna looked well rested after her previous day's adventures. Mary asked Donna how she liked the U.S. so far and Donna told her that everything was so big here and it seemed that everyone had plenty. Donna described the escalator adventure and the bus ride, just for them, to Mary.

Alan and Deloris decided that they would take Donna to Disney World and they would stay overnight at a nice hotel in Orlando. Donna was in awe of Disney World but refused to ride any of the rides except for the Tea Cups. No amount of tempting would get her on a Ferris wheel or roller coaster. Donna seemed to be as curious about the people who were also enjoying the Theme Park that day as she was the rides.

That night when they got to their hotel, Deloris accompanied Donna to her room and told her to pay close attention to the little details that she found in the room, such as the availability of a hair dryer, complementary coffee service, and how neat and tidy everything was. They hoped that this would impress on Donna the necessity for paying attention to detail when it came to the hotel that they hoped to create.

When they met for breakfast the next morning, Donna seemed to have the most questions, about what type of people who could afford to stay here. She seemed amazed that some of the travelers were alone. Deloris explained that those travelers were probably business people who were not traveling for vacation but that this was a part of their work schedule. Donna ask, "Why don't a lot of them stay together in one room, then?" Deloris tried to explain that Americans did not usually share a room unless it was family. Deloris had already been told that Belizeans are accustomed to putting 5 or 6 people in one hotel room to save money when they did travel, another cultural difference.

That afternoon they traveled back to Jacksonville. Deloris hoped that Donna had learned some things that would help her when Paradise was up and running.

Alan and Deloris took Donna with them to the animal hospital the next morning. On the way to the office they pointed out places of interest. When she was given a tour of the Animal Hospital she said, "Dis hospital for animals is bedda den de ones for people in Belize." Deloris explained to Donna that the government had rules and regulations that they had to follow. She told her that if the government's standards weren't met, they could be fined, or even shut down until they were in compliance. However, the main point that Deloris was attempting to make was that they took pride in their businesses and wanted to make sure that their clients knew that they were important. She knew that in Belize, an animal hospital was a unicorn and not many existed. The whole idea of the tour had been to show Donna how important it was to make a business look professional, clean, bright and efficiently run. Deloris wanted Donna to understand how important she and Alan thought the first impression was for any business.

Deloris invited Amy and Ernie to join Mary, Donna, Alan and her at a buffet restaurant for dinner. They wanted Donna to see how a buffet was served since they were not common in Belize and Deloris had the idea that this may be the way she wanted to serve her guest. When they ask why Belize did not have buffet restaurants they were told that Belizeans would eat too much since it was advertised as "all you can eat". They insinuated that Belizeans would be inclined to take some of the abundance of food home for their family. Deloris did not know if she believed that explanation or not.

Donna and Deloris climbed into Deloris' Suburban to go on a shopping trip for Donna and her kids. When Donna looked puzzled Deloris ask, "What's wrong?"

Donna paused for a moment, then ask softly, "Is dis car yours too?" Deloris, realized that Donna was probably thinking how excessive having two cars was for one family. She was afraid that Donna would only think that they were spoiled Americans. "This and the Hummer belong to the company. We use them as we need to." Deloris said.

Deloris realized that if anyone else had asked, she simply would have said, "Yes." The message of what guests would have expected when they came to Paradise, was dwindling away, as Donna was so focused on all that her new bosses had. Deloris wanted Donna to understand that they had to work hard for what they had. She knew that she and Alan had worked their fingers to the bone to get what they had, but many people in Belize worked just as hard, if not harder and they have nothing. Alan and Deloris had taken huge risks, used the rules and laws to gain in wealth, as well as sacrificed time and money, but Belize, and many other countries didn't work that way. The typical Belizean couldn't get a loan for a business without competing with everyone else, including their own family for a little stake in the market. In an instant, Deloris was forced to examine this life and all that she and Alan had accomplished. She decided to play Scarlet O'Hare and worry about this question at a later date.

Deloris had given Donna money to buy clothes for herself and her two children. They arrived at the mall and spent several hours looking through the stores; however, the shopping only resulted in Donna finding a nice blouse, a dress, or numerous other things, only admiring them, then looking at the price tag and placing it back onto the rack. Donna returned to the same item again and again, finally trying it on and then looking at the price tag again and placing it back onto the rack. Deloris isn't a shopper, if she needs something, she goes and gets it. She doesn't linger and only shops as a matter of necessity. She never spent extravagantly, but has nice things because she knows where to get deals. Alan was the shopper in the family and could spend hours finding the best deal on what he wanted. Deloris called Alan and asked him to meet them for lunch, she had decided he should be the shopper, not her. When he arrived at the restaurant, she told him her plan of letting him go shopping with Donna. Alan and Donna trekked from store to store and back again. After several hours had passed, Alan called Deloris and arranged to pick up her and Mary for dinner. Deloris was curious to see what Donna had bought, since the stores in Placencia didn't offer much in the way of new styles in clothing and had a very limited selection.

When everyone was seated, Alan told Donna to get whatever she wanted to eat. Deloris accompanied Donna to the selection of food and told her that she can choose as many items as she wanted and encouraged her to try different foods. Deloris selected her fill of favorites and when she encountered Donna again, she noticed that Donna had only selected small amounts of very few items. She asked, "Is something wrong, Donna?"

Donna, looking a little confused, answered, "I don't know what mos dis stuff is, so I don't know if I like it or not."

This was understandable since the food in Belize was always the same dishes and although they tasted great, there was no variety like what was being offered on this buffet bar. Deloris described the ingredients of some of the dishes. She assured Donna that if she were to choose something that she didn't like, she could simply leave it and get another plate to select a better dish. Ernie and Amy talked easily to Donna to encourage her with suggestions of items that she should try. Amy asked Donna, "So how do you like the United States so far, Donna?"

Donna paused and looked around, then at Deloris and answered, "Every ting is so different here. I think Americans are very lazy and spoiled people." Then took another bite of her pea salad.

Shocked and almost insulted, Mary asked, "So you think that Alan and Deloris are lazy and spoiled?" Donna, realizing that she had offended, didn't back down, saying, "Well, instead of walking de stairs, dey have stairs dat move for you. In de airport, de toilet, dey flush by demself. I can see now why Americans are so fat, look at all dis food; you could feed my whole village here, but dey is only a few people eating. Den here, everyone has two cars, most people in Belize do not have even one car." Looking around and searching everyone's face, she felt a bit relaxed as they all began to laugh at her explanations of why they were lazy. Americans have these things because they have the opportunity. They take that opportunity and work hard and develop ways that will make life easier. Because there are good jobs here, people make enough money to buy these conveniences so they are able to make their lives easier. Good jobs provide the ability to have an easier life. "Yes, Ms. D. but having a job that makes you a lot of money means that you must go to work every day whether you want to or not. If you want to go fishing or go pick up shells you can't do that, you have to go to work." Sometimes you just shouldn't have to go to work.", said Donna. "That is why we have vacations" said Deloris. "That is when we get away to relax."

Later that night, after everyone was in bed, Deloris said to Alan, "I'm not sure that bringing Donna to the U.S. was such a great idea after all."

"What do you mean? ", ask Alan. "We brought her here to show her how Americans live and what they expect, but I am afraid that the message that she is taking away from it is that Americans need an overabundance to be happy.", sighed Deloris.

"She's in a whole new world at the moment, Deloris. Those are her first impressions." "You know how important first impressions are", Deloris retorted.

"She only sees the results of our hard work. She has no idea how many eighteen, or twenty-hour days we have worked to have this life. She has no idea how many times we have been flat broke in our life and lost everything, having to start over again. She has no idea of how many nights I have laid awake and worried about how we were going to make payroll so that our employees could feed their families or how after making payroll, there was no money left for us to pay our own bills. She has no idea of all of the planning, worry and energy that we have spent to get to where we are now." Deloris complained as she turned to look at Alan, who had drifted off to sleep while she vented. She then realized that she had been rambling on about things he already knew. He was her sounding board, but his switch had been moved to "off" while she was still talking. She gently crawled out of bed to turn off the lamp. As she got back into bed, she continued to think about what Donna had said and realized that what Donna had said was true to a certain extent. She also realized that they had become successful from all the hard work and all the risks that they had taken over the years, but knew things could have turned out very differently. The difference here was not just a difference in attitude about what is most important in life, but here there is unlimited opportunities with hard work. Belize had a major shortage of opportunity. Nonetheless, she did see that people who didn't live this way, could perceive it as being spoiled. They had never lived the carefree life that most Belizeans live daily. The Belizeans that they had come to know, in Placencia, set small goals for their lives. They worked to eat, have a cell phone and watch T.V. occasionally. Time to do the things that they found enjoyable was at the top of their list in importance. Of course, there are exceptions to this rule, but worrying about the future did not seem to be a major pastime in Belize. This was the difference in the two worlds. She realized that it was an unobtainable goal to reveal a different culture to someone in a short week's time.

The next morning, Deloris and Alan left Donna at the condo with Mary for the day. When they first arrived in Jacksonville they had given Donna a calling card so that she could call her family in Belize. That afternoon when returned home from their meetings, Mary called Deloris into the other room. Mary told Deloris, that Donna had used the entire calling card in that one afternoon.

"The whole fifty dollars' worth?" Deloris almost shouted.

"Yes, I told her that she should save some for later, but she told me "that is okay, they will buy me another one." I was shocked! I think you may have a problem, now that you've brought her here. She thinks that you have all the money in the world and she may try to take advantage of you.", warned Mary.

Now, Grandma Mary was a wise woman and when she felt as if something was a bad idea, it generally was. Deloris agreed with her about the ill effect of bringing Donna to the U.S. may have caused. Donna perceived Americans as lazy and spoiled. Would she see the guest in a good light now? Would this trip make her strive to take advantage of the opportunity she was being offered or would it just make her resentful of Americans? If they wanted Donna to be a part of making Paradise successful, it must be the former.

Chapter 12

Paradise was landlocked except for that small path that passed between houses leading from Sunset Point Road to the hotel. This path was the vital easement to the property. While it was designated to be eight-foot-wide, fences around the yards with their abundant trees and flowers encroached to make the path only about six-foot-wide which would prevent Hans from bringing his trucks directly onto the property. Hans was able to arrange with the owners of the property next door to use their easement and bring his materials in over their property. However, when construction was over they would need to deal with the problem that this narrow easement would present for getting guest and their luggage to the hotel.

Over the next few months the usual ups and downs of construction continued. Hans would email them and describe an issue or problem and then wait for a decision from Alan and Deloris. They had been warned, by Hans that with a remodel that they must expected problems along the way that would have to be dealt with. Issues arose when it was required to make such changes as moving a wall. That change might reveal plumbing problems or wiring problems that Hans had no way of anticipating. Then the time and expense of rerouting or recreating a way to conceal certain items would have to be handled. They had done enough remodeling over the years to realize that this might happen, but dealing with it long distance, through an email, when they could not actually see the problem presented its own set of issues and challenges. In the states, the problems that you encountered were usually predictable because of building codes that were in force and strictly adhered to. Here George had his own set of rules that he had followed and as one might expect, this sometimes lead to some unexpected issues, however, they were not unsolvable problems. The rule, however did seem to be that if it could go wrong, it did, Murphy's Law, you know, was in full effect even here in Belize. They were already passed the estimated 8 months to complete this project and were now in the midst of the season for 2008. The construction had already been going on for 10 months.

Most of the old rooms were small and to make the most of the space, Deloris insisted that no space be wasted. There were often problems with communication because of the mixing of Kroil and English. Belizeans often forget that Americans and Canadian do not always understand the "Belizean Kroil". For example, Deloris received an email one day from Donna that said, "They start on cor' a door which paint?" Deloris tried to decipher what that meant without emailing back, but finally decided that she had no idea what the questions was. She emailed back, "I do not know what (cor a door) is. Which door are you referring to?" The reply from Donna was "The thing that run from the front door to back door in front of rooms."

Deloris realized that she was being ask what color to paint the hallway that runs through the hotel. This question was being asked even though she had left a detailed list of the colors for the hallway and each room before she left the last time. Which hall they were discussing, still had not been determined so another email was necessary to determine that information. Deloris had learned, with failed attempts, never to send an email covering more than one point at a time. If she had several points to make, or questions to ask, an email must be sent for each topic and another topic couldn't be broached until the first one was finished.

Alan made frequent trips to Placencia to check on the construction. When he was there he always seemed to run into Ms. Louise and would tell her of the progress with Paradise. She always asks when Deloris was coming to Placencia so that she could meet her.

Deloris loved plants but admittedly knew very little about them, or how to make them grow. Before construction began, she went around and selected some of the trees and bushes and ask that they be transplanted to the back of the property, where they were less likely to be damaged by the construction traffic. She had been assured they could be moved and replanted again when construction was finished. There were lots of the smaller palm trees that Deloris really liked and wanted to save. She realized that she couldn't save all of them, but she was determined to save as many as possible. She knew that she needed to save these so they would fit into the small area for trees that would be left after the addition of the restaurant and rooms. She loved the large, beautiful hibiscus plants in the reds, yellows and pinks that were abundant on the property, as well as many of the smaller palms and larger plants. Finally, the workers told her that there was a limit to the number of plants they could put in the small area, so she sadly agreed that those that were left, would have to fall to the destruction of progress.

Shortly after that decision, Deloris received an email from Donna saying, "Dem cut down da lime tree and everyone is angry with you. He told everyone that you said it was alright to cut down."

Deloris did not remember even seeing a lime tree, let alone saying that it was okay to cut one down. When she questioned Donna, it seemed that it was more of a bush than a tree and had not had any limes on it when Deloris and Alan had last been in Placencia. However, Deloris was now being told, in no uncertain terms, that the lime tree that was now destroyed, had been the "community lime tree" and they all depended on this tree to supply this community with limes. Now Deloris' construction had destroyed it. The once famed "Community Lime tree" was now just a pile of sticks. Deloris, of course, felt awful. If she had known it was important, she certainly would have saved it, but she had no idea that it was even there. When she emailed Hans, he simply said that he needed to move it so he could pour the footing for the fence while he had the concrete truck there and it was not one of the plants she had wanted to save and transplant, so it was not moved. He did not seem to be upset by the community's disapproval. However, Deloris had already changed from a rebuild to a remodel and now all the good will was destroyed by her not spotting a lime tree and somehow knowing it was a "community lime tree" that was on her property.

After the conversation with Hans she realized that she also did not know what wall Hans had been talking about. She remembered that Hans had mentioned that they would need to put up a fence, but she assumed that would be done after the construction was finished and would not be a priority. She asks Alan if he had discussed a fence with Hans. Alan thought Deloris was taking the cutting down of the lime tree much too seriously, but he also did not remember talking to Hans about a fence, especially one that required a cement footing. He told Deloris not to worry about it, he would talk to Hans about it when he got to Placencia. He did remember that Hans had told him that it would be necessary to establish a very clear property line since neighbors like to stretch out into other property if they needed a foot or two for something.

She knew he was right because of what she had witnessed with the easement path.

Both Deloris and Alan assume that this was something that Hans could have done at the end of the project. However, it appeared that Hans was establishing it now, so there would now be a wall on their property. Soon Hans started requesting draws of $50,000.00 to $100,000.00 every couple of months. He always sent an itemized breakdown of the labor and materials that had been used, so this helped Deloris understand much of the expenditures. When Deloris and Alan reviewed them, they knew they were correct, but the costs were adding up and adding up fast. It began to dawn on Deloris that at this rate they were looking at a major cost overrun. She knew that Alan would not want to hear that she was worried, but she had to talk to him about it. They were ten months into what had been estimated to be an eight-month project and they had already advanced three quarters of the estimated funds for the project. It appeared to Deloris that they were no more than half way through this project. However, Hans had made it clear that it was cost plus, so this should have been expected. When Deloris asked about what was left to do, it seemed that Han's confirmed that the project was at its half way point. She knew they were in way too deep to stop now, but she had to look at ways that they could afford a major cost overrun and somehow adjust the budget. They had been prepared to handle the original cost out of funds they had saved, but it looked like they might have to find a way to get twice that amount. Deloris knew that their business plan had been to operate the hotel on a part time basis, but the U.S. economy was getting worse and some of their affluent friends were cutting back on their traveling and more expensive vacations. Their dive clubs had already cut the "Big Trips" from twice a year back to once a year. Their U.S. businesses were still prospering and while they did not yet have any financial problems she knew that with bank loans getting tighter and borrowing money in Belize was impossible, they could face a cash flow crunch if the cost of the hotel continued to escalate.

She decided that she needed to sit down with Alan and they needed to plan for the inevitable that she could feel coming. One night after work they went to their favorite restaurant and Deloris brought up the subject. After presenting the problem in very factual terms, Alan agreed that they would need to get funding from a U.S. bank, so that the project could continue. He had expected this apparently and bluntly ask how far they could go without getting into serious debt with this project. Deloris already had the answer since she knew it would be one of the first questions Alan would ask. She had laid awake many nights figuring out the answer to his second question, which was, "If forced to borrow the balance do you have an idea how to make it work?"

She did, but she did not know if the bank would agree that it was a safe investment for them to take before the board and request the funds. She knew that she could put together, a strong case, but she had heard that many banks were being unreasonable at this time, because of the lending restrictions that were being implemented by the government. After she explained her plan to him, Alan agreed that under normal conditions there should be no problem, but he too knew that these were now, anything but normal, financial times in the U.S., during mid-2008, when nothing financial was normal.

Alan suggested that they plan another trip to Placencia to have a heart to heart talk with Hans. When they arrived, they found that the new construction was going well and Deloris could walk through the new rooms and picture the furniture she would design to go in each room. She loved the bathrooms Hans had started in their apartment. She had spent hours deciding exactly what colors she wanted in each room and each bathroom. She chose a royal blue and an off shade of her beloved yellow as accents to the beautifully painted accent tiles with geckos, for the bathroom in their apartment. It was coming together very nicely.

Hans had outdone himself with a marvelous walk in shower that did not require a curtain and a well-lit vanity. He has also allowed for a huge closet. Deloris had won the battle of closets against Han. She would have her closet, at least in their apartment. Hans explained that since they were doing a closet he had made it large enough so that they could store their valuable items and the most valuable equipment there while they were away. He claimed that it would be a selling point when they got ready to sell the hotel to another owner. It was obvious to Deloris that Hans thought that they would have the hotel up for sale within a few years.

Deloris had a great laugh when Belizeans would ask her why they had put an extra bedroom inside their bedroom. She realized that this closet was indeed as large as many of the bedrooms in Belizean homes, so she understood their confusion. Belizeans normally did not have closets, but used a chest or they would simply keep clothes in what they often refer to as barrels, which is what one might think a barrel looks like, only made of cardboard. These are the heavy cardboard shipping containers that are used to ship supplies to Belize. They are repurposed and serve as storage in many Belizean homes.

One day when Donna had on an outfit that Deloris had never seen, Deloris commented that it was a very cute dress and asked Donna if it was new. Donna replied no that it was just from "the bottom of the barrel". When she asked for an explanation, Donna told her that she kept her clothes in a barrel and because it had been raining all week, she had not been able to wash, so she was using things that were at the bottom of her storage barrel. This, of course made Deloris laugh and she said, "Oh, is that where that saying, "bottom of the barrel" comes from." Donna simply looked at Deloris and it was clear that she had no idea what Deloris was asking or why she was laughing. This was yet another example of when to simply smile and nod in the moment.

Hans told Alan and Deloris that he had purchased some unusual bathroom sinks that he had found in Mexico, he wanted them to see. He thought that Deloris might want to use them to create more style in at least a few of the rooms. Even though a little more expensive than the generic ones, they would create a unique look for those bathrooms. They were simply beautiful! Deloris loved them immediately. She knew they were there to try and keep the cost in line, but she really wanted these sinks in Paradise. She kept her love of the sinks to herself and would discuss it with Alan first, but she really liked them and ended up with them in the end.

The next night they met Hans at a Mexican food restaurant that was just north of the village. After a filling meal, they talked about finances and time of completion. Hans gave them an estimated completion date, which was still months and months away, as well as a projection of what he believed the additional cost would be. It was as bad as Deloris had feared it would be. He explained that material cost had skyrocketed and with the cost of gasoline rising, this pressed everything to cost more. Belize's gasoline prices were over $12.00 BZ per gallon in Belize.

It was decided that Hans would build all the beds for the hotel room. This would save a little, but not near enough for her to relax. He would also build the cabinetry which would save them some money as well. This would mean that the beds would all be the same, as well as the armoires, which would be standard in each of the rooms. There would be no closets in the rooms, just the armoires. Deloris had lost the battle of having a closet in each room because Alan agreed with Hans about it being a waste of space for people on vacation. Hans building these furniture items would also cut the waiting time. There was also the advantage of not having to make that trip to Cayo, with a machete in the back seat or having to forge a river, to get the beds. We all remember how that trip went for her. They did decide to go with the beautiful Mexico sinks and they decided to go with them in each room. They were worth the extra money.

Hans explained that he needed them to go to Belize City to a store called Benny's and pick out the tile they wanted to have installed throughout the hotel. He gave them the total square footage but told them he wanted Jose to give them the square footage of each area. They did not question why they might need this breakdown on different areas, but of course should have known there was a reason. When something sounds 'strange' in Belize it is best to ask for an explanation so you can plan ahead for the problem you will soon be facing.

Since they were going to Belize City, they decided to make a quick trip to Spanish Lookout, the Mennonite settlement just west of Belmopan. There they hoped to find a stove for their apartment and perhaps one for the restaurant as well. When they were traveling along the Western Highway they passed a small lean-to under which there were a large number of carvings. Deloris shouted for Alan to stop so that she could see what was available. As soon as she got out of the truck, she spotted five Iguana Fruit Bowls and five Turtle Fruit Bowls sitting on display. It had been almost 6 months since she had seen the craftsman at the Art Festival, and told him of her desire for the fruit bowls. When he walked out to greet his customers, he smiled a huge smile and said, "I had hoped you would come along and see that I made your Fruit Bowls". Deloris was shocked. "I thought you were going to bring the bowls to me in Placencia when they were finished. "I was, but my friend's truck no longer runs so I had no way to come. I had hoped you would come along soon.", said the craftsman.

As I told you earlier, Deloris got her fruit bowls, but not in a typical way.

Another example of how things are done in Belize happened with another craftsman from this same area of Belize. While Amy was building their condos, she met a craftsman selling his goods in Placencia from the back of a truck. Amy told him she needed two large carved poles as supports to a porch she was building. She specified that the poles should be at least 24 inches in diameter and 9-foot-tall, she called them her totem poles. She asks the craftsman to stop by and measure the area to be sure of the exact height. He did so and refused a deposit and told Amy he would deliver the supports as soon as he had them done. They would require a full mahogany tree trunk for each pole. A year, an entire year, went by and Amy, gave up waiting for the man to bring her "totem poles" so she had a local carver do the supports for her. Then one day after Paradise was completed and in operation, this same craftsman showed up at the condos with two gorgeous dark mahogany, beautifully carved "totem poles". Amy and Ernie were not there so the caretaker directed them to go to Paradise and talk with Alan. The caretaker knew that they were friends and thought, perhaps Alan knew something about the "totem poles." Alan of course, didn't but after a call to Amy, he knew what had happened. He told the craftsman that since it had been a year that Amy had already gotten her "totem poles". "But I told she that I would be back.", cried the craftsman. "They are very heavy and I do not want to take them back to San Ignacio", he continued. Then the craftsman looked around and his face brighten. "You can use them here", he said as he pointed to areas in the restaurant of Paradise. So, if you visit Paradise, look for the "totem poles" in the restaurant. You will then know the story. There is always a story in Belize.

Now back to our story of the trip to try and "cost control" the building of the hotel. They continued to Spanish Lookout. They turned off the Western Highway and drove the road to the heart of Spanish Lookout. They saw rolling farm land, pasture with livestock and they also saw oil wells, pumping away, producing the oil that had been found in Belize. The area is home to both traditional Mennonites who still wear the traditional garb and use a horse and buggy to get around, but also to progressive Mennonites who have started businesses that now offer tires, tools, auto repairs services and many of the mechanical items that are hard to obtain in other parts of Belize. As they shopped in Spanish Lookout, they found it was possible to get many of the items to complete equipping the restaurant. They found the stove for their apartment and a refrigerator for the hotel. This store would deliver these items to them.

After the side trip to Spanish Lookout, they made their way into Belize City and they found the store that they had been referred to. They were pleasantly surprised to find it was up to date and items were neatly displayed. Deloris even spotted the tile she wanted after looking for a very short time. They told the salesman how much they needed, and he stared at them in surprise as he spoke slowly, "We not have near dat much in stock."

Deloris, forgetting she was in Belize, asked, "How long would it take you to order the additional supply?"

"Well no take long to orda it. Getting it here da would be da problem. If we did da and orda, we could hope for it in 6 to 8 months.", replied the salesman.

Deloris, now knowing that was code in Belize for 'One year or never,' calmly asked that he show her which tiles they had in the appropriate quality.

He quickly told her that they didn't have any tile in that amount. She was surprised because this amount was only for the new addition and did not include the old building. They were only tiling the restaurant, bar, office and the three new rooms as well as their apartment. It seemed like a relatively small amount. In the states, this would not have been a big project at all. She then asked the salesman to show her the tile which she could buy just two styles and have enough tile for the entire project. She requested that it be contrasting if possible. Alan noticed the look that Deloris got from the salesman, which almost shouted, "stupid gringo!" Fortunately, Deloris missed the look because she was busy recalculating where the two tiles could connect and how to make the tile flow in the additions. The salesman left and soon came back with the news that with three choices that he had in stock, they had just enough tile to meet the square footage requirement. However, Deloris noted unhappily, that two of the styles were much too similar to use together, and they were not the same size. The colors were just different enough to make it look mismatched, but not enough to give her the contrasting look that she desired. The third choice was a light salmon color and while not bad, it was in the smallest quantity that the store had in stock. She looked at Alan to get his suggestion and true to form, he just gave a shrug and said, "What other choice do we have?"

To reassure Deloris, Alan reminded her that Hans had insisted she bring the square footage of each area. She used the information about each tile in stock and her square footage information from the hotel to quickly calculate the amounts of the different styles that she could use in the different areas. It looked like with some careful planning, it might just work. "Do you think we should check and maybe buy all the tile they have in each style so we won't run a few pieces short in any style. They don't have too much of any of these styles. We will be able to use it in storage areas later if any is left over."

Again, Alan shrugged and said, "Might as well."

They had the salesman calculate the additional cost and decided it was worth the additional price to go ahead and get the extra tile. Since Hans had an account with this store they were able to put the order on his account and arrange a delivery time. This trip to Belize was to determine where they could save some money and so far, they had spent more than they had planned on sinks and tile alone, and had only saved a little on getting some of the furniture made by Hans, rather than having Elisa build it for them.

Upon return to Placencia, Deloris spent a great deal of time calculating and deciding where each type of tile should go and how the transitions should look. There were stairs and balconies to include and with some planning she was sure a good transition could occur. She carefully drew up a plan in a very rough drawing and was satisfied with the outcome that she could picture in her mind. The next day when Jose came in, she attempted to show him her plan, but soon realized that this was the brother that did not speak English. He was the one that would be supervising the project for the next 10 days. Deloris made a copy of her sketched plans and gave it to Donna, so that she could give it to the English-speaking Jose before they started on the tile.

After having received the good news and bad news about the progress of Paradise and realizing that Hans planned on having the project finished by Christmas, Deloris decided it was time to choose some furniture for their apartment. She knew she would import their living room seating because she insisted on having a comfortable couch and chairs. She had yet to see anything built in Belize that was truly comfortable, so this was the logical choice. Alan would be very unhappy with most of the rigid chairs and couches that are favored in Belize so he would agree with her decision to import those items from the U.S. She wanted to design the furniture in the hotel in the natural Belizean flavor and wanted to utilize the wood that she had come to love so much. She knew that she wanted to have a large, wonderful, wooden bed made for their apartment. She had heard from Amy that there was a man in the village who was making handmade pieces and he was reasonably priced. He lived a short distance from the hotel, so they decided to walk over to his house. They had received directions and when they arrived, found a shed surrounded with chain link fence. The house was set further back on the property. There didn't seem to be any work going on in the shed or on the property at all.

A slightly built man with sun-touched skin, came out of the small house, and as he walked toward them, asked if he could help. He told them that his name was Isaiah. He seemed to be a happy old man. When they told him they wanted a bed, he said that was his specialty and he could make whatever they wanted. He took them into the shed and showed them several beds that he was in the process of building. Deloris liked them, but they were all too heavy and masculine for her taste.

Deloris's imagination had created the bed that she wanted, and after seeing what he was capable of building, she thought he could produce just what she wanted. She had imagined something that had its own shelf built into the headboard so she could put a lamp there to read before she fell asleep at night. She loved sleigh beds but did not know how to explain the design to Isaiah. Since she could not draw a straight line to save a burning orphanage, she excitedly told Isaiah, with excessive hand motions, what she wanted. Isaiah watched intently and nodded his head. Seemingly prehistoric communications were being used by Deloris to try to relay her ideas to Isaiah. Alan couldn't help but think that Deloris was in for another disappointment when she couldn't explain her design in concrete terms. He, himself had no idea what Deloris was asking Isaiah to do, and he had been married to her for more than 40 years, so how in the world was this man supposed to decipher her plans? Isaiah ask Deloris if she would like to have the headboard carved with a design as well. She was intrigued with the idea of having her own creation and having it with a carving as well. Isaiah ask her what her favorite sea creature was and Deloris promptly told him that it was sea horses. Isaiah said that he could put sea horses on her unusual headboard and would be glad to build her creation. Alan dreaded hearing the cost of this mythical and elaborate bed. He knew that custom built furniture in the states had become outrageously expensive. When Isaiah quoted her $250.00 U.S. they were both shocked! What Deloris was describing would be many times that in the states, if it could be done at all. Alan was now really convinced that Deloris was in for another hard-learned lesson about what occurs when two cultures try to communicate ideas. They gave Isaiah a small deposit, and told him to contact Amy or Donna when it was almost finished so that they could make arrangements to complete the payment and take delivery of the bed.

Belizean men tend to be well under 6 foot in height and women were naturally under five foot five so designs were done with that fact in mind, so as they were leaving, Deloris turned and asked Isaiah if he could raise the height of the bed by about two inches, since she and Alan were both taller than normal Belizeans, who stand at a normal height of five-feet, four-inches or so. She and Alan preferred the extra height of the taller bed and, always being the planner, it also meant extra storage space under the bed. After all, storage space was premium in Belize. Isaiah told her that it would be no problem to raise the height of the bed and told them that he'd get started right away.

As they walked back to the hotel, Alan looked forward and said, "You think he understood all that you want him to do?"

"I certainly hope so. I'd love to have the bed that I have pictured in my head. Maybe I should learn to draw.", she quipped.

Alan laughed and they made their way through the village to the hotel. They were ready to see where this new adventure would take them.

Chapter 13

After returning home to Florida, they were soon back in the pressure cooker of business in the United States. One evening before dinner, they talked about the timing for hiring the staff for the hotel. They agreed that the staff would need at least a month to be trained. Deloris felt that November looked like a good time to start and felt that December would be the grand opening. Did they feel confident enough to tell people that the hotel would be ready by Christmas? They certainly didn't want to book reservations if there was a chance that the hotel was not going to be completed by then. It would be a disaster to have guests plan a vacation and the hotel not be ready. In Belize, the task was only finished when it was finished and schedules changed like the clouds do. They had held up any advertising because they simply did not know when to start booking guest. They also talked about what kind of advertising since attracting dive and fishing clubs was becoming nearly impossible with the state of the economy in the U. S. After discussing the challenges, they agreed that it was best to get started hiring the staff soon, so they'd be ready as soon as the hotel was completed. They hoped that at the beginning they could draw some of the "walk-in" business. They had been assured by others in Placencia, that there was a "walk-in" market for rooms in Placencia and they would have the restaurant to draw people as well as the tour operation that would rent out kayaks and snorkel gear or as Donna and the other Belizeans insisted on saying, snorkel gears. Many of the people who come to Belize on a regular basis have adopted the Belizean notion of just not planning but assuming that they will be able to find a room when they needed it. This attitude has created the walk-in market for hotel rooms.

One morning, while Deloris was in her office, she received a telephone call from Donna. She knew immediately that it must be urgent. Donna said in a panicked voice said, "Miz D, dey done putting de wrong tile in de wrong rooms!" "Tell Jose to go by my plan." "Dis de Jose dat don speak English.", she rebutted." "Tell him again and maybe he'll understand.", cried Deloris. "I tella he a thousand time, he jus look at me when I speak.", whined Donna.

"Okay, call Hans and explain to him what's happening." Deloris instructed.

"I dun thought of dat he not in town. He phone ring and ring." Donna retorted.

"Oh my, well I guess there's nothing we can do, but wait and see how it turns out. Just call me after they have the tile placed and let me know what's going on." "Okay" Donna said, then 'click'. Deloris wasn't sure why they'd been disconnected, so she called Donna back.

"Paradise! How can I help?" Donna answered quickly. "Donna?", Deloris asked solemnly.

"Yes?" "We got disconnected. Did you have any other questions?" "No dat is why I hang up."

Deloris paused for a moment and then realized that Donna had ended the call without saying "goodbye" or any other common words, just because she was finished with what she had to say. Deloris said "Okay, I assumed since you didn't say "goodbye" that we had gotten disconnected."

"No, I was finish, but I will say goodbye." Donna confirmed. Just as Deloris was going to reply, the line went dead again.

She bit her lip for a second, then hung up the receiver realizing that the barriers between Belizean and American communications were a train wreck. She knew that she'd need to instruct the office personnel in the proper phone etiquette. She imagined the confusion of an American trying to get a room and then being abruptly hung up on.

Deloris briefly discussed the tile issue with Alan but wanting to keep the burden on herself, didn't explain that it was the 'no English speaking' Jose who was laying the tile. She found her mind racing in the wee hours of the morning. She realized she needed to sleep and implored her Scarlett O'Hare technique to avoid the issue until morning, or should I say "dawn".

Her mind raced over the next two days until, finally, Donna emailed and expressed that everything looked alright. She said that Hans had come and talked to Jose about the tile. Deloris thought about scolding Donna for not calling her as soon as Hans had come by, but chose only to say "Okay, that is good news."

Alan decided that he needed to return to Belize right after Thanksgiving to oversee the project and get started on hiring the staff. Deloris would follow suit and join him before Christmas. This way he could be there to help determine where they were in the process of building their personal piece of paradise. Alan realized that even when he felt that they were ready to open, Deloris would want to move pictures, have rooms repainted, or any number of things that she found necessary to complete one of their projects. They generally agreed on major decisions, but Deloris was the one who insisted on last minute details that others generally missed.

When Alan arrived, there was still minor areas that were not complete but the tile for the floors had been finished. He looked at the tile and although he did not know exactly what Deloris's ultimate plan was supposed to look like, he was certain that she'd be pleased with the way it had turned out. Jose, the English speaking one, approached him and told him that he needed his permission to break up a few pieces of tile on the apartment balcony, in order to create a design. He said that he was sure that Deloris would want the design done to pull two types of tile together. Although Alan was not sure that he understood the necessity, he gave his permission. That project was quickly finished and Alan saw that Jose had been forced to change the tile style from inside their apartment to the porch and he had made the transition flow better by creating a design with both colors in front of the doors. He did a wonderful job of making the transit appealing to the eye. Alan checked over many of the aspects of the hotel and was pleased with the outcome of it so far. He used his time there to start interviewing potential staff and to get last minute things organized and cleaned up.

When he began interviewing prospective staff members, he was shocked at the lack of suitable candidates. There were three who spoke no English, but at least they smiled very big during their interview. There were two men that arrived in torn and tattered clothes, but insisted they were good employees, but when ask what they could do, they assured Alan that they could do whatever job he needed for them to do. One woman had nine children, but swore that she could work while the kids waited in the restaurant. One woman he interviewed, wanted a waitress position, wore a mini skirt that was way too small for her, did not wear a bra and had no experience in being a waitress.

Alan began to lose hope in finding suitable staff for their new hotel. He quickly learned that he must ask very specific questions.

Everyone he interviewed assured him they could do everything, but very few had any experience. He was learning quickly that most Belizeans would assure you they could do anything that you needed done. It was necessary to distinguish those who had actually done this type of job before and those who just needed a paycheck. This was disheartening because a trained staff was necessary before the first guest arrived. They had to have two people for the office and he knew that at least two cooks must be hired and a minimum of 3 bartenders. There would need to be at least one housekeeper, with a backup for her days off. Then there was the need for a Manager for the whole operation. He interviewed kitchen staff, maid staff, waitresses, and bartenders. He suspected that many just wanted to see the new hotel. He had chosen only a few out of the many that he interviewed. He found that rumors in the village were growing with each bit of the hotel completed. Of course, Donna's synopsis of America and how rich the new owners of Paradise were helped fuel the rumors. There was a specific rumor that every person in America had their own home with multiple bathrooms, multiple cars, and when they ate, there was miles of food to choose from.

One day a young man, with no real office experience, but with construction and inventory experience, came by for an interview. His name was Ed Grant. He was a strong framed young man with a square jaw and clearly confident as he stood straight when he spoke. Alan realized that his experience in construction would be an asset to the hotel, as he knew that something would always need to be repaired. He also had experience working in the office of the construction company. The guy had a great charismatic personality and would do well making Americans feel welcomed, when they arrived. Then Karla, who had experience in front offices of several hotels and was experience in bookkeeping and filing government taxes and forms, was hired. Alan now had two cooks, two waitresses, a housekeeper and felt he had the staff he needed.

Deloris had been able to locate a shipping company in Florida that would come to her office and pick up whatever she had packed and ship it to Belize and actually deliver it to Paradise. This made it easier to get the things that they needed to equip the restaurant, bar and the rooms. It was not inexpensive, but they were finding that it was the only way to get good quality linen and other items that they knew they must have to make Paradise the kind of place they wanted it to be. For example, Deloris wanted lamps in each room and knew that she could have beautiful lamp bases made of wood carvings done right there in Belize, however, when she searched for lamp shades, they seemed unavailable. Therefore, a shipment containing lampshades arrived in Placencia, along with all the linen for the beds.

Three weeks before Christmas and one week before Deloris was scheduled to arrive, Alan received an excited call from Amy. She explained that Isaiah had just delivered their bed to Amy's house since he apparently did not know that Alan was in town. Amy gushed that it was the most beautiful thing that she'd ever seen. Could Isaiah have created what Deloris wanted with only her charades game as a blueprint? Did Isaiah really understand her requests?

When Alan walked into his friend's house, he saw a beautiful, solid mahogany bed with a roll top shelf at the top and a breathtaking aquatic scene, straight out of Jacques Cousteau's dream world. Isaiah certainly did understand Deloris's desires and he had actually made her vision come into being. There were several sea horses, of differing sizes, carved across the headboard, swimming among corral and a starfish that was nuzzled directly beneath a coral. He noticed the height right away and realized that Isaiah had created four huge sea horses as legs which blissfully tied in the design and supported the huge bed. He was very pleased and he knew that Deloris would be ecstatic. The fact that the bed had been inexpensive had made him happy; he was even happier now that he knew Isaiah had captured Deloris' vision. His only decision now was if he would tell Deloris how wonderful it was, or play his "oblivious" card and act as if it were simply a bed and let her discover its beauty on her own. He decided on the latter.

He wanted to move the masterpiece to their apartment so that she'd see it there for the first time. Amy however, insisted that before it was moved, she wanted to call all of her American and Canadian friends so they could come and see the bed. Alan agreed to leave the bed for a few days and set up a time that he and Ed would pick it up. That night when he and Deloris had their evening phone call, he simply told her that the bed was finished, but was evasive about it. He hoped that she assumed that it was nothing special. Over the next few days, he was told by several women, who had gone to see it, how beautiful the bed was. He worried that Deloris would hear from someone about the bed even though he had asked Amy to keep it a secret from Deloris. He just hoped that Placencia's "shush" did not extend all the way to Florida.

When Deloris arrived a week later, the first thing she wanted to see was the tile work; as expected, she was pleased with the way Jose had combined the tile and created a beautiful pattern. Deloris then said, "I'm surprised that the apartment is finished already." She had assumed it was finished because Alan told her that is where the bed had been placed.

Alan, looked at her and said, "Oh it's not finished yet."

"But you already put the bed in?", she asked curiously.

"They can finish the apartment with it in there.", Alan finished saying just as they had reached the door to their apartment. When Deloris looked down at the new tile pattern that Jose' had created at the entrance to their apartment she was stunned. She knew that he had used the salmon colored tile in their apartment and he had taken pieces of the salmon tile and inset it into a pattern just outside their front door. It was the perfect touch to introduce a new color inside the apartment. As she entered the apartment it was obvious there wasn't much more that needed to be done to complete it. She walked through the apartment to the bedroom. When she saw the bed for the first time, she literally gasped for air. Alan enjoyed seeing her surprised. She fell in love with it immediately. It was the bed that she had seen in her head and now, here it was reproduced in rich dark mahogany.

"I just realized that we haven't paid Isaiah the $250.00 for it yet. Isaiah didn't ask for the balance when he dropped it off at Ernie and Amy's. I forgot all about it." Alan shuttered.

"Let's go get him paid", said Deloris. As they walked, Deloris sang the praises of how beautiful the bed was and how impressed she was with Isaiah's workmanship and especially his interpretation of her desires for the bed's design.

"It is simply perfect!", she exclaimed. She would be walking on a cloud the rest of the day. She continued, "Oh, do you think we can have him build a matching chest or dresser?"

"Sure, we can. But I seriously doubt we'll get the same deal." Alan answered.

When they arrived, Deloris gushed about how much she loved the bed, covering Isaiah with praise again and again. Alan laughed to himself as he thought how untypical this behavior was for Deloris. Generally, she would have negotiated the price of the additional pieces before telling Isaiah how much she liked the bed. Alan enjoyed seeing her excited and happy about designing her own furniture. It meant a lot to her to have an artist create her vision. Belize was truly good for her spirit. He knew from the beginning that Belize would be good for him, but was concerned as to whether or not Deloris could adjust. He loved her new-found excitement and the new flexibility from her normal "all business" persona.

Deloris explained to Isaiah about her newest vision for a chest of drawers, as she still seemed to dance around in excitement over the bed. She wanted a large chest with five drawers and on top, a cabinet with a minimum height of three feet, with two doors that opened wide. Isaiah again seemed to follow her hand gestures and motions. Isaiah quickly explained to Deloris that it could not be a plain chest and must match the bed's carvings. Deloris quickly agreed. Isaiah suggested that they pick a different sea creature to adorn the three-foot-tall doors on the chest. Deloris said that Alan's favorite was the whale shark and it was soon decided that a whale shark would be the design. Isaiah asked about the drawers and Deloris said, "Isaiah surprise me. You do such good work that I want you to design it as if it were for yourself."

This seemed to please Isaiah, immensely. When Alan asked the price, Isaiah thought for a moment, then said "How about $500.00 U.S.?"

"That sounds like a deal!" Alan quickly answered. Elisa had quoted $1500.00 U.S. for a plain, much smaller chest. They were all set with a bed and soon, a chest of drawers with an upper cabinet.

When they returned to the hotel, Alan told Deloris that he had promised to call Ms. Louise when she was back in Placencia. He did so and Ms. Louise said that she would like to come over around lunch time the next day and meet Deloris. The bar was ready to serve drinks and beer, only the bar stools had not yet arrived. The kitchen was equipped except that one of the refrigerated units that they had purchased in the Spanish Lookout had not arrived. Deloris decided that she would make lunch for the three of them. It would be the first time that their kitchen or restaurant tables had been used.

That night, Ernie and Amy accompanied them to the "Purple Space Monkey" for dinner. This was the restaurant they'd visited on their very first night in Placencia. Sitting there, Deloris thought about the journey they'd taken. They came to Belize almost under duress. Now they owned a hotel here and even felt themselves to be a part of this village in a third world country. Belize now felt more like home than they could have ever imagined. They were still interested in their businesses in the states and continued to plan, for the future of those businesses, but Paradise-the hotel- was the new exciting relationship in their lives. The promise and allure that Paradise offered was unmistakably a fountain of youth for this couple. They had never been so seduced by an idea or a location in their life. Deloris stared at the Bird of Paradise cuttings that were in a small vase on their table as she pondered if the attraction and allure of this place was real and lasting, or if this seductive dream had manipulated their experienced perspective. Did they know what they were getting themselves into? Alan was excited and happy and so was she; so maybe the journey is the ultimate goal and the destination should take second place to the experience of getting to Paradise.

Amy broke Deloris's concentration by saying, "Hey! Where are you? Come back to us here in reality." Everyone began to laugh and Deloris joined them in laughter and began to explain, "I guess I was just under the spell of "tropical fever" and influenced by all of the events that have taken place since we first came to Placencia. All of these things are unbelievable, looking back. We would never have made those choices without being influenced by some mystical power. Ha, we were so hesitant to come on that first trip to begin with, that this almost never happened. Of course, now we are glad that we came. We own an almost finished hotel and we love it."

Deloris decided to order the Chicken Placencia, since that was what she'd ordered on her first trip. It was just as good this time and Deloris, remembered how strange "Purple Space Monkey" sounded when she had first heard it, but oddly how familiar it was to her now. She felt so comfortable now and believed that there were a lot of good times ahead. She laughs softly at her "Pollyanna attitude" as if she believed this idealism that she had seemingly just found was true.

Walking back down the potholed road toward Amy and Ernie's house, Deloris said to Alan "Let's plan on staying at Paradise tomorrow night." "But it is not finished.", cautioned Alan.

"I know, but let's find pillows, sheets and enough things to stay the first night in our owner's suite as Hans called it." I will prepare a lunch for the three of us tomorrow in our new kitchen and then we will spend the night at Paradise."

They went on to discuss how much needed to be done to each of the rooms to have them completed and what date they could assure guest that everything would be ready. The kitchen, bar and restaurant were almost complete and the remodeled rooms were close to completion as well, only the chests for each room were still missing. The three oceanfront rooms still had sanding and painting to be done and about half of the air conditioners had not yet been delivered. They had ordered bar stools from a furniture maker in Spanish Lookout and they were to be delivered tomorrow. Deloris had designed them and they were dark mahogany with a slightly curved back, ample seats and a comfortable foot rest. She would send cushions for the seats in the next shipment down. Alan, Ed and one of the bartenders set up the bar, deciding that they would open the bar this weekend. Tables and chairs that could endure the open-air conditions of the outdoor restaurant had been imported from the states, accompanied by soft cushions for each chair, and they were ready for restaurant guest.

The next day they had requested that the entire staff come in and they used the time to finalize the menu and talk with the staff about service. Alan and Ed along with Donna and Karla were in the office while Deloris was in the kitchen putting together a simple lunch of cheese and onion enchiladas and a guacamole salad for Ms. Louise's visit. Once she had everything ready, she walked around the restaurant trying to decide what additional decorations they needed. She heard a voice behind her and turned to find a black woman in her seventies with twinkling eyes and a Mona Lisa smile. She carried herself in the self-confident manner that a truly beautiful, successful woman aspires to. Deloris immediately knew that this was Ms. Louise. Her good humor showed in her eyes, but Deloris could immediately tell that this was a woman who knew what she wanted and would not be shy to ask for it. Deloris greeted Ms. Louise warmly and told her that she really had been looking forward to meeting her. They took one of the tables in the restaurant and one of the staff that had been hired for bar tending came over and ask if she could get them something to drink. When the waitress left to get their drinks Ms. Louise said, "So where is Alan?" Deloris told her that he was with the staff in the office. "If he were my husband, I wouldn't have him working when I was here.", smiled Ms. Louise in a playful manner. At that moment Alan came out of the office and joined them at the table. He told Ms. Louise that she would be the first guest in their restaurant and that Deloris had made them his two favorites. After a pleasant lunch, during which Ms. Louise told them interesting facts about the village, and the interaction of some of the people in the leadership positions. It was obvious that she wanted them to understand the local politics in the village. Ms. Louise shared some of her experiences while she was working in Chicago and how she had come to be friends with the Prime Minister and other government officials in Belize. Alan was called away to deal with some questions about the menu, but Deloris and Ms. Louise continued their conversation without a break. Deloris shared some information about their businesses in the states. She told Ms. Louise about her mother living with them in the states. She wanted Ms. Louise to understand why she had to remain in the states while Alan was here getting Paradise started. It was a very interesting discussion and Deloris immediately felt close to this woman. She could see her strength and her compassion for the young girls in Belize. She understood the lack of opportunity for those that choose to stay in Placencia but she wanted them to be the best they could be. Deloris talked to her about how she and Alan wanted to do a small part by offering their employees an opportunity not just a job. Their hope was they would take part in building a business that could be their future. She sought Ms. Louise's advice about how to motivate employees and the best way to teach employees to be service oriented. Ms. Louise had a wonderful sense of humor and it took Deloris some time to determine when she was kidding her and when she was serious. Dry humor is not something that Deloris had found in Belize so far. In fact, she had found that words are taken literally most often. After a long pause, Ms. Louise looked at her and said," I had decided that I was going to take Alan away from you, but you are such a nice person, that I have decided that we can share him. I will take care of him while you are not here and you can take care of him when you are here".

Now I can tell you that she said that in the most loving way, for in the years between that day and the day that Ms. Louise died, both Alan and Deloris knew that they had someone who understood their desire to make Placencia better, not different, just better and she was always there to offer advice on ways to do just that.

Paradise was not just to be a hotel. There was a bar and restaurant, a dive and tour operation and they rented kayaks, bikes and snorkel equipment. To keep track of everything a computer program was necessary. Even here in Belize. To get the Guest Reception area and Front office operational, Deloris installed Quick Books on the new computer they had brought down from the states and attempted to teach Donna how to input the data. Quick Book's is user friendly and Deloris felt that it would be possible to teach Donna the program and it was one that Karla already knew. Donna always had an excuse not to sit down and input data while Deloris was there. She was put off again and again for one reason or another. Donna assured Deloris that both she and Karla knew how to do everything necessary to efficiently run the accounting and reporting of guest information to the proper authorities. The reservations were still filled out by hand so that the BTIA (Belize Tourism Industry Association), the Belizean government entity who audits hotel rooms income, would receive it in the form they requested. However, Deloris kept insisting that she wished for this information also to be kept on the computer so that it could be emailed to her when she was in the states. She wrote down careful instructions for both Donna and Karla describing how she wanted the information input into the program. She wanted them to input all the information from the first day they had a guest in the hotel after they purchased it. It was not a lot of information and if they did it daily when they made the bank deposits, it would be easily accomplished. With each scoff, Deloris became less sure of Donna, but she kept assuring Deloris that she knew what to do. Deloris impressed on both of them, how important it was that this be done since she had heard horror stories about audits from the BTIA.

The bar was now serving drinks and some rooms were ready for guest, so they accepted the walk-in business that occasionally wandered down the path and found Paradise. The kitchen was almost finished and so Alan and Deloris ate in the restaurant and tested the items on the menu. A problem arose in the states and it was necessary for both Alan and Deloris to return for a short stay. The decision was made that the staff would continue to operate the hotel for the short period that they would be gone. Two days before they were scheduled to leave, Donna was approached by a tall, handsome Belizean man who walked into the office and asked to speak to the manager. He was looking for a venue to hold a wedding. Donna brought him out to talk to Deloris. The story that he told was that he was a wedding planner from Belmopan and he had a wedding scheduled for the following weekend, but the venue he had chosen was no longer available to him and he was desperate for a new venue. He told Deloris that the bride and groom would be arriving in Placencia in 5 days and they no longer had a place to stay and there was no longer a venue for the wedding. The bride was from Placencia and the groom was American and this was his first visit to Belize. The wedding was to be attend by about 75 people. These were people who lived in Belize except for about 6 or 7 and all, but the bride and groom and the groom's parents, still had places to stay, so the problem was a honeymoon suite for the bride and groom and a room for the parents as well as a place to hold the wedding. He went on to explain that he had a staff to cook and present the food. What he wanted was to reserve two of their best rooms and he wanted to have use of the entire hotel, restaurant and bar for Saturday and Sunday of the next weekend. Neither Alan nor Deloris thought that this was a good idea, but the entire staff insisted that they were capable of handing the event, without Alan or Deloris being there. The rooms were no problem. Since the restaurant was no yet serving food, to obligate it was not a loss. The wedding planner agreed that if he was allowed to use the venue, that Paradise could keep all the income from sales of drinks for the bar. He would need Paradise employees during the wedding to help serve drinks and food. He assured the reluctant owners that he would supervise the employees and it would be great training for them. Reluctantly, they agreed to help the wedding planner by allowing him to use Paradise. Two days after Alan and Deloris were back in Florida and the day before the wedding, Donna called them and told them that the "shush" around the village was that the wedding planner's original venue had been cancelled because he had failed to pay for the rooms that they were using and failed to give them the required deposit. The local shush was that he had spent the deposit the wedding couple had paid him and was not able to pay the hotel. Since Paradise was not supplying anything other than the venue they were still safe, because the rooms had already been charged to the groom's credit card. However; they certainly could not do an open bar for the wedding guest, unless payment was made by someone prior to the wedding. The bride and groom were arriving shortly and it would be left up to Donna to handle this painful discussion. Donna assured Deloris that she would simply tell the wedding planner that she had to have money for the drinks in advance. Her statement was, "He Belizean, he knows da he got to pay before we serve he drinks. I no give drinks without money. He understands." Donna had the required talk with the wedding planner. When the American groom arrived, the Wedding

Planner brought him into the office and the groom gave Donna his credit card for a large deposit for the drinks. He instructed Donna that she could make additional charges on the day of the wedding if the bar bill was more than the deposit. It would seem that he had worked something out with the wedding planner, so the wedding would proceed.

Florida is two hours ahead of Belize during Daylight Saving Time, so on the morning of the wedding, Deloris checked her email at what would be 5 a.m. in Placencia when she saw an email from Belize Electric, Limited. The email said "There will be an interruption of Electrical Service in the entire village of Placencia from 8:00 a.m. to 1p.m. We apologize for any inconvenience".

The wedding was scheduled for 1 p.m.; however, before the wedding there were plans for a hair dresser to come to Paradise and do the Bride's and all the Bridesmaid's hair. Deloris quickly called Donna's cell phone. When she answers it is apparent that she is already awake and there was panic in her voice. As soon as she realized it was Deloris she blurts out, "It is pouring rain, Ms. D and it is flooding. How can we have a wedding in this rain?" Deloris had nothing to offer Donna, because she now had to tell her about the power outage. When Deloris explained the plans for cutting the power, Donna started to panic even more. Alan ask to take the phone. He said to Donna, "Calm down, we have a generator. Tell Ed to get it out of the storage room. It has never been used but the instruction manual is with it. Tell Ed to call me when he is ready to start it." Eight a.m. Placencia time came and went. At 10 a.m. Placencia time, Alan still had not heard from Ed. He attempted to call the hotel but there was no answer. At 10:30 when he tried to call again, Donna grabbed up the phone and answered with a panicked voice. When she realized that it was Alan she said, "I tella he, I tella he to call, generator catch fire."

"On fire" shouted Alan, "is it still burning"

"De fire done out already de just de smoke", answered Donna.

"Put Ed on the phone", demanded Alan.

"I don't know how it catch fire, de no my fault" was Ed's explanation.

After Alan determined that the fire had been short lived and no one was hurt, he scolded Ed for not calling him prior to trying to start the generator. He then asks to speak to Donna again. "Donna, what else is going on there", asked Alan.

"Well de bride done broke down already. Her won't stop crying."

"Is it still raining there?", ask Alan.

"Yes, da water is coming in the downstairs hall, but Ed, he cleaned it up after he outed the fire."

Both Alan and Deloris felt helpless. What a disaster for the first event at Paradise. At 10 after 1p.m., Placencia time, they placed another call to Donna. This time her voice sounded much lighter. The power had come back on, the sun was out and the hairdresser had arrived, although she did complain about having to wade through water to get there. The bride had quit crying and the guest had begun arriving just as the rain quit about one o'clock, so the groom decided to go ahead and open the bar prior to the wedding since it was postponed until 3 p.m. He wanted everyone to enjoy themselves while they waited on the bride to get ready for the wedding. At this point the groom decided it would not be wise to rush her.

At 3 p.m. under a bright tropical sun, the two were married on the dock over the water with all the guest a little light headed from all the drinks that had been consumed during the waiting time. The reception went on until the wee hours of the morning, but the two love birds had a wedding that they will never forget.

The next morning, when Alan called Donna, she answered the phone sounding groggy. Alan ask, "What's wrong now?"

"Oh, nothin is wrong, just we all got de Goma.", replied Donna.

"Goma? That's a hangover! Did you drink at the wedding?" asked an incredulous Alan.

"Ya, de groom insisted that we all drink since it had been such a bad day." replied Donna. "But you were working!" said Alan.

"No, Mr. Alan, we weren't working we were at the wedding.", explained Donna.

Alan was lost for words. Deloris would not believe this. They returned to Paradise in a few days and sat the whole staff down and explained that when you are "on the clock" and serving guest you do not drink. This seemed to surprise the entire staff. They were offered drinks and they did not understand why they would have to refuse. Understand or not, the rule at Paradise was now that employees did not drink while they were being paid. The employees thought this unfair but Alan and Deloris were resolute in this matter.

After handling that problem, Deloris decided it was time to review the progress the staff had made with QuickBooks and be sure that the daily records were being done correctly. Imagine her shock when she discovered that none of the information had been posted in QuickBooks. When she asked Donna why it had not been done, she was met with a shoulder shrug. Karla said that Donna told her it was not necessary so she had not done it either. "When I ask you why I was not getting the daily reports you told me that you did not know how to email them to me, you did not tell me you were not doing them", said an exasperated Deloris. "I don't want to do dis if I have to deal with dat computer", said Donna. "I want to be a cook.", said Donna. "A cook?" said a bewildered Deloris. "Yes, I can cook good. You will not be sorry.", said Donna.

At this point, Deloris just walked away saying, "I need to process this. I will be back." She didn't want to say something that she would later regret. She and Alan sat down and she calmly told him the situation. Since accounting was her problem and not his, he told her he would back her in whatever she decided.

Now I can tell you that if this were a business they were operating in the states, Deloris would have nicely dismissed the employee, did the job herself until she could replace the employee, then made sure the next employee did the job correctly. However, it was different here. This was a small village. Donna had two kids to feed and no matter what she did, Deloris would be viewed as the uncaring American that was being unreasonable. Donna had been a part of this hotel for many years and so the decision was made to see if she really could move to the kitchen and be a valuable part of the staff there. Deloris and Karla sat down and discussed how they were going to rectify the situation. The daily income that had been deposited into the bank, was broken down to show how much had been received from the bar and restaurant. Therefore, the difference in income deposited must be from rooms. They had the numbered, hand-written registration forms they could use to break down the room income. It would require a lot of work, but it could be done. Over the next few days Karla and Deloris carefully tried to input the information. However, when it was completed there was approximately $5000.00 Belize dollars deposited into the bank that could not be accounted for. All the room registration forms had been put in. They called Donna and Ed in to see if either of them could imagine what this income was for. Neither had any idea, but knew that some was probably from the rental of kayaks and snorkel gear. Apparently, there was no record kept of those rentals, the money was simply put into the cash register and then deposited in the bank the next day. Donna said that sometimes they just forgot what was sold so they just made sure, that they put all the money in the bank that they received on any day. Deloris ask if the numbers they were given for bar and restaurant were the correct ones. Ed and Donna shared a look and then Donna said, "Well sometime we have extra and so we jus put in the deposit too." "Why didn't you change the reports to show that more money was deposited.", asks Deloris. Ed and Donna again shared a look and all Deloris got was a shoulder shrug.

Christmas, 2008, was fast approaching. It had been two and a half years since they first came to Placencia. In that time, they had fallen in love with this little village and the slow-paced way of life that it represented. They had purchased a hotel that they had no concrete plans for and now realized that their lives must change drastically, in order to make it a success. They had spent the last 18 months trying to get Paradise remodeled, added on to and back in operation. They still did not have all the equipment for the restaurant, but aside from little details the hotel was ready to start hosting guest, however, they did not have any room bookings until after the holidays so Alan and Deloris decided to give the staff Christmas Eve, Christmas Day and Boxing day off, because going forward, they hoped that Paradise would be very busy on Holidays. The bar was only serving a few beers and rum drinks to locals who happen to pass through. The two of them would stay at the hotel over the holidays and handle whatever came up while the staff was on vacation for the three days to celebrate with their families.

The restaurant was to be their living and dining room since Paradise would be their home, when they were in Belize, so they may as well get used to it. As the couple sat at the table and listened to the gentle waves on the beach, less than forty feet away, they discussed the hotel's future. They knew now that their original plan wouldn't work. The failing economy in the states simply wasn't robust enough to allow enough clubs to set up trips to support Paradise. They had not marketed rooms in other ways because they were unsure when everything would be ready. Now they needed to make a decision of how the hotel would operate. The cold hard facts were beginning to set in and no matter how "Pollyannaish" her attitude, she couldn't hope this dilemma away any longer.

They had businesses in the U.S. and another business in Belize, Central America. They couldn't be in two places at once, but all the businesses needed their supervision. If that had not been evident before the recent problem with the deposits certainly demonstrated it. There was no one to handle the entire operation. They had never spent much time apart in all of their forty plus years of marriage. They had worked together for most of those years. They drove to work together, ate lunch together and spent their evenings together. There was only one day in their entire marriage that they gone more than twenty-four hours without at least talking on the phone; that time was because Alan was on a live abroad boat in the Galapagos Islands and they couldn't get a connection on the Satellite phone. They usually spent hours a day talking. The thought of being apart to run the businesses was something that didn't seem workable or manageable to them. The couple discussed how it could work and finally settled on a plan to return to the states and launch an aggressive advertising campaign. Alan would spend two weeks in the states and two weeks in Belize. While not a perfect solution, it did seem logical. Deloris realized that this would mean while Alan was away for half of the time, she would have to assume his responsibilities in the U.S.; never one to complain about a little extra work, she was sure that she could handle it. She could join Alan in Belize when she could get away and on special occasions.

She would work towards being able to do some of her work from the states online.

On Christmas Eve, with no guest in the completed hotel and no staff there, Alan invited Ernie and Amy for dinner. Deloris went into the restaurant kitchen and cooked a simple, yet delicious meal. While the four of them enjoyed dinner, they discussed the fact that they had no bookings. The advertising to fishing and diving clubs, had resulted in expressed interest but there just did not seem to be enough members to put together those big trips that were normal when this project had begun. The U.S. economy had just changed too much in the last year. They had spent twice their expected budget on the construction of the hotel and only had a handful of people to run it. Ernie and Amy confided that they too had spent twice their expected budget on the condos, but moreover, now they had an issue with getting separate titles for each condo and this is what they had promised their prospective buyers. Building four condos on a single title property meant they'd have to obtain new titles for each condo. This would not be easy in Placencia. This created the dilemma of either holding the property until they had obtained the title or finding buyers who trusted the titles would be approved.

It looked like all four of them had fallen victim to the fate of so many gringos in Belize. It is the unknown that will get you here in Belize. Deloris remembered the song that they had heard on one of their first visits to Placencia. She jumped out of her seat, ran upstairs and in a few minutes returned with a CD and a player. She plugged it in and played "Gringo in Belize" by Jerry Jeff Walker, and the four sang along. It seemed that this amusing song now meant something to all four of them.

Chapter 14

Deloris had set up a small Christmas tree for the dinner with Ernie and Amy. Now it was Christmas morning and that little tree was all the Christmas, that could be found at their new hotel. They had already noticed that no one else had decorated around Placencia. While Deloris loved Placencia, she was not willing to sacrifice Christmas decorating completely. She did like the idea that people in Belize did not give gifts. She has always felt that gifts should be given when people desired to, not on command. Alan and Deloris were placing hard Christmas candy into small bags that Deloris had brought from the states. The bags were decorated with Christmas stickers and each bag held a small toy. Alan watched a little boy playing in the sand on the beach. He would occasionally jump off the dock and splash around happily in the blue Caribbean Sea that had always been his front yard. He appeared to be about 6 years old. It surprised the couple that children here in Placencia were allowed to play alone or in groups without noticeable adult supervision, especially in and out of the ocean. Alan walked out and asked if the boy had friends who would like some Christmas candy. The boy said, "Of course dem like candy!"

Alan sent him off to gather up some friends and return for the candy. Soon there were fifteen or so young children ranging in age from 2 to 12 asking for candy. The couple smiled and handed out the small bags of candy. The only gift that most of these kids would get today. They each thanked them enthusiastically with broad smiles. The thanks they received from the children was a gift to their hearts. Soon the bags were all given out and the children, after sampling their candy and examining their gifts, left their bags on the sand and all ran to the dock and began jumping into the water to splash and play. The older kids looked out after the younger ones. They laughed, jumped, shouted and splashed. The kids played, enjoying the simplicity of life and each other. They were truly being children enjoying a Christmas Day.

After the kids ventured elsewhere and their laughter died, it was quiet in their little hidden area of Placencia's Peninsula. A single young woman wandered down the beach and entered the open-air restaurant which was adjacent to the path that lead down the beach from the main road in the village. She asks if she could rent a kayak. Deloris and Alan outfitted her with all the equipment she needed and Deloris asked which direction she was going, in case they needed to come get her. Of course, everyone but Deloris thought that was a joke.

The afternoon came and with it came a group of local Belizeans, in their forties and fifties, they welcomed the newcomers to the community. This group was moving from house to house and bar to bar, spreading Christmas cheer and having drinks. Of course, this involved lots of hugging, drinking and laughing. The good cheer was so contagious that it had become a tradition in Placencia. Starting on Christmas Eve the group started their celebration and wouldn't rest until after "boxing day" thus was the tradition. One member of the group told Deloris that this was her first time to take part in the celebration because in the past her mother had done the honors, but her mother had passed away this past year, and she was carrying on the tradition. The celebration does not have a name, but the lack of nomenclature did not dampen the spirit. The couple did not understand why the group would stay awake for all those hours, or why the tradition had started, but they could clearly see that the group was having a great time, but they did not envy the crash that was sure to follow. The group would only remain in a location for an hour or so and then move on to the next. Because Placencia is a small village, this entailed visiting some venues more than once during the celebration. Deloris suspected that the determination of which venues were visited more than once, might be determined by the strength of the liquid refreshments that were served.

After the drinking group left, Deloris reminded Alan that the girl hadn't returned with the kayak. After an hour or so, a small skiff with a 15-horsepower motor operated with a tiller for steering, pulling the Paradise kayak behind it, arrived at the dock. A clearly relieved young woman explained that she had paddled around the end of the Peninsula into the lagoon, but when attempting to return, the tide and the wind prevented her from getting out of the lagoon. Despite her determined efforts to paddle against the incoming tide she couldn't break free. The young bare-chested Belizean with beaded dreadlocks had spotted her and come to her aide, delivering her safely back to Paradise. She laughed as she and the Belizean boy sat at the end of the bar. She had promised the savior, operating the rescue vessel, endless beers for the evening, if he'd promise not to leave her alone until she was safely back at Paradise. She had been confident and carefree when she'd rented the kayak, yet when she returned, it was clear that she felt she had struggled with the remarkable power of mother nature and felt that the young Belizean had been the reason that she was able to win this battle. After a few beers, she seemed to forget the traumatic experience and enjoyed the company of the young rescuer. Both in their mid-twenties, the lull of the magical and intoxicating spell of the tropics, seemed to speed along romance as they enjoyed a Christmas they'd not soon forget.

As the evening progressed, local villagers as well as some expats started to wander into the bar. Alan explained that, although they hadn't officially opened, he could serve them beer and simple rum drinks as well as chips and his special salsa. Alan and Deloris took their place at their special table, the one where they had first had lunch with Ms. Louise and soon there was a constant flow of people to sit with them and tell them their stories. Several of the people ask to see the rooms because they had guest visiting them soon and they wanted to see what Paradise was like so they could refer them to Paradise for lodging while they were in Placencia. Although off for the holiday, Karla and her husband, Ringo came in. When Karla saw all the people in the bar, she insisted that she and Ringo would stay and serve drinks and make items such as nachos, cheese stick, or fish fingers for the guest. That way Alan and Deloris could visit with all the guest that came in. When Deloris said, "But you are not a cook or bar tender."

Karla just laughed and said, "But I am Belizean so I can do a little of everything." That night she proved that she was indeed a good cook and, surprisingly, an efficient bar tender as well. Thus, was the opening of the restaurant and bar for Paradise. Also advertising the rooms was accomplished once several guests saw the rooms. The village shush would do the rest and soon anyone who had guest visiting would know that Paradise was an option for accommodations. That night they visited with several people who had come to Placencia and found just what they were looking for. There was the couple who had been there for 15 years and could not imagine living anywhere else. They were an integral part of the keeping the village safe from fire. They insisted that they would never return to the states. There was the woman who came 10 years ago with her Belizean husband and although the marriage did not last, she now only feels at home when she is in

Belize. She works with the children and cannot imagine doing anything else. There was the couple that sells real estate and feels that Placencia truly is their Paradise. There is another couple who found Placencia while they were sailing around the world and by happenstance were stranded when their sailboat was damaged in a storm. After staying in the village long enough to get their sailboat repaired, they decide that they wanted to stay and they gave up their life of sailing constantly and were building their dream home in the village. There were several others who had gone through the unexpected hardships but had conquered those battles and now lived in peace and harmony in Placencia. They also visited with several couples who lived on the sailboats that were anchored out in the harbor. They learned that these people lived on those boats year-round and Placencia was a place they visited each year for several months. While they may not live on the land in Placencia, they considered Placencia as being a part of their world. They all were very interesting and Deloris loved to talk to them and get their perspective of life. In fact, Deloris decide then that one of the things that she loved most was sitting around this table and have people from all walks of life, tell their stories of why they were in Placencia and what their views of the world were. Whether she agreed with them or not, she found these perspectives to be intriguing. That night as they entertained, they realized that this had been the least stressful Christmas Day ever. They decided that this was the way to do Christmas.

After Christmas, Deloris returned home while Alan remained in Placencia. The first of the year arrived and shortly after, Deloris received a call from Karla telling her that the BTIA was in the office to do an audit. Deloris's fear had come true. Oh well, they had grouped the mystery income into a lump and she had instructed

Karla to pay the highest tax rate on that amount of money since they were unsure of what type of income it was. Belize taxes different types of income at different rates. Deloris assumed that she would be safe if she assigned the highest rate to that income. Logical, right? Well, remember this is Belize. The auditors went over the books and Karla carefully explained that Ms. D was the person who handled the setup of the books. Karla patiently explained that they had diligently tried to reconstruct the income that had come in, but when they were unable to do that the remainder was posted and they paid the highest rate when reporting the income. This did not satisfy the auditor. Since Alan had not been involved in how this was handled, Deloris did not want him talking to the auditors. If they were not being logical she did not think Alan would make a good impression at all. Finally, Karla put the auditor on the telephone with Deloris. She again carefully explained that the employees did not follow her original instructions in reporting money collected and deposited in the bank. On her last visit, she had attempted to fix the problem and make sure that all the taxes were properly paid. However, they had probably overpaid since they assigned the mystery income to the highest rate. The auditor said that if she did not know where the income came from perhaps there was more income that she did not know about. Deloris tried very patiently to be logical with the auditor but he insisted that a large fine was the only thing that would rectify the situation. Deloris was shocked at the size of the fine. She asks the auditor if he would allow her some time so she could return to Placencia and once again try to fix the accounting problem. He granted her a short time to do so. She did come back and search as she would, she could not identify all the income. She called the auditor and ask what would it take to satisfy him. A fine and a letter stating that it would not happen again were finally agreed on. What choice did she have? She now knew that the horror stories of these audits were not exaggerated. Belize is determined to know who occupies each room and for how long and at what price. They are not strict about a lot of things, but this is one thing they are very determined to have accurate records on, at least from the gringos.

Since Deloris was back in Placencia, she decided to stay for a couple of weeks and be sure the office was running smoothly before she left again. Alan had his hands full with the kitchen, restaurant, dive shop, and tours operations. Amy dropped by and told them that they were planning on making a trip to Honduras in a couple of days and wanted them to accompany them on the trip. She explained that they would go by boat to pick up some carved doors they had ordered and they'd probably stay overnight in Guatemala. Deloris had no desire to travel in a boat to Honduras, she didn't enjoy the sway of boats at all. However, the allure of seeing carved doors, the jungle views and all of the other wonderful things that Amy had assured her they would see, quickly swayed her to agree to come along.

There was never a doubt that Alan would enjoy this long boat journey to Honduras and Guatemala. Deloris decided that maybe it was time to do a wild and non-typical thing, the kind of thing she'd sworn off before. Amy and Ernie had been doing these things for years, so she decided she was worried for nothing.

Chapter 15

The day for the trip arrived and the couple explained to Karla, Donna and Ed that they'd be away overnight since they'd be traveling to Honduras with Ernie and Amy. The three primary employees agreed to continue as if they were still there. Donna was really a good cook and was doing well in the kitchen. She would see that the food quality remained high and Karla seemed to be doing a good job in the office and now knew the importance of keeping accurate records. Ed was in charge of helping in the restaurant and fixing anything that did not operate properly. With their fingers crossed they met Ernie and Amy at their house. They had packed only for overnight, as they knew there would be limited space in the boat.

Deloris, trying to be the optimist, felt her heart sink when she saw that the boat was only twenty-three feet long and had a flat bottom. Then there was the fact that there was only a small canopy over the driver, leaving the remainder of the boat open. Fred the fishing guide, would be the captain and Larry, the boatman from Soul Shine, that they met on their very first trip to Placencia would also accompany them. Larry would be their Spanish translator in Honduras and Guatemala.

Amy, in an attempt to take Deloris' mind off the coming journey told Deloris about the quiet Christmas time they had shared with Fred and his family at his home in Independence. Seven of Fred's eight children were there for a meal and Amy had lots of good stories from the visit. Then Amy explained that as a gift to the family, they would take two of the eight children to the U.S. for a year or so. They had already been working on visas and they were finally approved. This would allow them to expose the children to life in the states. Ernie and Amy's kids were in college but were home often and that would help the Belizean teens to assimilate in the Americanized social group. Deloris thought this was a great idea, but couldn't help to be concerned after her experience with Donna being in the U.S. She wondered if the teens being cultured by other adolescence, would help with the cultural differences. She kept her concerns to herself, but would keep up with this experiment and how it worked for all involved. Amy and Deloris couldn't express how much different and more relaxing this Christmas time had been for them and how different from the hectic one they would have spent had they remained in the states for Christmas.

Deloris and Amy climbed aboard the boat and made their way to the rear of the boat. Deloris took a deep breath. Not only did she dislike the sway of the boat, but the wind in her face tormented her. She felt that no canopy would see her sun burned by the end, and she had no idea what was in store for her on this journey. She decided it best to try and relax and enjoy this adventure. Although she didn't drink alcohol, today she wished she did. She continued to tell herself, "This is just a boat ride."

Ernie had insisted that she go out in the boat with them each time she and Alan were in Placencia, so she'd gotten used to enduring the bouncing and wind for a short distance until they had reached a beautiful cay where she and Amy would relax while their husbands fished so she knew what to expect with a ride on the open ocean.

Fred and Larry had already taken all of their passports to Big Creek's immigration office to check them out of Belize, this way they could simply leave the dock and head south out to sea. They were scheduled to stop in Livingston, Guatemala, where they'd fill up with gasoline and stay overnight. The next leg of their journey would take them just south of Puerto Barrios, the next morning.

The wind in her face was enough to steal her breath. The constant bouncing of the flat bottom boat, reminded her of breakfast. She closed her eyes and tried to relax. She tried to convince herself that this is something that most people loved to do and many would never get to experience it.

It was a long fifty-three miles to Livingston, but she had no idea how fast they were going. They seemed to be going a hundred miles an hour, when in reality, they were going about eighteen miles per hour. The sting of the wind on her face was deceptive and after an hour of being on the open ocean, it seemed that not much progress had been made. The constant view of the mountains off to the west made it seem as if they were not making much progress. After what seemed forever to Deloris, the boat slowed and they pulled into the port of Livingston, Guatemala. Livingston is a Garifuna town that is located on the Rio Dulce River. The Rio Dulce is part of a lake system and many of the people who live on sailboats year-round, sail up this river to Lake Tzabal where they stay during Hurricane season each year. Deloris and Alan had met quite a few of these sailors during their time in Placencia and everyone had described how beautiful this area was.

As they approached the dock in Livingston the beauty of the place was in full evidence. A very steep hill with steps cut into the rock, lead up to the village. The land was beautiful with majestic mountains in the background. Ernie told Alan and Deloris to remain in the boat while the rest of them went to check the group into the country. As the others began the climb up the hill, the dock filled with men speaking Spanish. They were standing all around the boat and they were pointing at the cooler that Ernie had in the boat. Their demeanor was almost menacing. Deloris leaned into Alan and whispered, "Do you think there's beer in there and that is what they're after?"

Alan was not often accused of being a patient man and after several minutes he shouted at the men. Deloris was certain that the locals didn't understand the four-letter words he had used, but the tone was what encouraged them to reluctantly withdraw. Unlike Belize, she didn't feel the same love and respect here. It seemed much more third world and open to begging.

Soon the three men of their party returned and Deloris looked past Ernie to find Amy, but didn't. She asked, "Where's Amy?" "She's getting us a place to stay." Ernie answered.

Deloris raised her eyebrows, she couldn't imagine Amy was safe after Alan had to shout at the men to get them to leave them alone.

After the men returned the crowd gathered again and after some discussion, Ernie opened the cooler and handed out a few beers. With that, Ernie was able to dismiss the crowd and then explained that Fred and Larry would be staying with the boat and keeping it and the cooler safe and they would seek a room in town.

Ernie grabbed his and Amy's bag and told Alan and Deloris to come with him. As they climbed out of the boat, Ernie explained that there was bad news because Livingston port is out of gas so they couldn't refuel there. Deloris couldn't believe her ears. After all, a boat on the ocean without gas is as handy as a paper bag in a windstorm. Ernie assured her that they had enough gas to get to Puerto Barrio and perhaps even back to Placencia. He explained that he simply wanted to fill up with gasoline there because it was so cheap. This being said, Deloris wasn't sure she believed it or not.

They were soon climbing the steep steps clambering up the hillside toward the town. They met Amy coming down after a short distance. She looked upset. She quickly explained that although she had been told that this particular hotel was safe, it did not look safe to her. Ernie suggested that they go find somewhere to eat and perhaps get a reference for a safe hotel. Amy expressed that she didn't feel safe even eating there. Ernie shouted, "But I just paid $100.00 U.S. to check into Guatemala. Are you suggesting that we leave now?"

"Yes, I think it would be best if we tried to reach Puerto Barrio before dark." Amy said as she gave Ernie a puppy eyed look. Deloris quickly chimed in "How far is it?" "It is only about thirteen miles. We can make it by dark." Ernie answered.

The plan seemed made now and the four returned to the boat. Larry and Fred seemed relieved to see them. Ernie explained the dilemma and asked Larry to find out if they could get gasoline in Puerto Barrio. Returning to the boat, both men seemed assured that they could reach Puerto Barrio and fill up there before dark. They were soon back on the open ocean and headed south. Soon they could see the mountain range to their west. When they approached the coast of Honduras the boat slowed and the men seemed to be looking for something. Deloris couldn't hear the conversation over the wind and the motor, but she could tell there was obviously a problem. She motioned for Alan to come to her. She wanted to see if he was worried. She'd decided that if he wasn't worried; she would try to remain calm. She was so far out of her normal, in control and compartmentalized lifestyle that she needed reassurance that this would end well. Alan seemed interested, but not worried. It seemed that they needed to beach the boat in a small village just west of Puerto Barrio and although Fred had been there before, he was having trouble locating exactly where they should go into shore.

Soon they began moving toward the shoreline and ended up beaching the boat on a nice sand beach at a small village. Amy grabbed all of the passports and volunteered to go and find the immigration officer. She asked Larry to come and translate. Although it was clear that no one should exit the boat before being cleared by immigration, Amy and Larry were off to solve the problem. Deloris realized that this was a side of Amy that she'd only witnessed while furniture shopping in Cayo. Even then she had a machete in the back seat. Now she only held their passports. She seemed fearless as she stormed the beach in Honduras to have their passports inspected and them to be granted entry into the country. Deloris realized that she'd be hard pressed to ever act in such a way.

After being eaten by bugs and sitting in the blistering sun for a while, Ernie decided he would get out of the boat. Again, a group of locals surrounded the boat and Ernie in very strained, broken Spanish was attempting to communicate. Fred wasn't much help, but there seemed to be some sort of conversation between him, Ernie and the Meso-American locals. Alan and Deloris clearly had no idea what was taking place. After conversing with several men, Ernie wondered off with the locals down the beach. Deloris scrutinized the crowd and realized that there were two young boys, about six in age and wearing only underwear. They watched as the villagers lead their host away. One boy picked at his belly button and stared at Deloris as the other tugged on his ear as if it hurt. Flies swarmed the boy's mouths and Deloris knew that their feet must be hot in the burning sand. These two boys were obviously Maya Indians and were a bit different from the majority of the village. They were obviously very curious about the strangers who had arrived on their shores. Deloris wished that she could talk with them but knew not a word of Spanish.

Amy returned while Ernie was still gone and was white as a sheet. Now Deloris realizes that it is getting dark, one host is missing, perhaps kidnapped, and the other host just returned looking clearly distraught, it was time to panic. Deloris asked "Okay, what happened?"

Amy remained quiet for a few moments, as she looked around for Ernie. He chose that moment to reappear still accompanied by the group of locals.

Amy said "We asked for directions and found the immigration officer's house, he wasn't there, so his wife took us to where he said he'd be in an English class, but he wasn't there. She was clearly pissed about that as she drove us back to their house. She ran over a dog and wouldn't even stop to let us help the poor thing. The immigration officer's wife kept all of our passports and said to find a hotel for tonight and leave the boat moored at the dock or beached here, whichever we want. She assured me that the immigration officer would find us and bring our passports as soon as he gets home."

"Okay, so that is not so bad, all but the dog being ran over," Ernie replied.

"Yes, it is, Ernie! When he gets home, his wife is going to tear him up about lying to her about taking an English class. They won't even think about us until all of that is over and she has our passports. Hell, we can't even enter back into Belize without our passports!" an exasperated Amy replied.

"Let's just get a hotel and we'll handle this later." Ernie answered to calm his near hysterical wife.

Deloris looked down at her side to see the little Maya boy standing close to her. He didn't smile as he looked up at her, but Deloris felt something, something very ancient when she looked into his eyes. The clamber and noise of her companions faded away for a moment. She remembered that she'd brought a bag of left over Christmas candy with her. She reached into her purse and handed the hard candy to the little boy. He quickly took the candy and darted away. But before he disappeared behind a large bush, he turned and gave Deloris a big smile. Deloris wasn't generally the mushy type, but her heart warmed at the little boy's smile.

Apparently, the conversation that had been occurring between Ernie and the locals, a bit ago, was for the boat to be taken to someone's house and be stored overnight. Ernie, Fred and Larry stayed in the boat and told Alan and the girls to follow on shore to where they'd dock the boat. Soon they arrived at the man's house but the pitch black of night was upon them. Deloris was past frightened now, as she clinched her husband's hand tightly. "You are crushing my hand!" Alan gently reminded her. She eased her grip a little, but refused to let go. The locals assured Ernie that the boat would be fine and for them to go ahead and find a hotel. Amy was well versed in hotels that were available in many countries and happen to know the name of a hotel in this village but of course they did not have reservations. Fortunately, they were told that the hotel was not far from where they were. They followed Amy and one of the locals who was showing the way, down a long, dark path, through low-hanging trees. Deloris was a bit taller than Amy and Fred so twice she found herself fighting through spider webs. Any other time this would have bothered her greatly, but tonight she only wanted to see a place to stay. The sight of the hotel was a welcomed relief. Alan, trying to get a laugh from the guys said, "I think I heard that guy that just walked out say, No more rooms."

Deloris smacked his arm and said, "Please don't kid like that, Alan it is not funny!" Alan giggled softly.

All but Amy and Alan agreed to wait outside while the two of them went into the small hotel's lobby. When they returned Amy said, "They are full and have no rooms."

Deloris had enough of the jokes and said "Amy, quit kidding, I'm tired, full of salt and I just want a place to shower and sleep."

One look at Amy's face and Deloris knew that she wasn't joking. Her heart sank. Ernie, being the host of this voyage, decided that it was time to get his group back in the right state of mind, and said, "Okay, let's just find something to eat and maybe we can come up with a plan on a full stomach." One of the locals who spoke some English said, "Come with me, I know where you can get food."

The group followed him down another dark path to a restaurant that was obviously closed. Deloris was not amused by their luck this far on the trip for this famous set of doors. The local guided them to the door and knocked on it. Soon a man answered the door of the closed restaurant. After a hurried conversation in Spanish, the man opened the door and invited them in. The owner agreed to make food for the six of them. However, when they sat down there were eight of them. The man who led them to the restaurant and his friend would be joining them for dinner. The invitation was assumed. The menu was in Spanish, so Alan asked Larry to translate it. Although Larry could speak Spanish, he couldn't read it at all. Deloris spotted the word "pollo" and knew that was chicken, so she simply pointed at that. Alan and the others soon followed suit. Larry talked with the locals in an attempt to find rooms for the six of them. They were told that there were engineers working on a project and had all the rooms booked. However, in the conversation, the local man said that he had a relative with three cabanas for rent. They were mainly rented by locals but he knew that they were empty for the night.

Alan asked, "How is the immigration officer going to find us?"

"It is a small village; we stick out here. He won't have any problem finding us." Ernie answered.

Ernie had faith that the passports would be returned. Alan, clearly did not share his optimism. Ernie asked the English speaking local, "Can you also help us find a van to take us to San Pedro first thing in the morning?"

"I will go find someone while you eat.", answered the man.

"Okay, but it needs to be big enough for six of us and to bring our large doors back with us", said Ernie.

"Okay, senor, I will find what you need." Then he disappeared out of the restaurant.

Deloris, so worried about where they'd stay and what would happen in the morning and about their passports, barely touched her dinner.

After they'd eaten, Ernie decided he should go check on the boat and Fred would accompany him. Deloris felt that everyone should stay together, but knew that her nervous fears weren't welcomed, so she kept it to herself. While Ernie and Fred were gone checking on the boat, the local came back and let them know that they could rent the three cabanas and they should follow him. The immigration officer had not yet arrived and it was getting late. They paid the very kind restaurant owner with a large tip and stood to leave.

Just then the immigration officer walked in. Amy quickly had Larry help her communicate with him. It appeared that the passports needed to be stamped by someone other than him and that would require him to travel several miles to have them stamped. He would charge an additional fee for that. Ernie arrived as Amy and the man were discussing this. Ernie assured the immigration officer that he'd make it worth the effort if he got the passports stamped properly and returned to them tonight. The man agreed and off he went. As the immigration officer was walking away, the English-speaking local told him, in Spanish, where the six would be staying. He nodded and headed out. Again, when they were ready to make their way to the cabanas, the local, finding a van, returned with a German national in tow. They were introduced to Dieter, who quoted Ernie a price for the van rental. He found out where they were staying and told them he'd be there at 7 a.m. to drive them to San Pedro where the factory was located that made the doors that they were seeking. They set out to find the cabanas. It was necessary that they walk down several dark pathways and soon arrived at a run-down house with three small concrete rooms behind it. The local told them two had air conditioning and one did not. They accepted the price without even seeing the room. Amy told Deloris to take the first room and she would take the next. She also knew that Fred and Larry weren't used to air conditioning, so they'd be fine in the third room.

Amy, searching Deloris's eyes for life said, "Why don't you and Alan get some sleep? I will stay with Ernie until we get the passports all taken care of." "Okay, I just want a shower and some sleep.", said an exhausted Deloris. "Okay, we'll be leaving here at 7 a.m. for the drive to San Pedro." Said Ernie.

Deloris nodded her head and thought, this is as bad as I could've imagined so far. When Deloris walked into their room, it got even worse. There were four single beds scattered throughout the room and none had linen. There was a small pile of what appeared to be clean sheets on a bed in the corner. She walked into the bathroom she saw a single pipe sticking out of the wall that had no shower head on it. When she turned it on, she realized that to hope for hot water was unrealistic. This didn't detour her though; even without hot water, the thought of ridding herself of the sea salt was appealing enough to tolerate the cold water. Feeling desalinized, she stepped out of the cold water to find there were no towels. She couldn't ask for one now, she called for Alan to bring her something from their bag to put on. She assumed that she'd dry quickly as the air conditioner was blowing air, but not cold at all. While she was in the cold shower, Alan had moved beds around so that one bed blocked the door. He discovered that there were only enough linens to make up one of the beds. So, they decided that they'd use the others to block the door that didn't lock. After Alan had his cold shower, he joined Deloris on the tiny bed and although Deloris believed it would be impossible to sleep, there were soon both asleep. They both woke when they heard Ernie and Amy returning to their room. Deloris couldn't help but laugh out loud when she heard Amy's reaction to their room. As she drifted back off to sleep she took comfort in the fact there were no windows and with the door blocked, they were probably safe.

The next morning, they were awake and dressed before 7 a.m. Since they hadn't heard anyone else stirring, they stayed in their room. Soon they heard a horn honk outside. They opened the door to Dieter, in a big white van that looked only to be a few years old. Both breathed a sigh of relief as they looked at the van. Although they hadn't heard the others, they all soon emerged from their rooms and all six-people piled into the van. Dieter explained that it was a little more than a hundred miles to San Pedro and if they could wait, breakfast would be better there. The roads were good and they were soon approaching San Pedro. It seemed to be much more modern than anything in Belize. Dieter parked the van and the group walked into a Burger King. Although Deloris didn't generally eat fast food, the sausage biscuit that she ate that day was surely the best thing she'd ever tasted. Alan seemed to agree because he ordered himself a second one. After breakfast, they were back in the van and headed toward the doors.

When they arrived Dieter and Larry both helped translate for everyone. While Amy was talking with the sales person, Deloris wandered around in awe. She was captivated by the carved doors; cabinetry and she fell in love with the wooden creations of color. She wanted everything she saw. Amy called her over to tour the factory to help pick out four different carved doors. The factory had six styles and the women clearly loved each style. In the end, Amy chose four and the men loaded them. Alan could tell that Deloris loved all the carvings and would love to have something from there. He asked her if she could have only one item, what would she choose? She promptly knew that it was a battle between three items, the screen, a coffee table, and a beautiful trunk, carved with beautiful tropical scenes and painted to perfection.

Alan told her to choose one and he'd make it a gift for her. He could tell that she was torn and helped by reminding her about the limited room in the van and boat. She really wanted the dressing screen, but knew that she had no obvious place to put it. She really wanted the beautiful and colorful trunk, but realized it was not practical so she chose the round coffee table with the beautiful carves fish all around. She chose it because they needed one in their apartment and it was the most practical choice. They wrapped the coffee table and loaded it in the van. Alan could tell that she was happy with her new gift. He also knew that she'd always want the other two items. He liked carved wood, but Deloris had a deep appreciation that he did not understand.

They were soon back in the van and made their way back to Puerto Barrios. On the way, Dieter told them that he was traveling to Latin America and that he'd already traveled Europe. When he came into a country and he couldn't speak their language, he immersed himself in the culture and language, and was soon fluent. He'd always find a niche where he could make enough to live and save enough to move on to the next country. He had been in Guatemala for two years and when he left, he planned to follow the path of the famed explorer Marco Polo. Deloris listened with intent and wondered if there were a lot of people in this world who wandered as Dieter did. She realized, yet again, that there was so much more out there that she'd never considered. She wondered why people would want to live the kind of life that this middle-aged German clearly relished. She decided at once that she wanted to talk to as many of people as she could. She was curious about their thought process and how they came to think in such a way. She told herself that when she had a guest at the hotel who lived a different lifestyle, she'd pay close attention to what they had to say. This would help her understand how they thought.

When they arrived in Puerto Barrio, they found their boat still moored safely at the man's house. They asked about getting gas for their trip back to Belize and were told to try here, or there, but no one was sure who had gasoline. The men measured what was left in the tanks, and after some debate, decided that they had plenty to make it back. Deloris who never let her car get below half a tank, didn't want to hear about this. She loved the carved items she'd experienced and her new coffee table, but wished she was back in Belize, that would feel like home after this trip. After heading North across the bay of Honduras they saw black thunderstorms heading toward them. Fred adjusted the course to avoid the down pours and Deloris worried more with each mile. Getting wet was the least of her concern at this point. Finally, it was over and they pulled into a port at Ernie and Amy's dock. She felt as if she could kiss the ground. She probably would have, if everyone had not been close enough to see. What a trip! Alan looked at her and could clearly see her relief.

He said, "We'll go back and get the dressing screen and chest when you are ready to make that trip again."

Deloris stopped in her tracks, turned and looked to see him smiling and clearly teasing her. She gave him a jolly laugh and finally realized that they were safely back in Belize and she could breathe again.

Now I can tell you, readers, I visited Paradise a couple of years after this story ends. If you think the stories up to this point have been unbelievable just wait until we tell you the other stories that have happened and the things that we learned as they sat around that darn table at Paradise Resort Hotel. Or better yet, just make a reservation and sit at the table and hear those stories first hand. Oh, but be careful there is no cure for "Tropical Fever".

Made in the USA
Columbia, SC
18 February 2022